Halliday, Frank Ernest

The cult of Shakespeare

THE CULT OF SHAKESPEARE

Untouch'd and sacred be thy shrine,
Avonian Willy, bard divine,
In studious posture leaning!

Garrick and the Shakespeare Statue
by R. E. Pine, 1784

THE CULT OF SHAKESPEARE

by

F. E. HALLIDAY

GERALD DUCKWORTH & CO., LTD.
3 *Henrietta Street, London, W.C.*2

Printed in Great Britain by Richard Clay and Company, Ltd.,
Bungay, Suffolk

CONTENTS

LIST OF ILLUSTRATIONS

All but the last three illustrations are reproduced by permission of the Shakespeare Birthplace Trust.

PREFACE

The Cult of Shakespeare is a survey (not over-solemn, I hope) of the fortunes of Shakespeare from the time of his death to the present day; an account of the rise of bardolatry and the more frenzied excesses of the devotees of his cult: of the liberties that have been taken with his work and the follies that have been committed in his name. Few people, I think, are fully aware of this history and of the power of the spell that the great name has exercised throughout the centuries.

Yet, when the Stuarts were restored to the throne in 1660 there was no magic in the name. Even before the theatres were closed in 1642 Shakespeare had been overshadowed by Beaumont and Fletcher and Ben Jonson, and when they were reopened at the Restoration he was remembered not very vividly as a once-popular dramatist who wrote before the age of enlightenment. His plays as they stood were unacceptable to an age polished by its contact with France, but, as there was a dearth of new drama after twenty years without demand, they might be made to serve if skilfully adapted. And so we get the refined classical versions of Davenant, those strange outrageous hybrids with which the modern popularity of Shakespeare began. The refining process was continued by Dryden, Tate, Cibber and others, until at the beginning of the Georgian era poets and scholars began to return to what Shakespeare had really written, and to wrangle about the restoration of his text. The Pope-Theobald-Warburton-Hanmer squabble is not the least diverting episode in this history.

Then, in the middle of the eighteenth century, came the great showman Garrick, who did more to popularise Shakespeare than all his predecessors, and by his Jubilee at Stratford firmly established the Shakespeare Cult as an integral part of the English way of life. The latter half of the century was further enlivened by the mischievous antics of George Steevens.

After the patronage of 'the wild irregular genius' by the ages of enlightenment and reason there followed the orgies of romanticism, of exploitation in Stratford, the forgeries of William-Henry Ireland, the

Shakspeare Gallery affair, and the prim expurgatory labours of Thomas Bowdler.

The Victorians added their own peculiar follies. The first Shakespeare Society was brought to grief by the frauds of its founder, J. P. Collier, and the New Shakspere Society, under the ebullient leadership of F. J. Furnivall, contrived to bring science into the service of sentiment as well as of scholarship. Sentimental superlative was piled on romantic hyperbole; the illiteracy of the Stratford background was exaggerated, and Shakespeare recklessly lauded as an inspired peasant, the son of an ignorant butcher, who by his native genius became the greatest poet and dramatist of all time, and an omniscient philosopher to boot. Not unnaturally some people, like the nautical American, Joseph C. Hart, began to wonder how such an untutored genius could have achieved all that was claimed for him, and to ask, Who was this Shakespeare? His countrywoman, Delia Bacon, found him in her namesake, Francis Bacon. And so, based on the rickety foundations of a muddled and antiquated view of Shakespeare's life and art, have been erected the crazy structures, the final follies, of the Baconians, Oxfordians, Derbyites and the rest. Some of their literature, it is true, is comparatively restrained, some of it scholarly when not perversely distorted, and some of it downright dull and dreadfully verbose, but its highest flights of fantasy make the most entertaining reading of all in the history of the Cult of Shakespeare.

It is a pleasure to have this opportunity of thanking all those who have helped me in obtaining material for this book. Mr John Summerson gave me the free run of Sir John Soane's Museum, of which he is Curator, and showed me all the Shakespeareana, books, pictures and curios, which it contains. Mr Levi Fox, Director of Shakespeare's Birthplace, put all the resources of the Birthplace and Memorial Theatre libraries at my disposal, and supplied most of the prints for the illustrations that are here reproduced. I am particularly grateful to his archivist, Mrs Berry, and to Miss Robinson, the librarian, for their invaluable help; no sooner had I mentioned a book than it was on the desk beside me. Then there is Mrs Harvey of the Morrab Library, Penzance, Q's 'library in a garden by the sea'. Owing to lack of funds the catalogue is sadly inadequate, but Mrs Harvey spared no pains in tracking down the treasures that I was after. And there is considerable treasure to be found there, for Halliwell-Phillipps left it many of his books and rare pamphlets, most of them annotated. There can be few other libraries that possess, for example, so many quartos of Elizabethan plays, the *Shakspeare Papers* of Samuel Ireland, and guidebooks to Stratford of 1806, 1824 and 1864.

A list of the books to which I am mainly indebted will be found on page 210.

F. E. H.

St Ives, Cornwall
   April 1957

SHAKESPEARE ECLIPSED

W H E N Shakespeare died in the spring of 1616 there were neither newspapers nor periodicals to record the event and publish an obituary. Even if there had been it is quite possible that the death of a retired actor and playwright in an obscure provincial town would have passed unnoticed. He was, it is true, highly regarded as a poet and esteemed as the most popular dramatist of his day, but plays, at least contemporary English plays, were scarcely acceptable as literature; Sir Thomas Bodley would have nothing to do with such 'idle bookes and riffe raffes' in his new library at Oxford, and even the dramatist Thomas Heywood twitted Ben Jonson for his presumption in calling his plays 'Works' in the folio edition published in the year of Shakespeare's death.

There had been numerous appreciative references to 'friendly Shakespeare' and his work since the time of Henry Chettle's apology for Greene's attack at the beginning of his career. As early as 1598 Francis Meres had called him the best writer of comedy and tragedy in English, but he had retired to Stratford some five or six years before his death, and nobody knew better than Shakespeare that in that fiercely competitive and rapidly changing age

> to have done, is to hang
> Quite out of fashion, like a rusty mail
> In monumental mockery.

When he died, therefore, there would be comparatively few in London who were aware of the event. By those few his memory was cherished as a friend and as a writer of more than common merit, and by a wider public he was remembered as the author of a number of plays, now, however, becoming somewhat old-fashioned and giving place to the work of the younger men, Beaumont and Fletcher. There was no adulation of the author, no suggestion that he was a man of extraordinary accomplishments; rather the reverse, for Beaumont had written that he wished to keep his lines as free from learning as Shakespeare's best.

When Beaumont himself died, a few weeks before Shakespeare, he

was buried in the south transept of Westminster Abbey, close to
Chaucer and Spenser. But then he was the son of Sir Francis Beaumont, Justice of the Common Pleas, and, having married an heiress, a
very wealthy man. His friend Richard Corbet, chaplain to King
James, wrote a valedictory epigram, and young John Earle an elegy,
concluding,

> When thou'rt of Chaucer's standing in the tomb,
> Thou shalt not share, but take up all, his room.

It is just possible that there was talk of moving the remains of Shakespeare to the Abbey, for shortly after his death William Basse wrote a
sonnet:

> Renowned Spencer, lye a thought more nye
> To learned Chaucer, and rare Beaumont lye
> A little neerer Spenser to make roome
> For Shakespeare in your threefold fowerfold Tombe.

But almost certainly Basse meant merely that the poet was worthy of
burial in Westminster Abbey, for he concludes,

> If your precedency in death doth barre
> A fourth place in your sacred sepulcher,
> Under this carved marble of thine owne
> Sleepe rare Tragœdian Shakespeare, sleep alone.

And so Shakespeare was left quietly interred in the church of the Holy
Trinity at Stratford, in the grave beneath the 'carved marble' monu-
ment on the wall, with its Latin inscription comparing him to Nestor,
Socrates and Virgil.

These things remained then: the monument, an elegiac sonnet,
and his published work. But by no means his complete work. Of his
thirty-seven plays only eighteen had been published, and of these the
texts of two, one being *King Lear*, were deplorably poor, and of four
others, including *Henry V*, hopelessly corrupt. It is true that there were
numerous reprints of some of the more popular plays; there were, for
example, five quarto editions of *Richard II*, *Richard III* and 1 *Henry
IV*, but nineteen remained unpublished, among them *Twelfth Night*,
Macbeth, *Othello*, *Antony and Cleopatra* and *The Tempest*. If this had
been the end of the story, the material might have been too scanty to
fire posterity with a desire to know more about Shakespeare than his
contemporaries, about the prolific Fletcher, for example, or the enterprising Jonson. Fortunately, it was not the end of the story.

In the summer of 1618 Ben Jonson set out on a walking-tour to Scotland. There he met William Drummond, who invited him to spend Christmas at Hawthornden, his country home a few miles from Edinburgh. Drummond, a shy and gentle poet of the old school, was overwhelmed by his vigorous, egotistical, touchy and hard-drinking guest, yet he was so fascinated by his conversation that he made notes of his most striking, provocative and outrageous remarks. Amongst other things Jonson told him that he disliked Spenser's *Faerie Queene* and Drayton's *Polyolbion*, that Daniel was no poet, that Donne deserved hanging for his irregular metre, and that 'Shakespeare wanted art'. Moreover, 'Shakespeare in a play brought in a number of men saying they had suffered shipwreck in Bohemia, where there is no sea by some hundred miles'. Jonson had just written the preface to his translation of Horace's *Art of Poetry*—he read it aloud to Drummond —and it was this art that Shakespeare so lamentably lacked; the man would not imitate the ancients and follow the precepts of Aristotle, but insisted on going his own easy, unofficial English way. Perhaps, after all, Shakespeare was more truly contemporary than Jonson.

While Jonson was enjoying himself at Hawthornden, living in the element of drink and mischievously shocking his susceptible host with anecdotes and epigrams about his contemporaries, in London another man was taking even greater liberties with the name of Shakespeare. This was the publisher Thomas Pavier. At the beginning of the century Pavier had secured the copyright in three of the pirated editions of Shakespeare's plays, parts 2 and 3 of *Henry VI* and *Henry V*, the last of which he had reprinted in its mutilated form. Then in 1608 he had registered 'A booke Called A Yorkshire Tragedy, written by William Shakespere' and published it with the name 'W. Shakspeare' on the title-page. *A Yorkshire Tragedy* is a short melodrama, based on the story of Walter Calverley of Yorkshire, who had recently stabbed his wife and murdered two of his children. It was acted by the King's Men at the Globe, where Shakespeare may have given it a few final touches, but that he should have written this crude thriller at the time when he was writing *Macbeth* and *Antony and Cleopatra*, or indeed at any time, is inconceivable. Obviously Pavier ascribed it to him because, like every other publisher, he knew that his name was sufficient to sell a play.

Two years later Pavier went in for piracy in a much bigger way. He already had the copyright in three of Shakespeare's plays, that they

B

were 'bad' quartos was no matter, and nobody had seriously questioned the authorship of *A Yorkshire Tragedy*. Why not add a few more, and publish a small collected edition? It had never been done before, and such a volume, in large quarto size, would be sure to sell. Pavier therefore approached the printer William Jaggard, who had a tenuous claim to the copyright of two genuine plays of Shakespeare, and they set to work. There were to be ten plays. To Pavier's *Henry V*, two parts of *Henry VI* and *A Yorkshire Tragedy* Jaggard contributed *The Merchant of Venice* and *A Midsummer Night's Dream*, which had originally been printed by his predecessor in his business. They added another 'bad' quarto, *The Merry Wives of Windsor*, two poor quartos, *Pericles* and *King Lear*, and as a crowning act of impudence Pavier slipped in the first part of *Sir John Oldcastle*. He knew quite well that this was not Shakespeare's, for he had himself published it in 1600, though fortunately without a name on the title-page. It had in fact been written in collaboration by a group of playwrights, including Anthony Munday and Michael Drayton, for Philip Henslowe and the Admiral's company as a counterblast to Shakespeare's *Henry IV*. It was well known that the original name of Falstaff had been Sir John Oldcastle, and that Shakespeare had been compelled to change it when Oldcastle's descendant, Lord Cobham, complained. The historical Oldcastle had been a friend of Henry V, a courageous soldier, but a convinced Lollard, for which heresy he had eventually suffered martyrdom. This was the story that Munday, Drayton and their colleagues set out to tell in *Sir John Oldcastle*, prefacing their play with the lines,

> It is no pamper'd glutton we present,
> Nor aged counsellor to youthful sin,
> But one whose virtue shone above the rest,
> A valiant martyr, and a virtuous peer . . .
> Let fair truth be graced,
> Since forged invention former time defaced.

It is an admirable play—with episodes borrowed from *Henry V*—and was deservedly popular. But it was not Shakespeare's, and Pavier knew it.

His scheme, however, came to nothing. At the beginning of May, 1619, Jaggard had just finished printing *Henry VI* and *Pericles* when Shakespeare's old company, the King's Men, heard of what was afoot, and Lord Chamberlain Pembroke wrote to the Stationers' Company ordering the staying 'of any further impression of any of the plays or interludes of His Majesty's servants without their consents'. Pavier, therefore, had to abandon his design of a collected edition, but he was not to be beaten, and by issuing the plays separately with false dates he passed them off as copies of the original impressions.

No doubt the Lord Chamberlain's order had long been forgotten when, in 1622, another stationer issued sixth editions of *Richard III* and 1 *Henry IV*, and Thomas Walkley published the first quarto of *Othello*, confident that 'the Authors name is sufficient to vent his worke'. Another play of Shakespeare's had been given to the world, yet half of them remained unpublished. But not for long. A genuine collected edition was already in the press, curiously enough William Jaggard's press, and towards the end of 1623 some thousand copies of 'Mr William Shakespeares Comedies, Histories & Tragedies' were on sale in the London bookshops. This was the First Folio, edited by Shakespeare's friends and colleagues in the King's company, John Heminge and Henry Condell. They were the only men who could have tackled the job, for they were the only men who had worked continuously with Shakespeare since the beginning of his career, they alone knew which plays should be included as entirely or substantially his, and they were in charge of the manuscripts from which most of them were printed. For the plays were 'Truely set forth according to their first originall'; that is, not only the previously unpublished plays, but those already issued with bad texts, those 'stolne and surreptitious copies, maimed, and deformed by the frauds and stealthes of iniurious impostors', were set up from the jealously guarded manuscript copies, some of them in Shakespeare's hand, in the possession of the King's Men. It was, as 'I.M.' wrote in a prefatory poem, 'a Re-entrance to a Plaudite'.

There were other commendatory verses prefaced to the volume, by Hugh Holland and Leonard Digges, but pride of place was given to the noble and generous elegy of Ben Jonson 'To the memory of my beloved, the author Mr William Shakespeare, and what he hath left us', in which he developed the theme of Basse's sonnet:

> My Shakespeare, rise; I will not lodge thee by
>   Chaucer, or Spenser, or bid Beaumont lye
> A little further, to make thee a roome:
>   Thou art a Moniment, without a tombe,
> And art alive still, while thy Booke doth live,
>   And we have wits to read, and praise to give.

Shakespeare was alive again, and the scene set for the birth of a legend.

The first folio was sold out within a few years and reprinted in 1632 with an additional 'Epitaph on the admirable Dramaticke Poet, W. Shakespeare':

> What needs my Shakespear for his honour'd Bones,
> The labour of an age in piled Stones,
> Or that his hallow'd reliques should be hid
> Under a Star-ypointing Pyramid? . . .

It was the first published poem of young John Milton. Charles I bought a copy of the second folio, and wrote in it an alternative title to *Much Ado: Benedicte and Betteris*, the name by which it was known when he first saw a performance at Court as a boy of twelve.

It was at about this time that Jonson wrote his most considered opinion of Shakespeare. Himself a notoriously slow and careful writer, he thought Shakespeare altogether too rapid and careless, and, though admittedly his virtues redeemed his vices, too often he failed to control his pen and fell into ridiculous excesses and laughable errors. The criticism was a fair one, but as some thought it malevolent he justified his candour by maintaining that it was doing Shakespeare a disservice to praise him for his greatest fault, to consider it a virtue that 'he never blotted out line' when he should have revised and altered a thousand, adding that he himself loved the man and honoured his memory, 'on this side idolatry, as much as any'. According to Jonson's severe standards uncritical idolatry was already in the air. Perhaps his shaft was directed primarily against his young rival for favour at Court.

William Davenant was now thirty. He was the son of John and Jane Davenant of the Crown Tavern, Oxford, where Shakespeare was said to have broken his journeys between London and Stratford, and to have become so friendly with the couple as to agree to stand godfather to the baby William. After some terms as an undergraduate at Lincoln College young Davenant had gone to Court as page to the Duchess of Richmond before entering the service of Fulke Greville, Lord Brooke, after whose murder he became, like his reputed godfather, a dramatist. His first plays were produced in 1629–30, but soon came a chance of more rapid advancement. For almost thirty years Jonson and Inigo Jones had collaborated in the production of Court masques, Jonson supplying the words, Jones the costumes and ingenious scenery. The partnership was an uneasy one, for the two great men were equally arrogant and irascible, each convinced that his contribution was the more important. When, therefore, a particularly violent quarrel broke out and Jonson wrote ironically of his colleague's 'carpentry', Jones invited Davenant to supply a script, and *The Temple of Love* was performed at Whitehall by the Queen and her ladies early in 1634. The ailing Jonson could scarcely be expected to look with favour on this young supplanter, who openly maintained that Shakespeare was a greater dramatist than he. When he died in 1637, joining Chaucer, Spenser and Beaumont in the Abbey, Davenant succeeded him as Poet Laureate, and in the following year published his first volume of poems, containing an 'Ode in Remembrance of Master William Shakespeare'. Poets in search of inspiration are warned to avoid the Stratford countryside in spring, for there the flowers hang the pensive head, the stunted trees cast a night rather than a shade, and the river has long since wept itself into a shallow brook. Davenant took a personal interest in Stratford, for after all it might almost be called his native town. He felt the spirit of Shakespeare working strongly within him. Perhaps he was more intimately related to his godfather than he knew. What if he were not merely the godson, but the very son of Shakespeare?

In 1639 Davenant became manager of the small Phoenix theatre in Drury Lane, though he was, of course, precluded from producing the plays of Shakespeare, as these were the property of the King's Men, still acting at the Globe and Blackfriars theatres. Sometimes, however, unscrupulous companies would attract an audience by putting on a Shakespeare play, and the Master of the Revels, Sir Henry Herbert, made a satisfactory addition to his income by forbidding such piracy in return for a douceur from the King's Men.

How popular and profitable Shakespeare's plays were, or had been twenty years before, is witnessed by verses prefacing an edition of Shakespeare's *Poems* in 1640. It was a strange volume. *Venus and Adonis* had gone through sixteen editions, and *Lucrece* eight, but the publisher confined himself virtually to the *Sonnets*, which had only once been printed, arranging them in a different order and so altering them that they appeared to be addressed to a woman. Leonard Digges was the author of the prefatory poem, written probably at about the same time as the commendatory verses that he had contributed to the first folio. After praising Shakespeare for his originality, his refusal to borrow from the Greeks and imitate the Latins, he asks,

> But oh! what praise more powerfull can we give
> The dead, than that by him the Kings men live?

'How could the Globe have prospered,' he asks, if half the plays had vanished with his players? Then he describes the crowds who, neglecting the tragedies of Jonson, thronged to hear Shakespeare at the Globe:

> So have I seene, when Cesar would appeare,
> And on the Stage at halfe-sword parley were
> Brutus and Cassius, oh how the Audience
> Were ravish'd, with what wonder they went thence,
> When some new day they would not brooke a line
> Of tedious (though well laboured) *Catiline*;
> *Sejanus* too was irkesome, they priz'de more
> Honest Iago, or the jealous Moore . . .
>   when let but Falstaffe come,
> Hal, Poines, the rest, you scarce shall have a roome
> All is so pester'd: let but Beatrice
> And Benedicke be seene, loe in a trice
> The Cockpit, Galleries, Boxes, all are full
> To heare Malvoglio that crosse garter'd Gull.

By 1640, however, the day of the open public playhouses was almost over. It was here, at the Theatre, Curtain, Rose and Globe, that the Elizabethan drama had been born and nourished, drama on the titanic scale of Marlowe and Shakespeare, of *Tamburlaine* and *Lear*, when miniature armies had room to deploy, and actors declaimed their lines from the apron stage to an audience of a thousand and more, drawn from all sections of society. But shortly before Shakespeare retired the King's Men had opened the small, intimate Blackfriars theatre, which had proved so profitable that others had followed suit and built the Phoenix in Drury Lane and Salisbury Court near White-friars. It was to these comfortable and expensive little theatres that people of fashion now resorted to see the sophisticated drama that they demanded. Shakespeare's last four plays, from *Pericles* to *The Tempest*, had been written for the Blackfriars stage, but almost all those of Beaumont and Fletcher had been written for this private theatre, typically, sentimental tragi-comedies spiced with bawdy innuendo, which appealed to the taste of the age. It was for this reason that the King's Men were now producing three plays by Beaumont and

Fletcher for every one by Shakespeare. Records have survived of twenty-five performances of Shakespeare between 1616 and 1642, most of them at Court, and the choice is an interesting one. *The Winter's Tale* was given four times, and 'likt', *Othello* was presented once at Court and twice at Blackfriars, *Pericles* once at Court and once at the Globe, and the one Court performance of *Cymbeline* was 'well likte by the kinge'. Adultery, jealousy and a young heroine's humiliating exposure to vice are the popular themes, and no doubt Fletcher's unpleasant little sub-plot in *The Two Noble Kinsmen* accounts for the inclusion of that play.

The last recorded performance of a Shakespeare play by his own company is that of *The Merry Wives of Windsor* at Court in November 1638. Four years later the Civil War broke out, the theatres were closed and remained closed until the Restoration of Charles II in 1660. Not only were Davenant's plans foiled for a new theatre with a stage that would accommodate Inigo Jones's elaborate contraptions for changes of scene, but most of the existing theatres were destroyed or allowed to decay. A few years earlier William Prynne, the militant Puritan, had denounced plays as pomps of the devil and had his ears cropped off for his pains, but now, after a struggle that had lasted since the first London theatre had been ⎿built, the Puritans had won.

The Swan playhouse was already in a ruinous condition, the Hope, or Beargarden, occupied mainly by 'wild beasts and gladiators', and then, incited by the sectaries, soldiers sacked the Phoenix, Fortune and Salisbury Court. But the Globe, 'the *Continent of the World*, because halfe the yeere a World of *Beauties* and brave *Spirits* resorted unto it', was the first to go, being razed on Monday, April 15th, 1644, to make room for houses, a fate that overtook the Blackfriars theatre ten years later. The Curtain seems somehow to have survived the Commonwealth period, as did the Red Bull, apparently converted into a roofed playhouse, and though some of the other old theatres were usable as makeshifts at the Restoration they were soon replaced by new private theatres. The Elizabethan heritage of the public theatres perished in 1642.

The acting companies were broken up and the players scattered, but before they were finally dispersed the King's Men, emulating Heminge and Condell twenty years before, issued a folio edition of the manuscript plays of Beaumont and Fletcher in their possession. It was

dedicated to the 4th Earl of Pembroke, to whom, with his dead brother
the 3rd Earl, the Shakespeare folio had been dedicated:

> Directed by the example of some, who once steered in our quality, and so
> fortunately aspired to choose your Honour, joined with your (now glorified)
> brother, patrons to the flowing compositions of the then expired sweet swan
> of Avon Shakespeare; and since, more particularly bound to your Lordship's
> most constant and diffusive goodness, from which we did for many calm years
> derive a subsistence to ourselves, and protection to the scene (now withered,
> and condemn'd, as we fear, to a long winter and sterility) we have presumed to
> offer to yourself what before was never printed of these authors.

It was the final curtain of Shakespeare's old company, formed just half
a century before. One of the ten signatories of the dedication was John
Lowin, who had played with Shakespeare in *Sejanus* as far back as
1603, another Joseph Taylor, who had joined the company as their
leading tragic actor after the death of Burbage in 1619.

But although the theatres were closed and the public performance
of plays forbidden it was impossible to stop all forms of dramatic
entertainment, and in the more settled period of the Commonwealth
'drolls' were commonly performed in the provinces. These were
adaptations of comic scenes from the Elizabethan and Jacobean drama
attached to some legitimate form of diversion at fairs and similar
festivities. One of these was *The Merry Conceited Humours of Bottom
the Weaver*, and another *The Bouncing Knight*, a running together of
the Falstaff scenes in 1 *Henry IV*. A third was *The Gravemakers*, in
which the 'Actors Names' are given as, 'Grave-maker and his Man,
Hamlet and his Friend'. The scope of the action is indicated by the
Argument: 'While he is making the Grave, for a Lady that drown'd
herself, Hamlet and his friend interrupt him with several Questions,'
and the droll is virtually Act V Scene i as far as Hamlet's improvised
lines about 'Imperious Caesar', ending with tantalising inconclusive-
ness before the entry of Ophelia's funeral procession. No doubt it was
the frequent performance of these concentrated comic scenes, in booth
and makeshift theatre, that helped to establish their immense popularity.

During these eighteen years of dramatic sterility Davenant was not
idle. Although he was an active royalist, knighted by the King after
the siege of Gloucester, and more than once imprisoned, he contrived
to publish two plays before the Civil War was over. His last imprison-
ment was in the Tower on a charge of high treason, from which he

was eventually released, possibly owing to the intervention of Milton, and by 1652 free to carry out his schemes for the production of a modified kind of play. It was an ingenious plan. The government was prepared to sanction musical entertainment provided it was elevating, and Davenant obtained permission to produce an 'opera', a new and inoffensive word to describe the declamation of verse 'in recitative music'. And so, in 1656, the first English opera was staged at Rutland House, *The Siege of Rhodes*, the libretto by Davenant and music by Matthew Locke and Henry Lawes. But Davenant introduced more than Italian opera to the theatre-starved English; he presented women on the public stage for the first time, and contrived changes of scene with devices similar to those that had been developed by Inigo Jones in the Court masque.

When, therefore, the theatres were reopened in 1660, the conditions for the production of Shakespeare's plays, which Davenant was burning to introduce to audiences that had never been to a theatre, were very different from those that had prevailed in 1642. The theatres were now roofed, with expensive seats in the 'pit' where once the groundlings had stood. The apron stage was merely an extension beneath a proscenium arch within which much of the action took place, and instead of the rapid and thrilling Elizabethan tempo, made possible by the use of three stages, two levels and a minimum of scenery, productions were cramped and retarded by changes of scene, laboriously contrived spectacle and operatic music. Finally, women's parts were beginning to be taken by women, though the change did not come all at once, for though Margaret Hughes played Desdemona in December 1660, in August Pepys saw fifteen-year-old Edward Kynaston as the Duke's sister in Fletcher's *Loyal Subject*, 'the loveliest lady that ever I saw in my life'.

It was in August that Charles II sanctioned the formation of two companies of players, the only companies allowed in London: one, the King's under his own patronage, the other the Duke's under that of his brother, the Duke of York. The King's company was to be formed by Thomas Killigrew, the Duke's by Davenant, each authorised to build a theatre, and by 1661 the Duke's were in their playhouse in Lincoln's Inn Fields, significantly known as 'the Opera', and soon afterwards the first Drury Lane theatre was ready for the King's. Although Killigrew formed his company mainly from the older actors, to begin with they were more interested in Jonson, Fletcher and the new men than in Shakespeare; but Davenant *was* interested in Shakespeare, and asked the King for the exclusive right to produce a number of the plays. He chose four comedies, four tragedies, and a spectacle: *Twelfth Night, The Tempest, Much Ado about Nothing* and *Measure for Measure*; *Macbeth, Romeo and Juliet, Hamlet* and *King Lear*; and *Henry VIII*. To these were added later *Troilus and Cressida, Timon of Athens*, and *Henry VI*. But Davenant did not ask merely for the right to perform these plays, he asked for the right to *reform* them as well. Before the closing of the theatres he had had no authority to produce Shakespeare, while they were closed he had had no chance to produce them; he had waited eighteen years for this opportunity, he was now fifty-four, and there was no time to be lost. But first he had to collect his company of young and inexperienced actors and teach them how Shakespeare should be played. He was fortunate in finding young Thomas Betterton, whose first appearance on the stage had been rapturously received, and he set to work to groom him. According to John Downes, the company's book-keeper and prompter, Davenant had seen Joseph Taylor play Hamlet at Blackfriars, and as Taylor had been instructed by Shakespeare himself he was able to give Betterton the authentic Shakespearean touch. Although this is improbable, for Shakespeare was dead when Taylor took Burbage's place, it was no doubt true that Davenant got information from John Lowin, who was still alive in 1660, and really had been coached by Shakespeare, apparently in the parts, among others, of Falstaff and Henry VIII. Within a few months Davenant was ready, and on August 24th, 1661, Pepys went 'to the Opera, and there saw *Hamlet, Prince of Denmarke*, done with scenes very well, but above all, Betterton did the Prince's part beyond imagination'.

How then did Shakespeare's reputation stand in 1660, forty-four years after his death and eighteen after the last performance of his plays? Not very high; not so high as Jonson's, and well below the level of that of the more sophisticated Beaumont and Fletcher. All had been published in folio, but they were awkward and bulky volumes, discouraging to any but the most earnest reader, and an educated man of thirty-five might well be quite ignorant of their plays. John Evelyn, aged forty and a bookish man if ever there was one, had not mentioned any of them in his Diary. Then Shakespeare, the oldest of the group, belonged to the barbaric, almost medieval, Elizabethan world, so different from the polite and polished age that was just beginning, illumined by the rays of the Roi Soleil across the Channel. He slept peacefully in Stratford church, undisturbed by curious pilgrims, and by anything more agitating than local gossip, now fast withering, for few remained who could remember him. His daughter, Judith Quiney, was still alive, an old lady of seventy-five, who no doubt had a few stories to tell about her father, and his nephew, Thomas Hart, was living in his birthplace, but the new vicar had never read any of the plays, and made a note 'to peruse and bee versed in them, that I may not bee ignorant in that matter'. William Davenant was even more determined that England, or at any rate London, should not be ignorant in that matter.

II

SHAKESPEAR REFORMED

PEPYS was so enchanted by *Hamlet* that a fortnight later he went again to the Opera to see *Twelfth Night*. He was disappointed and, though he saw it twice again, found no reason to change his opinion that it was 'but a silly play' and one of the weakest that he ever saw. *A Midsummer Night's Dream* was even worse, 'the most insipid, ridiculous play that ever I saw in my life', and he made a vow, one of the few that he kept, never to see it again. But worst of all was *Romeo and Juliet*, which he saw at the beginning of 1662. It was the first performance, with Betterton and his wife, Mary Saunderson, as the hero and heroine; they fumbled their lines, but it was not for this that Pepys condemned it as the very worst play that ever he heard. So much for three of Shakespeare's loveliest plays, in the opinion of one of the most able men of the day. The poetry and delicate fantasy of Elizabethan times was not for the young men of the new age, and on December 26th, 1661, the day after Pepys paid his second visit to *Hamlet*, Evelyn wrote in his Diary, 'I saw *Hamlet, Prince of Denmark* played; but now the old plays begin to disgust this refined age, since his Majesty's being so long abroad.' Davenant had feared as much, but had something up his sleeve to the purpose, and when Pepys went to the Opera early in the new year he saw *The Law against Lovers*, 'a good play and well performed, especially the little girl's, whom I never saw act before, dancing and singing'. Evelyn saw it at Court the following Christmas, but made no comment.

The Law against Lovers was Davenant's name for *Measure for Measure*—with a difference. He had been licensed to perform and reform Shakespeare, to present him, that is, in a refined and elevated guise that would make him acceptable to an age so much more civilised than the Elizabethan, and this was the first of his reformations. The essential thing was to get rid of the low comedy to which Shakespeare so often descended; obscenity was permissible, desirable even, but not vulgarity, and Mistress Overdone, Froth, Elbow, Pompey Bum and the rest had to go, and with them one of the funniest, perhaps the funniest of all, scenes in Shakespeare. The Mariana sub-plot, too, could go, and to fill the gap Benedick and Beatrice could be transferred from *Much Ado*—without Dogberry and Verges, of course. So plot and characters were rearranged. Benedick is Angelo's brother, and Beatrice Julietta's cousin and sister of young Viola, much given to dance, song and playing the castanets. The scene, for some reason or other, is removed from Vienna to Florence.

The play begins something in the manner of *Measure for Measure.* The Duke leaves Angelo as his deputy to enforce the long-neglected laws while he professes to set out for Spain, but remains in Florence disguised as a friar to see how Angelo acquits himself. Claudio is arrested for getting Julietta with child; both are imprisoned and Angelo condemns Claudio to death. Isabella intercedes for her brother, and Angelo promises to spare his life if she will yield to his passion. She refuses, as does Julietta to play the part of Mariana. Meanwhile Beatrice and Benedick plan the escape of the lovers, and in desperation Benedick raises a revolt against his brother. The Duke reveals himself, pardons everybody and, as Angelo has been merely testing the virtue of Isabella, the proceedings end with their betrothal, and of course with the promised nuptials of Benedick and Beatrice.

It makes a fair tragi-comedy of the emasculated Beaumont and Fletcher variety, occasionally flaring into real significance and passion when Davenant retains Shakespeare's lines, but this is what he makes of Claudio's appeal to Isabella, 'Ay, but to die, and go we know not where,' when she tells him that she will not sacrifice her virtue for his life:

> Oh sister, 'tis to go we know not whither.
> We lie in silent darkness, and we rot;
> Where long our motion is not stopt; for though
> In graves none walk upright, proudly to face
> The stars, yet there we move again, when our
> Corruption makes those worms in whom we crawl.
> Perhaps the spirit, which is future life,
> Dwells salamander-like, unharm'd in fire:
> Or else with wand'ring winds is blown about
> The world.

And then Viola, the 'little girl' who so transported Pepys, passes through the play like a tiresome and irrelevant Pippa, indefatigably singing her silly songs, 'Wake all the dead! what hoa!' Clacking her castanets she dances a saraband in which all join, and instead of 'Take,

O take those lips away', there is a quartet with chorus sung by Lucio, Beatrice, Benedick and Viola.

Davenant followed up his success with another reformation called *The Rivals*. Pepys was not greatly impressed, and if he had read the original English version of the story in Chaucer's *Knight's Tale*, or even *The Two Noble Kinsmen* that Fletcher had written with Shakespeare's help, we can understand why. Yet it was played for nine days to a crowded house, a long run for the period, and became one of the principal stock-pieces of the company. Downes's lyrical description of its first performance gives some idea of the play: 'A play having a very fine interlude in it, of vocal and instrumental music, mixt with very diverting dances; Mr Price introduced the dancing by a short comical prologue which gain'd him an universal applause of the town. The part of Theocles [Arcite] was done by Mr Harris; Philander [Palamon], by Mr Betterton; all the women's parts admirably acted, chiefly Celania, a shepherdess, being mad for love; especially in singing several wild and mad songs—"My lodging is on the cold ground", &c. She performed that so charmingly that, not long after, it raised her from her bed on the cold ground to a bed royal.' When Pepys saw it, Celania (Mary Davis) had already danced herself into Charles II's bed (though not before Nell Gwynn had given her a calamitous purge), for he notes that there was 'good acting in it; especially Gosnell comes and sings and dances finely; but, for all that, fell out of the key, so that the musique could not play to her afterwards; and so did Harris go out of the tune to agree with her'. Pepys had an ear. He also had a particular interest in Gosnell, for she had recently been his wife's maid, and he had first seen her on the stage on the occasion of his third visit to *Hamlet*, though to his disappointment she neither danced nor sang, indeed, she did not even speak. Celania, of course, is not the vulgar gaoler's daughter of *The Two Noble Kinsmen*, but elevated into the daughter of a Provost, Master of the Citadel, and though she loses her reason she recovers it and her lover as well. All that is best in Shakespeare's work has gone, in particular the invocations to Mars, Venus and Diana, and the play is on the verge of opera, almost indeed, though unintentionally, of comic opera.

Having so successfully reformed two comedies, Davenant turned to the improvement of tragedy. *Macbeth* appeared to be the one most in need of his attention; moreover, the witches offered irresistible operatic possibilities, and in his mind's eye he already saw them flitting over

Lincoln's Inn Fields on the wires of his ingenious contraptions. So he employed Matthew Locke to write the music, and by 1664 all was ready. As this version of *Macbeth* held the stage, to the exclusion of the original, for almost eighty years, it is worth considering in detail what the age of enlightenment understood by the improvement of Shakespeare.

The first three and a half acts follow Shakespeare's pattern fairly closely. The witches appear aloft, in the foggy filthy air, to the accompaniment of thunder, lightning and shrieking owls, and then are whisked offstage. At least they speak approximately what Shakespeare wrote, but the first words of the next scene prefigure what is to come. Shakespeare's Duncan, it will be remembered, meeting 'a bleeding Sergeant', bluntly asks 'What bloody man is that?', but when Davenant's Duncan meets 'Seyton wounded' (Seyton's part is neatly and economically extended to embrace half a dozen minor characters), he enquires 'What aged man is that?' This gives the formula: the vulgar word and low expression are to be purged and replaced by language altogether more elevated, so that 'Fortune on his damned quarrel smiling, Show'd like a rebel's whore', becomes 'Fortune with her smiles obliged awhile', and Macbeth, instead of carving out his passage till he faced the slave, now cuts his passage to the rebel's person.

Again the witches are whisked across the stage to alight on the heath and greet Macbeth, and when they vanish the astonished Banquo asks,

> Were such things here as we discours'd of now?
> Or have we tasted some infectious herb
> That captivates our reason?

Shakespeare had written,

> Were such things here as we do speak about?
> Or have we eaten on the insane root
> That takes the reason prisoner?

Like Seyton, Macduff is given a much bigger part, becoming indeed the virtuous and conventional hero of the play, and it is he, instead of the superfluous Ross and Angus, who comes to congratulate Macbeth on his new title. 'Why am I then perplext with doubt?' Macbeth asks himself; and then aloud, 'I was reflecting upon past transactions.'

On the change of scene to Inverness we find that Lady Macduff is staying with Lady Macbeth. They have been comforting one another while their husbands were at the wars, but now Lady Macduff's presence is embarrassing, for Lady Macbeth is holding an unread letter in her hand. She turns to her guest with womanly concern:

> Madam, I have observ'd, since you came hither,
> You have been still disconsolate. Pray, tell me,
> Are you in perfect health?

The stratagem fails, eliciting merely a panegyric on Macduff and a commentary on the vanity of martial glory. 'I willingly would read this letter,' mutters Lady Macbeth, 'but her presence hinders me. I must divert her.' So almost impatiently she suggests,

> If you are ill, repose may do you good;
> Y' had best retire, and try if you can sleep.

Lady Macduff takes the hint and withdraws, and her eager hostess exclaims, 'Now I have leisure to peruse this letter.'

When she hears that the King is coming to stay under her battlements she makes her great invocation to the powers of evil, great, that is, as Shakespeare wrote it, but now a mere travesty of the original, concluding,

> make haste, dark night,
> And hide me in a smoke as dark as hell,
> That my keen steel see not the wound it makes,
> Nor heav'n peep through the curtains of the dark
> To cry, hold, hold!

Shakespeare wrote, 'pall thee in the dunnest smoke of hell', 'keen knife', and 'blanket of the dark'. It is the classic example of refinement, defended by Dr Johnson almost a hundred years later. 'The efficacy of this invocation', he wrote, 'is destroyed by the insertion of an epithet now seldom heard but in the stable, and *dun* night may come or go without any other notice than contempt.' Again, the feeling of terror 'is weakened by the name of an instrument used by butchers and cooks in the meanest employments; we do not immediately conceive that any crime of importance is to be committed with a *knife*; or who does not, at last, from the long habit of connecting a knife with sordid offices, feel aversion rather than terror?' Finally, this utmost extravagance of human wickedness 'is so debased by two unfortunate words, that while I endeavour to impress on my reader the energy of the sentiment, I can scarcely check my risibility, when the expression forces itself upon my mind; for who, without some relaxation of his gravity, can hear of the avengers of guilt *peeping through a blanket*?' Such insensibility, or sensibility as Davenant and Johnson would have called it, is almost incomprehensible today, but it explains why these refined versions held the stage so long, and it is important to realise that Shakespeare's reputation was built up largely on the basis of these travesties.

This queasiness over the homely word and image, to which Shakespeare's poetry owes so much of its energy, accounts for the omission of Banquo's 'There's husbandry in heaven, their candles are all out', and for the substitution of 'Sleep that locks up the senses from their care' for 'Sleep that knits up the ravell'd sleave of care'. And Macbeth's fearful vision of his hangman's hand that will 'the multitudinous seas incarnadine' is reduced to

> Can the sea afford
> Water enough to wash away the stains?
> No, they would sooner add a tincture to
> The sea, and turn the green into a red.

The shockingly low scene of the drunken porter is omitted, and in its place we are treated to a few observations about the weather:

> Good morrow, my lord. Have you observ'd
> How great a mist does now possess the air?
> Rising this morning early, I went to look out of my
> Window, and I could scarce see farther than my breath.

Then, to round off the second act and give a certain symmetry to the play, Davenant inserts a completely new scene. Lady Macduff, accompanied by a maid, a servant and her sleeping children, is discovered waiting for her husband on the edge of the haunted heath. As he arrives they hear a hellish song. It is the witches. They prophesy again: 'He will, he shall, he must spill much more blood.' Macduff is shaken, but Lady Macduff remains confident in her innocence. After another song the witches enter dancing and their next prophecy seems 'to foretell some dire predictions':

> Saving thy blood will cause it to be shed.
> He'll bleed by thee, by whom thou first hast bled.
> Thy wife shall, shunning danger, dangers find,
> And fatal be to whom she most is kind.

'Nothing but fiction,' exclaims the courageous lady as they hurry from the scene.

c

We meet the Macduffs again when they have reached the comparative safety of their castle, and another brand-new scene in elevated couplets reveals their secret thoughts:

> *Macduff.* It must be so. Great Duncan's bloody death
> Can have no other author but Macbeth.
> His dagger now is to a sceptre grown;
> From Duncan's grave he has deriv'd his throne.
>   *Lady M.* Ambition urged him to that bloody deed:
> May you be never by ambition led . . .
> I am afraid you have some other end
> Than merely Scotland's freedom to defend.
>   *Macduff.* What if I should
> Assume the sceptre for my country's good?

There is a familiar ring about that, but on the whole the sentiments are irreproachable, and make an admirable foil to the following scene between the guilty couple. 'Duncan is dead! He after life's short fever now sleeps; well,' Macbeth exclaims before delivering the improved version of his invocation to night:

> The crow makes wing to the thick shady grove,
> Good things of day grow dark and overcast,
> Whilst night's black agents to their preys make haste.

We now see the three murderers hiding in the bushes near the palace. Banquo and Fleance come in chatting about the weather. 'We must make haste,' Fleance replies to his father's remark that it looks like rain. 'Our haste concerns us more than being wet,' Banquo warns him as they hurry towards the castle to be in time for the royal feast. The murderers pursue them, a clashing of swords is heard within, and Fleance reappears pursued by one of the murderers, crying 'Murder! help, help, my father's kill'd!'

After another rhyming episode, in which Macduff leaves his wife for England, comes the central scene of the play, the scene to which all else has been but prologue; or rather scenes, for the next two gatherings of the witches are run together. When Hecate has finished her couplets, and music and song are over, the machine descends, that is, a foggy cloud accommodating familiar spirits is let down from the flies, and with it the necessary wires and apparatus for the witches. To the cry 'Come away', Hecate replies, 'I come, I come with all the speed I may.' 'With all the speed I may,' she repeats as she buckles on her harness. 'I will but 'noint and then I mount, I will but &c.' she chants cryptically as she tests the straps. Then away she goes on her besom. A spirit descends for a sip of blood, and one of the witches takes off:

> Now I am furnished for the flight,
> Now I go and now I fly,
> Malkin, my sweet spirit, and I.

The others follow, singing,

> O what a dainty pleasure's this!
> To sail i' th' air,
> While the moon shines fair;
> To sing, to toy, to dance and kiss;
> Over woods, high rocks and mountains,
> Over hills and misty fountains,

and over the audience in the pit. After their aerial frolics they strike a more serious note and descend to the cave to prepare their charms. The ingredients of their cauldron are those of the original recipe, except that, instead of a tiger's, a Dutchman's entrails are thrown in, to the great content of Pepys, engaged in victualling the fleet for the Dutch war. On Hecate's return there is more music and song, taken from Middleton's *Witch*, and Macbeth arrives to hear their further prophecies, delivered, curiously enough, without the aid of apparitions other than Banquo's ghost and a shadow of eight kings.

From now on Davenant shuffles the scenes shamelessly, so contriving to break up the tedious business of Malcolm and Macduff in England, though by delaying the murder of Macduff's family, which is merely reported, he sacrifices the Shakespearean irony. More unfortunate is the introduction of a scene in which Macbeth and Lady Macbeth upbraid each other for the murder of Duncan. In the original play there is not a word of reproach, and it is this, almost as much as their poetry, that makes the couple into truly tragic characters. No doubt the scene is good theatre, as it is certainly Davenant's best contribution, but he sacrifices the whole to the part, precisely what the neo-classic critics accused Shakespeare of doing. It is such intrusive scenes as this that reveal Shakespeare's plastic power and complete comprehension of a theme, and how dangerous it is to fiddle with any detail of the organic whole.

Lady Macbeth is pursued by the ghost of Duncan, and pleads with Macbeth to release her from the horror by resigning the crown:

> *Macbeth.* Can you think that a crime which you did once
> Provoke me to commit? Had not your breath
> Blown my ambition up into a flame
> Duncan had yet been living.
>
> *Lady M.*   You were a man,
> And by the charter of your sex you should
> Have governed me: there was more crime in you
> When you obeyed my counsels than I contracted
> By my giving it. Resign your kingdom now,
> And with your crown put off your guilt.
>   *Macbeth.* Resign the crown! and with it both our lives?
> I must have better counsellors.
>   *Lady M.*   What, your witches?
> Curse on your messengers of hell. Their breath
> Infected first my breath. See me no more.

How completely false it is to Shakespeare and his characters! The ghost appears again, Macbeth calls for his wife's attendants, and they lead her away. The sleep-walking scene is reduced to a few lines of verse.

Davenant is at his excruciating worst in the tremendous third scene of the last act. In the original play, when the terrified servant comes to report the advance of Malcolm and his forces, the half-demented Macbeth turns on him with,

> The devil damn thee black, thou cream-faced loon!
> Where got'st thou that goose look?

This is polished into,

> Now friend, what means thy change of countenance?

Macbeth's tragic meditation on his way of life, 'fall'n into the sear, the yellow leaf', is cut, as also his listless query, 'Canst thou not minister to a mind diseased . . .?' And why, oh why did Davenant change the line 'The way to dusty death. Out, out brief candle!' into 'To their eternal homes: out, out that candle!'?

Lennox plays the part of young Siward and is killed, and when at last Macduff confronts Macbeth he is able to answer prophecy with prophecy:

> *Macbeth.* I have a prophecy secures my life.
> *Macduff.* I have another which tells me I shall have his blood
> Who first shed mine.

They fight, Macbeth falls, and dies with a moral on his lips,

> Farewell, vain world, and what's most vain in it, ambition!

If Davenant's version were an original play it would pass as a remarkable Restoration tragedy, the sillinesses redeemed by flashes of magnificent poetry, and it is only when compared with what Shakespeare wrote that it is so deplorable. The greater part is no more than a pedestrian paraphrase in limp blank verse, and, by attempting to elevate, Davenant succeeds merely in depressing the poetry to his own level. He left nothing to his audience's imagination, and worst of all, perhaps, is his maddening trick of flattening Shakespeare's imagery into literal statement: 'Their daggers unmannerly breech'd with gore' —'being yet unwiped'; 'Screw your courage to the sticking-place'— 'Bring but your courage to the fatal place'; the list could be almost indefinitely extended. Yet it was one of Pepys's favourite plays, and he saw it at least seven times between 1664 and the end of 1668. Above all he liked the 'divertissement', the variety of dancing and music which, though he admitted to be a strange perfection in a tragedy, he considered most proper and appropriate in *Macbeth*.

While walking up Drury Lane on June 7th, 1665, Pepys was disturbed to see two or three houses marked with a red cross, and 'Lord have mercy upon us!' written on the doors. Plague, the worst visitation in its history, had descended on London. The theatres had been closed two days before, and it was not until the end of 1666 that they reopened. It was hard on Davenant; he had had to wait for the Restoration before he could produce Shakespeare, and now another eighteen months were taken from him. But the time was not entirely wasted. His semi-operatic version of *Macbeth* had been a great success, and if any other play of Shakespeare lent itself to similar treatment it was *The Tempest*; Ariel might have been created for Lincoln's Inn Fields, and there was no reason why he should be a solitary flyer; there was, indeed, every reason why he should not be; Shakespeare lacked the right classical balance, which simply demanded a pair of loving spirits. And why not a companion for Caliban?—and a man who had never seen a woman?—and a sister for Miranda? The possibilities were endless. And then he might kill two birds with one stone. Young John Dryden was making a reputation for himself as a dramatist at the rival King's theatre in Drury Lane, and if he could be induced to collaborate in an improved version of *The Tempest* he might change his allegiance to 'the Opera'. Dryden leaped at the opportunity, and soon after the theatres reopened the new *Tempest* was ready for the stage.

Pepys saw it at the beginning of November 1667. The King and Court were there, which always added to his enjoyment, yet the play had no great wit, and was the most innocent he had ever seen. 'Innocent' is not, perhaps, quite the word we should use to-day to describe this Davenant–Dryden version. Davenant's object was to popularise and elevate Shakespeare, to purge him of vulgarity even if that meant rewriting or paraphrasing his lines, and though he had no great objection to indecency he did not go out of his way to introduce or emphasise it. Dryden, on the other hand, had more respect for Shakespeare's poetry, but was only too willing to pander to Restoration taste and sauce his work with smutty innuendo. The version he wrote with Davenant—two girls who had never seen a man, a man who had never seen a woman—gave plenty of scope for the exercise of his talent.

But Lincoln's Inn Fields did not give sufficient scope for the 'divertissement', and when the Duke's company moved to the new Dorset Garden theatre a few years later, the Davenant–Dryden version was slightly altered by Thomas Shadwell, who had already made a competent refinement of *Timon of Athens*. He employed all the latest 'operatic' devices—for opera implied machines as well as music—to ravish the eyes of his audience, and as his version differs very little from that of Davenant and Dryden, and reveals Restoration adaptation in all its childish glory, it is the one described here. The music appears to have been written by John Banister.

The opening stage direction is more than commonly interesting, as it describes the first known experiment in moving the musicians from their box over the stage to a space in front, but then such a large orchestra as the 'opera' demanded could scarcely be accommodated in the old music room.

The front of the stage is opened, and the band of twenty-four violins, with the harpsicals and theorbos which accompany the voices, are played between the pit and the stage. While the overture is playing, the curtain rises, and discovers a new frontispiece, joined to the great pilasters, on each side of the stage. This frontispiece is a noble arch, supported by large wreathed columns.... Behind this is the scene, which represents a thick cloudy sky, a very rocky coast, and a tempestuous sea in perpetual agitation. The tempest (supposed to be raised by magic) has many dreadful objects in it, as several spirits in horrid shapes flying down amongst the sailors, then rising and crossing in the air. And when the ship is sinking, the whole house is darkened, and a shower of fire falls upon them. This is accompanied with lightning and several claps of thunder, to the end of the storm.

We can understand why a wit should write,

> Such noise, such stink, such smoke there was, you'd swear
> *The Tempest* surely had been acted there.

As we should expect from this sensational setting, the shipwreck is a more detailed and lengthy affair than Shakespeare's vivid sketch. We are introduced to Stephano the ship's master, Mustapho his mate, Trincalo the boatswain, and the mariner Ventoso. Their passengers are Alonzo, Duke of Savoy and usurping Duke of Mantua, his son Ferdinand, Antonio usurping Duke of Milan, and Gonzalo, a nobleman of Savoy. The guns break loose, the pumps are manned, they split, and all shift for themselves.

In the midst of the shower of fire, the scene changes. The cloudy sky, rocks and sea vanish; and, when the lights return, discover that beautiful part of the island, which was the habitation of Prospero: 'Tis composed of three walks of cypress-trees; each side-walk leads to a cave, in one of which Prospero keeps his daughters, in the other Hippolito: the middle walk is of great depth, and leads to an open part of the island.

All this is not very clear to the audience at first glance, but through the smother we can descry two figures, and the dialogue begins with Prospero's startling question, 'Miranda, where's your sister?' As Dorinda is watching the storm there follows a shortened version of Prospero's retrospective narrative. The verse is severely cut, but approximately Shakespeare's, except that we learn that there are two freckled hag-born whelps on the island, Caliban and his twin-sister Sycorax. Moreover, Ariel has a gentle spirit for his love, Milcha, who flutters down to his assistance. 'Hence, with diligence,' Prospero commands them, and they both fly up, crossing in the air, apparently a favourite aerobatic turn. Caliban enters cursing in prose, and when he and Prospero leave the stage, Dorinda joins Miranda. She describes the wreck, and then with artless innuendo the two debate the burning questions, What is a man? and how Prospero came to be their father. Miranda longs to see the effect of his great art, but Dorinda more longs to see a man.

The scene changes to the wilder part of the Island. 'Tis composed of divers sorts of trees, and barren places, with a prospect of the sea at a great distance.

According to Dryden, the comical parts of the sailors were written mostly by Davenant, the spicier ingredients no doubt being added by himself. Pepys found their scenes a little tedious, but, though they bear little resemblance to Shakespeare, they are very funny in places. Stephano proclaims himself Duke of the island, with his two rebellious subjects, Mustapho and Ventoso, as viceroys, but Trincalo, master of a butt of sack, refuses to recognise the regime, declares war, conscripts Caliban as his subject and strengthens his claim to the island by espousing the 'monstrous fair' heiress Sycorax.

Cypress Trees and a Cave.

Prospero has an interview with Hippolito to balance that with Miranda. The young man is the real Duke of Mantua, brought up in solitude since Alonzo tried to drown him along with Prospero and his daughters. As he has never seen a woman, Prospero warns him of these dangerous enemies of men, and Hippolito promises to shun them,

> But let them not provoke me, for I'm sure
> I shall not then forbear them.

The situation is tricky, for owing to the wreck Prospero has had to take Hippolito into his own cell, and when his daughters approach he warns them of the dangers lying in a wild young man. 'Do they run wild about the woods?' Dorinda asks. 'No,' Prospero replies, 'they are wild within doors, in chambers and in closets. No woman can come near them but she feels a pain full nine months.' The girls are prepared to risk that and Dorinda contrives a meeting with Hippolito, when both are overcome by strange and pleasurable emotions.

A Wild Island.

The central operatic entertainment now begins in earnest. Gonzalo, Alonzo and Antonio have spoken a few lines of more or less Shakespearean verse when they hear a flourish of music. It grows louder, the stage opens in several places, there is another flourish of voices under the stage, and three devils emerge singing 'Where does the black fiend Ambition reside?' It is a lengthy song, and after the fourth chorus Pride, Fraud, Rapine and Murder appear one by one, each with his appropriate lines. Devils and Deadly Sins take hands and dance round the miserable mortals before vanishing to a final chorus. But the worst is yet to come. As they stumble out a devil rises just before them and sings, 'Arise, ye subterranean winds!' Twelve winds rise and dance, after which some of them sink again while the remainder drive their victims off the stage. The music now changes from fiendish to celestial and Ferdinand follows the voices of Ariel and Milcha singing 'Come unto these yellow sands' and 'Full fathom five'.

The Cypress Tree and a Cave.

Prospero interviews Miranda and is relieved to find that, although she has seen Hippolito at a distance, she has not fallen in love. Dorinda, however, is a problem. Nothing will prevent her meeting Hippolito again, and Prospero can only warn her not to be too kind, for that is the way to lose him. 'I hope you have not cozened me again,' she says as she hurries towards her man.

A Wild Island.

Ariel and Milcha now show the castaways their whole repertory of tricks, flying in and out with tables of food, and changing bottles of wine into water, or 'mere element', as Trincalo calls it. Then when Ferdinand appears again Ariel repeats his last words—'Here I am', 'Follow me', 'One step further'—until Ferdinand tries if the echo will answer when he sings his sorrows to the murmurs of the brook. It does, and we hear this pretty song:

Ferdinand.	Go thy way.
Ariel.	Go thy way.
Ferdinand.	Why shouldst thou stay?
Ariel.	Why shouldst thou stay?
Ferdinand.	Where the winds whistle, and where the streams creep.
	Under yond willow-tree fain would I sleep.
	Then let me alone,
	For 'tis time to be gone.
Ariel.	For 'tis time to be gone.

And so on. Pepys found this 'curious piece of musick in half sentences' much the best thing in the play and so mighty pretty that he got Banister to write it out for him.

In the end all works out according to Prospero's plan, but not before Ferdinand has wounded Hippolito in a duel, for the ignorant young man, uncertain of what he wants with woman, desires them all, Miranda included. However, he is cured by Dorinda with a balsam fetched by Ariel; there is a grand reconciliation scene, the lovers are paired off, and all is set for the finale.

The scene changes to the Rocks, with the arch of Rocks, and calm Sea. Music playing on the Rocks.

Neptune, Amphitrite, Oceanus and Tethys appear in a chariot drawn by sea-horses, on each side of which are Sea-Gods and Goddesses, Tritons and Nereids. 'This,' comments Alonzo, 'is prodigious.' It is indeed: a masque to make Ben Jonson and Inigo Jones shift in their graves with envy. When, in a quartet, Amphitrite pleads for a calm voyage for the mortals, Neptune orders Oceanus to put on his serenest looks, and Aeolus to muzzle his roaring boys. Aeolus descends, singing, 'Come down, my blusterers, swell no more.' The winds fly down from the four quarters of heaven and are driven into the earth's entrails, while the chorus sings 'Send a calm', at each repeat of which the Tritons seem to sound their wreathed and shelly trumpets. After a symphony of music and more songs, choruses and dances the scene changes to the Rising Sun. Spirits appear in the air, and Ariel flies out of the sun towards the pit. Hovering over the audience, he and his attendants sing 'Where the bee sucks', though not without altering 'On the bat's back' to the more poetical 'On the swallow's wings'. Then in rhyming verse he bids farewell to his master. Prospero replies:

> Thou hast been always diligent and kind.
> Farewell, my long-loved Ariel! thou shalt find
> I will preserve thee ever in my mind.
> Henceforth this isle to the afflicted be
> A place of refuge, as it was to me:
> The promises of blooming spring live here,
> And all the blessings of the ripening year;
> On my retreat let heaven and nature smile,
> And ever flourish the Enchanted Isle.

Ariel is whisked back into the stage, the curtain descends, and the revels are over.

It is just as well, for this version of Shakespeare's loveliest play is one of the most unpleasant of the adaptations; all innocence is lost, and the delicate fantasy debased to a salacious musical comedy. The poetry is sacrificed to pantomime spectacle and to the nasty little Dorinda–Hippolito sub-plot, so that there is neither time nor occasion for Prospero's lines on 'this insubstantial pageant' or for his resolution to drown his book 'deeper than did ever plummet sound'. But again, it is just as well; the poetry would ring as false on the lips of this Prospero sunk to the level of Pandarus as it would be incomprehensible to any of the other characters. Dryden tells us that he never wrote anything with more delight, and doubtless the outrage is mainly his, though Davenant must share the blame, for he was ultimately responsible, and revised the work of his young collaborator.

Davenant died in April, 1668, shortly after his production of *The Tempest*. He was only sixty-two, and had had a bare six years in which to introduce Shakespeare to the new age. Yet his life's work had been accomplished. He had popularised his idol. He had produced nine of the plays, some of them, it is true, altered almost beyond recognition, and probably none of them completely escaped his reforming hand. *Henry VIII*, for example, appears to have been all gorgeous shows and processions, and *Romeo and Juliet* was presented in a very strange guise. This was a version by James Howard, who converted it into a tragi-comedy by preserving the hero and heroine alive, and so popular was it that when the tragedy was revived it was played alternately, tragical one day and tragicomical the next, for a considerable run. The King's Company in Drury Lane were not slow to profit from Davenant's success. They had already produced a few of the plays, and in 1669 secured a patent to perform those that were not already the property of the Duke's, and by the time the companies amalgamated in 1682 they had produced nine of them.

The reputation of Shakespeare had changed vastly between 1660 and 1668. Then his plays had been read by only a few, now they were seen, even if seen in mangled versions rather than heard in their original forms, by crowded houses who clamoured for more. This was mainly the work of Davenant. Moreover, he had handed on his work to the next generation. It was he who first taught Dryden to admire Shakespeare, as it was he who fired Betterton with the desire to emulate Burbage by playing all the great Shakespearean heroes, and to find out more about the dramatist to whose work he was indebted for his success. Dryden and Betterton had thirty to forty years of active life before them, time enough to consolidate and advance what Davenant had begun.

III

SHAKESPEAR REFINED

AMONG the first to profit from the pioneering work of Davenant and the Shakespeare boom were the Restoration booksellers. Anonymous old plays in their stocks were recklessly advertised as Shakespeare's, three of them being bound together in Charles II's library and labelled 'Shakespear, Vol. I'. And not only anonymous plays, but plays by Peele, Chettle, Fletcher, Marlowe, Middleton, Massinger and others were gaily fathered on Shakespeare in their play-lists. It was an old game, for even while he was alive enterprising stationers had published other men's work under the magic name, and it was their example that inspired Philip Chetwind to reprint the folio in 1664 with 'seven Playes never before Printed in Folio'. All of these had appeared in quarto in Shakespeare's lifetime, three with his name on the title-page, three with his initials and one anonymously. The last was *Sir John Oldcastle*, another *A Yorkshire Tragedy*, and a third *Pericles*, all of which Jaggard had proposed issuing in his abortive collected edition of 1619.

The only genuine Shakespeare play, at least in part, and incomparably therefore the most important of the seven, is *Pericles*, which Heminge and Condell had omitted from the first folio, presumably because they knew that Shakespeare had written only the last three acts. It seems to have been the first of his plays to be revived at the Restoration, and possibly the one in which Betterton made his name, for he acted in the production and Pericles was one of his favourite and most notable parts. To-day the play is seldom read and rarely acted, and yet it contains some of the finest of Shakespeare's late poetry, and the heroine, the silver-voiced Marina, is a worthy companion of Imogen, Perdita and Miranda.

The other four plays are of little value. Perhaps the best is *The London Prodigal*, a domestic comedy of a rascally son who is redeemed by the love of the wife he has won by fraud. *The Puritan Widow* is an anti-Puritan farce in which George Pyeboard and Captain Idle, by their fortune-telling and conjuring, almost win the hands of the widow and her daughter, and *Thomas Lord Cromwell* is an ingenuous chron-

icle history, a series of episodes with little motivation or plot, sympa-
thetically describing the rise and fall of Henry VIII's minister.
Locrine is an older play than any of the others. It was published in
1595 as a 'lamentable tragedy, no less pleasant than profitable', and
there are indeed passages of pleasantry, albeit unintentional. The verse
reads like a parody of early Marlowe:

> These arms, my lords, these never-daunted arms . . .
> This heart, my lords, this ne'er appalled heart.

Locrine, King of Britain, defeats Humber the Scythian King in
battle:

> But stay, methinks I hear some shrieking noise,
> That draweth near to our pavilion.

It is Humber's wife, Estrild:

> So fair a dame mine eyes did never see;
> With floods of woes she seems o'erwhelm'd to be.

Locrine takes her as his mistress, and his wife leads a rebellion in which
he is defeated and kills himself. There are two ghosts, and the profitable part of the tragedy is supplied by Ate, Goddess of Revenge, as
chorus. It is scarcely a Shakespearean piece, but then, when it was
originally issued the publisher claimed merely that it was 'Newly set
foorth, overseene and corrected by W.S.' It is just possible that W.S.
was Shakespeare at the beginning of his career, though as unlikely as
his having had a hand in any of the other plays, save *Pericles*. But
Chetwind knew his business; they had long ago been ascribed to
Shakespeare, and their inclusion in his third folio was an additional
inducement to buy.

Apparently the lively and eccentric Duchess of Newcastle lost no
time in reading the volume, for in a letter of 1664 she mentions *Henry
V* and *Antony and Cleopatra*, neither of which was produced at the
Restoration. Maybe she got her knowledge of some of the other plays
from the theatre, for was she not herself a dramatist, author of *The
Humorous Lovers*, according to Pepys, 'the most ridiculous thing that
ever was wrote'? But even if she was no more than a scribbler and a
pretender to learning and poetry, her letter is a remarkable effusion.
Shakespeare, she wrote in her irrepressible enthusiasm, was a natural
orator as well as a natural poet, who so expressed to the life all sorts of
people and all sorts of passion, that one would think that he himself had

been those people and suffered those passions. And she paid him the greatest compliment she could by suggesting that one would think he had been metamorphosed from a man to a woman, for how otherwise could he so have drawn Cleopatra to the life? Doubtless the Duchess tended to identify herself with the Egyptian Queen, a woman whose infinite variety custom could not stale, but there were others: Nan Page, Mrs Ford, 'Bettrice', Mrs Quickly and many more.

Pepys too was reading his folio, and spent the afternoon of Sunday, November 13th, 1664, learning 'to bee or not to bee' by heart. But presumably he had got hold of a quarto of *Othello* when, on that August morning of 1666, he read it on his way to Deptford by water. Unfortunately he had just read *The Adventures of Five Hours*, and after that *Othello*, which he had always thought a mighty good play, seemed but a mean thing. The Duchess of Newcastle was a shrewder critic of Shakespeare than Pepys. And yet when he saw *The Taming of the Shrew* a few months later he was sufficiently discriminating to consider that too but a mean thing. For it was not Shakespeare's play that he saw, but another, and particularly unpleasant, adaptation.

Encouraged by Davenant's successful reformations of Shakespeare for the Duke's company, John Lacy of the King's, Charles II's favourite comedian, tried his hand at the game. *The Taming of the Shrew*, the most boisterous and farcical of the comedies, was his natural choice, but as the role of Petruchio did not offer quite enough scope for the low comedy in which he excelled, he took that of his servant Grumio, changed the name to Sauny, expanded the part, and called his product *Sauny the Scot*. When it was published it was with the couplet,

> Then I'll cry out, swell'd with Poetick Rage,
> 'Tis I, John Lacy, have reformed your stage.'

Shakespeare reformed indeed! The verse is reduced to prose, the scene changed from Padua to London, Lucentio becomes the Restoration Winlove, Katharine, for some reason or other, Margaret, Christopher Sly is omitted, and the fifth act rewritten. All this in addition to the expansion of Grumio's part and his transformation into a Scottish Sandy—and yet, a Yorkshireman as much as a Scot, for Lacy came from Doncaster, and the gibberish that Sauny speaks has in it as much of the West Riding as of North Britain. Pepys, and presumably the greater part of the audiences, did not understand it, which was just as well. Yet in spite of this the wretched farce kept the original play off the stage, and lingered on for more than two centuries.

As an example of Lacy's reformation of Shakespeare, here is Sauny trying to dissuade the aged Woodall (Gremio) from wooing Bianca: 'You're troubled with a great weakness i' th' bottom of your bally. What sid ye dea with a young maiden?' Again, when Margaret protests that Petruchio's face almost turns her stomach to look at it, Sauny interjects, 'Gud, an your stomach wamble to see his face, what will ye dea when ye see his a . . e?' There is more in a similar vein with a similar vocabulary. Then, we are admitted to the bridal-chamber, where Petruchio orders Peg to undress. She asks him to send his men away and call for maids. 'Maids?' Petruchio cries, 'I have no such vermin about my house; any of these will do as well. Here, Sauny! Come hither, sirrah, and undress your mistress.' Sauny begins to do so, and the stage direction as much as his speech affords a glimpse of what a Restoration audience thought so funny.

The last act is altered almost out of recognition. Once Margaret is back in her father's house she becomes the shrew again: 'I'll make Petruchio glad to wipe my shoes or walk my horse ere I have done with him.' But her rebellion fails. Petruchio lets her talk until she can talk no more and relapses into sullen silence. Then he protests that she is ill, and calls a barber to draw a tooth. She drives the barber away, but as she does not speak Petruchio pretends that she is dead, and orders Sauny to fetch a bier on which she is tied. This is the breaking-point, and Margaret capitulates: 'Hold, hold, my dear Petruchio; you have overcome me, and I beg your pardon.' *The Taming of the Shrew* is itself an adaptation, and Shakespeare, had he been alive, could not, and would not, have objected in principle to the Restoration adaptation of his plays, though he might have read them a little ruefully and wondered at the havoc that well-meaning improvers made of his poetry. Yet even that most tolerant of men must have protested at *Sauny the Scot*.

But a far greater man than Lacy, far greater than Davenant who had inspired him, was at work on the improvement of Shakespeare. This was Dryden, whose version of the Antony and Cleopatra story, *All for Love*, appeared in 1678. Yet *All for Love* is scarcely an adaptation of Shakespeare's *Antony and Cleopatra*; it is at once a concentration and a diffusion. Shakespeare's tragedy is the most cosmic of all his plays, and this defect, as the age of enlightenment considered it, Dryden remedied by beginning the story after the battle of Actium and by a strict observance of the unities, particularly of action, so that no comic relief or other irrelevancy was allowed to intrude. Moreover the verse is Dryden's own, and though there are echoes of Shakespeare, as in the famous description of Cleopatra on Cydnus, *All for Love* is really an original play on a Shakespearean theme.

Troilus and Cressida, which soon followed, is another matter, and in his preface Dryden defends the practice of revising 'the divine Shakespear'. 'It must be allowed to the present age, that the tongue in general is so much refined since Shakespear's time, that many of his words, and more of his phrases, are scarce intelligible. And of those which we understand, some are ungrammatical, others coarse; and his whole style is so pestered with figurative expressions, that it is as affected as it is obscure.' That is a matter of opinion, and the present age is less confident of its own greater refinement, but it was the opinion that led Davenant to paraphrase Shakespeare's unintelligible phrases and laboriously unpick, or impatiently sever, the complex knots of his imagery. Yet it was not only the rusty language that needed polishing; *Troilus and Cressida* was even more of a muddle than most of Shakespeare's plays, so that Dryden 'undertook to remove that heap of rubbish under which many excellent thoughts lay wholly buried'. Accordingly, he remodelled the plot, threw out many unnecessary characters, and improved others that were imperfectly developed, such as Hector, Pandarus, Thersites and Troilus himself. Then he regrouped the scenes more coherently to suit the new picture-frame stage, and wrote another fifth act. 'I need not say', he added casually, 'that I have refined his language, which before was obsolete.'

Although the product of this ferocious treatment is the best of the Restoration adaptations, it is a poor substitute for the magnificent, though admittedly sprawling, play that Shakespeare wrote. Fortunately Dryden does not refine the poetry overmuch, but some of the best passages are omitted, and the main refinement is the character of Cressida, which accounts for the new tragic ending and alternative title, *Truth Found too Late*. Cressida is not Shakespeare's faithless wanton, and only dissembles love to Diomede so that she and her father can escape to Troy. But Troilus overhears her apparent surrender to Diomede and, when the three meet in the last scene, accuses her of infidelity. She protests her innocence, but the philandering Diomede swears that she is false; Troilus believes him, and Cressida stabs herself. Too late Troilus discovers the truth, and is about to fall on his sword when he remembers Diomede. They fight, and the engagement becomes general. Then Achilles enters with his Myrmidons; the Trojans are surrounded, but Troilus kills Diomede before Achilles kills Troilus. 'All the Trojans die upon the place, Troilus last.' It is good theatre, but conventional tragedy, and a remarkably unrefined catastrophe.

Dryden's entry into the refining business encouraged a host of smaller men. Shadwell, as he himself put it, 'made *Timon of Athens* into a play', and Edward Ravenscroft found another 'heap of rubbish' in *Titus Andronicus*, which he modestly claimed to have made into a real structure, 'the language not only refined, but many scenes entirely new, besides most of the principal characters heightened, and the plot much increased'. His chief addition is in the finale, when Tamora stabs her blackamoor child, and Aaron, stretched upon the rack, cries,

> She has outdone me in my own art—
> Outdone me in murder—kill'd her own child.
> Give it me—I'll eat it.

The curtain falls as flames envelop the racked and writhing body of the Moor.

Between 1680 and 1682 the rivalry of the King's and Duke's produced a further spate of adaptations. For the King's at Dorset Garden, John Crowne turned out *Henry the Sixth, the First Part*, and *The Misery of Civil War*, a version of Part Three and half of Part Two. Tom D'Urfey replied for the Duke's at Drury Lane with *The Injured Princess, or the Fatal Wager*, in which Pisanio's daughter is raped off-stage, while on the stage Pisanio himself is blinded by Cloten. One is almost tempted to question the so much vaunted refinement of the Restoration age. A still more curious piece is Otway's *Fall of Caius Marius*, which, despite its Roman title, is the story of Romeo and Juliet. Presumably classical Rome was more refined than Renaissance Verona. Lavinia (Juliet) wakes before young Marius (Romeo) dies of the poison, thus giving time for a lovers' parting, a pretty device that held the stage for a long time. Lavinia stabs herself, and the ruffling Sulpitius (Mercutio) dies last, to Shakespeare's prose and a triplet of Otway's doggerel.

There was even worse to come when Nahum Tate entered the ranks of the adapters. *Richard II* is his best effort because he made

D

relatively few alterations, though he could not resist exploiting the disappearing table of *The Tempest* just before Richard's murder. Nor are the alterations very serious in *The Ingratitude of a Commonwealth*, his version of *Coriolanus*—until he comes to the last scene. It is noticeable that all these refiners prided themselves on improving Shakespeare's final scenes. Coriolanus is murdered by the Volscians, but he does not die at once, nor before mortally wounding Aufidius, who has conceived a guilty passion for Virgilia. Owing to news of an imminent battle, the stage is deserted by all save the helpless Coriolanus, the not quite so helpless Aufidius, and Tate's new villain of the piece, Nigridius. Aufidius tells Coriolanus that Virgilia is his captive, and that his last act will be to ravish her before his eyes. But Virgilia has given herself 'a Roman wound', and dies shortly after her would-be ravisher. Coriolanus then asks the Gods for news of his mother and son, and Nigridius tells him how, having killed old Menenius, he threw 'the tortured brat, with limbs all broke' into Volumnia's arms. Tate knew his *King Lear* better than any of his contemporaries, and this accounts for his stage direction, 'Enter Volumnia distracted, with Young Martius under her arm.' He also knew his *King John*, and the grandmother Volumnia outraves the mother Constance before seizing a partisan and felling Nigridius. The play ends with the death of Coriolanus holding the body of his wife in one arm, the body of his son in the other. After this orgy of rape, murder, madness, suicide and torture, Shakespeare's play with its single assassination seems classically austere and singularly free from need of such refinement. Moreover, the carnage is strangely at odds with Tate's own dramatic theory: 'Otherwise I must have encumbered the stage with dead bodies, which conduct makes many tragedies conclude with unseasonable jests.'

The quotation is from the Preface to his adaptation of *King Lear*, and part of his apology for 'making the tale conclude in a success for the innocent distressed persons'. This happy ending necessarily followed from his introduction of a romance between Edgar and Cordelia (as there is no King of France in his version, she is unmarried and free), for it would never do if the heroine were to perish, and, though the old king himself was expendable, his death would sully the new-found happiness of his young daughter. Tate had found a treasure, 'a Heap of Jewels so dazzling in their Disorder' that he had set to work with such enthusiasm and so polished and strung them together that they shone again in his new comedy of *King Lear*.

The real object of the pious Tate, versifier of the Psalms, was to play up the love interest, not only the innocent love of Cordelia and Edgar, but also the unholy passion of Edmund for Goneril, Regan—and Cordelia as well. This had the advantage that the less interesting part of the play, the agony of Lear, could be reduced, and the Fool omitted altogether. When Lear disclaims Cordelia in the second scene (Shakespeare's first) he puts the matter in a nutshell:

> Now, minion, I perceive
> The truth of what has been suggested to us,
> Thy fondness for the rebel son of Gloster.

We soon discover that the king's suspicions are well founded, but, having just been rejected by the mercenary Burgundy, Cordelia mistrusts Edgar's advances and will have nothing to do with him. He meditates suicide:

> How easy now
> 'Twere to defeat the malice of my trail,
> And leave my griefs on my sword's reeking point;
> But love detains me from death's peaceful cell,
> Still whispering me, Cordelia's in distress;

and he disguises himself as a Bedlam beggar.

The main plot, if such it may still be called, pursues a course not unlike Shakespeare's, though grievously cut and mangled. Here is Lear in the storm:

> Blow, winds, and burst your cheeks! rage louder yet!
> Fantastic lightning, singe, singe my white head! . . .
> Rumble thy fill, fight whirlwind, rain and fire!

Edmund receives love-letters from Goneril and Regan, and witnesses Cordelia's appeal to Gloster to succour her father, while she and her gentlewoman, Arante, fly to find him on the heath:

> Bold in my virgin innocence I'll fly,
> My royal father to relieve, or die.

Edmund, who has been casting lascivious glances at Cordelia, overhears and confides to the audience:

> I'll bribe two ruffians shall at a distance follow,
> And seize 'em in some desert place; and there
> Whilst one retains her, t'other shall return
> T' inform me where she's lodg'd: I'll be disguis'd too.

> Whilst they are poaching for me, I'll to the Duke
> With these dispatches: then to th' field,
> Where, like the vig'rous Jove, I will enjoy
> This Semele in a storm; 'twill deaf her cries.

It is a favourite diversion with Tate, and indeed with almost all the Restoration refiners. But of course the ruffians seize Cordelia outside the hovel of Edgar, who drives them off and turns to their intended victims:

> O, speak, what are ye, that appear to be
> O' th' tender sex, and yet unguarded wander
> Through the dead mazes of this dreadful night,
> Where, though at full, the clouded moon scarce darts
> Imperfect glimmerings?

He reveals himself, and Cordelia, no longer bashful, cries, 'Come to my arms, thou dearest, best of men!'

As a nice dramatic contrast to this we hear Regan's invitation to Edmund to await her in 'the grotto within the lower grove', while his father's eyes are put out. 'And there', he leers, 'I may expect a comforter, ha, madam?' But few people would object to Tate's removal of Gloster's blinding from the stage to the wings.

As in the original play, the king's forces are defeated in battle, Lear and Cordelia taken prisoner, but then all suffers a rare Tatefication. We see the old king and his daughter in prison, the entry of the executioners with cords, Lear's felling of two soldiers with a borrowed partisan, and then—Enter Edgar, Albany and forces: 'Oh, my Edgar!' 'My dear Cordelia!' It only remains to tie up the loose ends into a happy knot. Albany, less generous than Shakespeare's duke, restores Lear to his kingdom, 'save what part yourself conferr'd on us', but Lear will have none of it and gives it to Cordelia:

> winds catch the sound,
> And bear it on your rosy wings to heav'n,
> Cordelia is a queen.

Cordelia herself he gives to Edgar:

> here's the fair amends . . .
> Thou serv'dst distress'd Cordelia; take her crown'd.

And Lear has a plan for his elderly companions, too. Gloster, Kent and he are to pass their remaining days retired to some close cell, calmly reflecting on their fortunes past, and cheered with relation of the prosperous reign of Edgar and Cordelia.

In spite of the protests of Addison, this silly novelette version of one of the world's greatest tragedies, this shopgirl's romance, held the stage until the middle of the nineteenth century, and was even defended by Johnson on the ground that Cordelia's death is merely shocking, and offends man's natural love of justice.

For almost twenty years after the amalgamation of the rival companies in 1682, and Betterton's move to Drury Lane, there was only one important adaptation of Shakespeare. This was *The Fairy Queen*, an operatic version of *A Midsummer Night's Dream*, put on in 1692 at the Dorset Garden theatre, which now specialised in spectacular forms of entertainment. How glorious the spectacle was is indicated by the stage directions; for example: 'The scene changes to a Garden of Fountains. A Sonata plays while the sun rises. . . . Before the trees stand rows of marble columns, which support many walks. . . . The stairs are adorned with figures on pedestals. . . . Near the top, vast quantities of water break out of the hills, and fall in mighty cascades to the bottom of the scene to feed the fountains which are on each side. In the middle of the stage is a very large fountain, where the water rises about twelve foot.' *The Fairy Queen* is still remembered for Purcell's music, but for more than two hundred years its childish mechanical marvels had a deplorable influence on the staging of Shakespeare.

Thus, when the next wave of improvements came in the first decade of the eighteenth century, Charles Gildon's *Measure for Measure*, George Granville's *Jew of Venice*, and Charles Burnaby's *Love Betrayed*, a dreary vulgarisation of *Twelfth Night*, were all slashed and mangled to make room for masques. One of the last adaptations of the period, not this time a 'musical' but a dull and smutty version of *The Merry Wives of Windsor*, was John Dennis's *Comical Gallant*, but the best was Colley Cibber's racy melodrama, *Richard III*. It is also the funniest, though unintentionally so, for it is a patchwork made up of half a dozen of the histories. Evidently Cibber was haunted by the opening of 2 *Henry IV*, where Northumberland hears of the defeat and death of his son Hotspur. Thus, in the first scene of his *Richard III*, Henry VI asks for news of his murdered son in almost identical words, though his lamentation is that of Bolingbroke in *Richard II* ('O, who can hold a fire in his hand / By thinking on the frosty Caucasus?') and of Richard himself ('Tell them the lamentable fall of me'). The next scene, that of his own murder, is taken from 3 *Henry VI*. A little genuine *Richard III* with Cibber's improvements is followed by the Lady Anne's quoting the first lines of 1 *Henry VI*, which after all can be made to apply just as well to the sixth as to the fifth Henry, though it is the fourth whom she next quotes, very much from memory, when her crowned head lies so uneasily. Richard's head is equally uneasy, but when he unburdens himself he returns to Northumberland with his 'fever-weakened joints'. The night before Bosworth is, of course, indistinguishable from the night before Agincourt; again 'The hum of either army stilly sounds', and before the battle it is only natural for Richard III to encourage his army with a paraphrase from Henry V:

> But when the blast of war blows in our ears,
> Let us be tigers in our fierce deportment.

It is a particularly felicitous touch that the dying Richard should resume his 'fever-weakened joints' speech, and expire with the words of Northumberland on his lips. Cibber's *Richard III* is still not quite dead—few actors can resist his famous line, one of the most famous in 'Shakespeare': 'Off with his head—so much for Buckingham'—and it well deserves its popularity, for it is as good as *Savonarola Brown*.

By 1710, when Betterton died, most of Shakespeare's plays had been refined according to the neo-classical rules of unity and symmetry. The worst was over, but the half-century since the Restoration had set a precedent for tampering with the texts that was not forgotten for another two, though the problem of the eighteenth and nineteenth centuries was to fit the plays into a stage for which they were not written, and into which they simply would not go: a picture-frame stage lavishly encumbered with scenic splendour. Yet, thanks to Davenant, Dryden and Betterton, Shakespeare had been not only refined but rediscovered; rediscovered perhaps only because he had been refined, and so made acceptable to Restoration taste.

Dryden, however, was active in the cause of Shakespeare not only as a refiner and populariser of his plays, but also as a critic, and by the time he succeeded Davenant as Poet Laureate his opinion in literary matters was scarcely open to question. There was, it is true, Thomas Rymer, who was charmingly ironical about *Othello, or the Tragedy of the Handkerchief* ('Had it been Desdemona's Garter the Sagacious Moor might have smelt a Rat'), which, though it has 'some ramble of Comical Wit, is plainly none other than a Bloody Farce'. Shakespeare could

turn out a tolerable comedy, but as for tragedy, alas, you see how 'tis—
a little o'erparted: his brains are turned, he raves and rambles without
any coherence or any rules to control him. Lack of rule (Jonson had
called it 'want of art'), that was the trouble, for how can you write
tragedy without following the rules of Aristotle? Rymer wanted 'regularity and roundness of design' and a Chorus, which would ensure
that the dramatist did not juggle with the unities. In short, he wanted
English tragedy to be shackled with all the neo-classical paraphernalia
that were paralysing most of the drama of Europe.

Dryden had some sympathy for Rymer, though not much. He, too,
believed in a classical coherence, lucidity, balance, symmetry and
unity, but rules are not sacrosanct, and English drama was not to be
perpetually bound by precepts laid down two thousand years ago.
Thus, though he admits what he considers to be Shakespeare's faults,
his bombast, obscurity, incoherence, and occasional insipidity and dull-
ness, they are largely the faults of the barbaric age in which he wrote,
and can be refined away—had he not himself done so?—and what remains is pure gold. Shakespeare had the largest and most comprehen-
sive soul of all poets, and many times wrote better than any poet in any
age. He is 'the divine Shakespear' who began dramatic poetry amongst
us and, 'untaught by any, and as Ben Jonson tells us, without learning,
by the force of his own genius performed so much, that in a manner
he has left no praise for any who come after him'. He admired Jonson,
but he loved Shakespear; as for Fletcher, he was but 'a limb of
Shakespear'. Dryden had spoken, and there was no more to be said:
Shakespeare was the greatest of the Elizabethans, the greatest poet and
dramatist in our language. But the perpetuation of Jonson's *obiter
dictum* that 'Shakespeare wanted art', in the uncritical and degraded
form of 'wanted learning', was to prove an endless source of misunderstanding and mischief.

Betterton agreed with Dryden, and his veneration for Shakespeare
induced him to make a journey to Stratford to gather what information
he could about the dramatist to whose plays he owed his fortune and
reputation as an actor. And so, at the beginning of the eighteenth century, almost a century after Shakespeare's death, the first earnest pilgrim arrived on the hallowed scene. Thomas Fuller, it is true, had been
there before him during the Commonwealth period, but that had been
in the way of routine, collecting material for his *Worthies of England*,
published in 1662. Fuller was fanciful rather than informative,

contenting himself with recording that the poet died in '16 . .', and had
many combats with Ben Jonson, in which he imagined Shakespeare as
a nimble English man-of-war, Jonson as a ponderous Spanish galleon.
And even in the 1690's Shakespeare's growing reputation had been
enough to attract curious sightseers. Thus, in 1693 a Mr Dowdall had
been shown over the church by an ancient verger who told him that
Shakespeare had been bound apprentice to a butcher, before fleeing to
London, where he was 'received into the playhouse as a serviture'. And
in the following year a young Oxford man, William Hall, 'went to
visit ye ashes of the Great Shakespear', buried, according to his in-
formant, presumably the venerable verger, 'seventeen foot deep'. Dowdall and Hall should be celebrated in Stratford as the first recorded
devotees of the Shakespeare cult, harbingers of the millions of pilgrims
who have since done homage at the shrine. But Betterton was the first
to come for something more than idle curiosity or devotional reasons.

He looked up the town records and church register, and found that
Shakespeare's family was of good social standing, being mentioned as
gentlemen, that his father was a considerable dealer in wool, and had
ten children. (Here he was wrong, for he was confused by the family
of another John Shakespeare.) William went to the grammar school,
entered his father's business, married 'the daughter of one Hathaway',
by whom he had three daughters (presumably he thought that Hamnet
was a girl), two of whom were married, Judith to Thomas Quiney and
Susanna to Dr John Hall, whose only daughter, though twice married,
died childless. It was a biographical beginning, and a demand for Shakespeareana had been created. The supply was not slow in forthcoming.

Betterton probably brought back to London the tradition of the
deer-stealing, which first gained currency at this time, and he would
certainly hear of the verses that Shakespeare was said to have 'fanned
up' on his friend John Combe, buried near him in Stratford church.
But apparently he did not know the anecdote recorded in his diary by
John Ward, the vicar who had made the note that he must read the
plays, that 'Shakespear, Drayton, and Ben Jhonson, had a merry meeting, and itt seems drank too hard, for Shakespear died of a feavour there
contracted'.

Then, there were traditions still to be gleaned from the old actors in
the London theatres. Davenant, of course, had been fertile in their
supply: the Earl of Southampton had once given Shakespeare £1,000;
he himself possessed 'an amicable letter' written to the poet by King

James, though unfortunately he had mislaid it; and in his cups he liked to hint that William Davenant might be more than the literary son of Shakespeare. The 'magotie-headed' antiquary, John Aubrey, extracted some of the information for his *Brief Lives* from Davenant, and most of the remainder from the old actor William Beeston. Though not very helpful biographically, it is at least picturesque. Shakespeare was a butcher like his father, and when he killed a calf he used to do it in a high style and make a speech. 'He was a handsome well shap't man,' temperate, and if invited to a debauch would plead that he 'was in paine'.

Dryden died in 1700, Betterton in 1710, just fifty years after the Restoration. Then, Shakespeare had been almost forgotten, most of his work accessible only in the cumbersome folios, read only by a few men of letters who might well never have seen a play of his on the stage. Now, on the threshold of the Georgian era, he was recognised as England's greatest poet and dramatist, his works not only read (the folio had been printed for a fourth time in 1685) but seen more frequently in some sort of version, than any others on the London stage. He was already on the way to becoming a legend, and as a trophy to his happy triumph his plays had just been edited and published in six handy octavo volumes. It was the first modern critical edition of Shakespeare.

IV

SHAKESPEAR RESTORED

THE editor was Nicholas Rowe, a dramatist whose only comedy is said to have amused no one except the author, and a future Poet Laureate as undistinguished as his predecessor, Nahum Tate.

Shakespeare's plays were sadly in need of an editor. Although Heminge and Condell had done their best to give their readers a good text, with no editorial tradition behind them their standard of accuracy could not be expected to be very high, and in addition to any laxity of theirs the printers involved themselves in innumerable muddles. What, for example, was to be made of Mistress Quickly's description of the dying Falstaff: 'his Nose was as sharpe as a Pen, and a Table of greene fields,'? or the report of Macbeth's success: 'as thick as Tale / Can post with post.'? It is true that there had been some correction of misprints and attempt to emend corrupt passages in the second and following folios, but as these were often wrong and further misprints were added the fourth folio was even more remote from Shakespeare's 'originals' than the first. Of course, an editor should have collated all the texts, or at least the first folio and the first good quarto, where one existed, but unfortunately Rowe worked almost entirely from the fourth folio. As he was the first professional editor in the field he was able to correct a vast number of obvious errors, and to make numerous conjectural emendations, some of which were later found to be the reading of the original editions. A happy example of his work is 'as thick as hail / Came post with post' for the *Macbeth* passage quoted above, a reading that has been generally accepted.

Although a text that was virtually a conjectural revision of the fourth folio left much to be desired, Rowe's work was a step in the right direction. Shakespeare was made not only more easily accessible in his six handy volumes, he was also made more easily intelligible. For Rowe completed the division of the plays into acts and scenes, and added explanatory stage directions and lists of *dramatis personae*. He also made his edition more alluring by supplying an illustration for each play. It is true that they were not uniformly helpful as interpretations of the poet's meaning, but at least they had the merit of being among the first contributions of the visual arts to the cult of Shakespeare.

Finally, Rowe introduced his work with a *Life* of Shakespeare. He got most of his information from Betterton, incorporated Davenant's stories, and seasoned the whole with a little picturesque surmise and anecdote, such as his description of Shakespeare's acting: 'the top of his performance was the Ghost in his own *Hamlet*.' The Restoration tragedian begins his critical remarks on a somewhat sour note, deploring the fondness of the English for tragi-comedy, which they seem to prefer to an exact tragedy. Nevertheless he admits that there is a great deal of entertainment in Shakespeare's comical humours. As for his tragedies, we must make allowance for the fact that he knew nothing of the rules of Aristotle, but 'liv'd under a kind of mere Light of Nature . . . in a state of almost universal License and Ignorance'. Ben Jonson was right: 'Shakespeare wanted art.' Until the end of the eighteenth century Rowe's was the orthodox view, as his *Life* was the standard biography. But his edition did not long remain the standard one.

The Shakespeare cult was attracting the scholars, but another poet was to anticipate them in editing the plays. Rowe's edition was published in 1709; in 1721 *Mist's Journal*, a violently Tory paper, announced, 'The celebrated Mr. Pope is preparing a correct edition of Shakespear's works; that of the late Mr. Rowe being very faulty.' Yet it was 1725 before the six handsome quarto volumes appeared. Pope had a first folio (with characteristic inaccuracy he ascribed it to 1621), according to him the source of almost all the errors of succeeding editions, so that the quartos were the 'only materials left to repair the deficiencies or restore the corrupted sense of the author'. He professed, therefore, to have collated the original editions, and gave a list of twenty-nine quartos that he had consulted. But he consulted them only at intervals, and his text is substantially that of Rowe's edition, based on the fourth folio. His emendations were according to his own fancy, his explanatory notes largely guesswork, lines that he did not understand were silently dropped, and passages that he disliked were degraded to the bottom of the page. Macbeth's 'Sleep that knits up the ravelled sleave of care' was one of these, and, as there was 'no hint of this trash in the first edition', the racked Othello's incoherent ejaculations were relegated to the margin. But it was the verse that most interested Pope, and by juggling with the words, ejecting one here, inserting one there, and transposing others, he made rough and recalcitrant passages as smooth as the eighteenth century could wish. For example, according to the first folio, Isabella in *Measure for Measure* says to the Duke:

> There haue I made my promise, vpon the
> Heauy midle of the night, to call vpon him.

This Pope polished into,

> There on the heavy middle of the night
> Have I my promise made to call upon him.

He set the fashion, and similar distortions of this and other passages may still be found in some modern texts.

Of course, it was not all as bad as this. Pope did make some able emendations, he improved on Rowe's scenic division, he threw out the seven 'wretched plays' of the third folio (he called them eight) including, unfortunately, *Pericles*, and he wrote a Preface. This is interesting because it was written by a great poet, but it is all very general, a variation on the theme of the wild irregular genius who has written better ('as he has perhaps written worse') than any other man, despite his small Latin, less Greek, want of art and lack of judgment.

Yet, when all has been said in its favour, Pope's *Shakespear* remains a deplorable failure. Although he was a creative genius Pope lacked all the essential qualifications of an editor: patience, diligence, accuracy and scholarship. His indolence left many passages as corrupt as ever, his ignorance led to wanton and erroneous alteration, and his misdirected industry refined the plays to such an extent that, as Malone said sixty years later, Shakespeare himself would not have understood his own works. One of Pope's contemporaries was thinking much the same thing.

This was Lewis Theobald, or Tibbald, a minor poet and dramatist, a translator of the classics, and an omnivorous reader of all things Elizabethan. His version of *Richard II* had had a run of seven nights before being deservedly forgotten, but he was now engaged on a much more exciting enterprise. It is a curious story. There are records of two Court performances in 1613 of a lost play called *Cardenio*, which, though never published, was registered by a dealer in manuscripts forty years later as 'The History of Cardennio, by Mr. Fletcher and Shakespeare'. Then in 1728 appeared 'Double Falshood; Or, The Distrest Lovers. A Play . . . Written Originally by W. Shakespeare; And now Revised

and Adapted to the Stage by Mr. Theobald.' It is based on the story
of Cardenio and Lucinda in *Don Quixote*, which must have been the
source of the original *Cardenio*. Is *Double Falsehood*, then, a version of
the play of which Shakespeare was said to have been joint-author?

In his Preface Theobald wrote that he had three manuscript copies
of the original, one of which was more than sixty years old, and that he
had been told that Shakespeare gave the play 'to a Natural Daughter of
his, for whose Sake he wrote it, in the Time of his Retirement from
the Stage'. When his 'adaptation' was put on at Drury Lane in 1727
it naturally excited a great deal of attention, and was received with
'unanimous applause' for ten nights. 'How would Shakespeare joy,' the
Prologue boasted,

> How cry with Pride—'Oblivion I forgive;
> This my last Child to latest Times shall live:
> Lost to the World, well for the Birth it stay'd;
> To this auspicious Æra well delay'd.'

The play might equally well have been called *The Two Gentlemen of
Andalusia*. Henriquez basely betrays the trust of his dear friend Julio,
for after violating Violante he is prevented only at the last moment
from forcibly marrying Leonora, beloved of Julio, who, not without
reason, asks,

> Is there a Treachery, like this in Baseness,
> Recorded any where? It is the deepest:
> None but Itself can be its Parallel:
> And from a Friend, profess'd!—Friendship? Why, 'tis
> A Word for ever maim'd; in human Nature
> It was a Thing the noblest. . . .

Yet there were sceptics. Some asserted that it was 'incredible that such
a Curiosity should be stifled and lost to the World for above a Century'.
Others less charitably maintained that the author was Theobald himself:

> Fired or not fired, to write resolves with rage,
> And constant pores o'er Shakespear's sacred page;
> Then starting cries, 'I something will be thought,
> I'll write, then boldly swear 'twas Shakespear wrote.'

Others again considered that both treatment and versification resembled Fletcher rather than Shakespeare. They were right. There is
nothing to suggest Shakespeare's hand, though of course it might have
been there before being improved by Theobald's refining muse. The

most likely solution is that Theobald really did get hold of manuscripts of *Cardenio* and, finding that it was written by Fletcher, titivated and presented it as Shakespeare's. This would account for the fact that nobody has ever seen any of his three manuscripts, and for his failure to publish the unadapted text, which would have been a scoop indeed, in his edition of Shakespeare. But whatever the explanation, fraud, forgery or innocent improvement, it is clear that the Shakespeare cult had got a firm grip by the beginning of the eighteenth century.

This then, Lewis Theobald, was the man who felt so strongly about the shortcomings of Pope's *Shakespear*. Stimulated by the deficiencies of Rowe's edition, he had for the last twelve years been studying and annotating Shakespeare's text, working mainly from the second folio, so that it did not take him long to put together the two hundred pages of the book that he published in 1726 as 'Shakespeare Restored, or a Specimen of the many Errors as well Committed as Unamended by Mr. Pope in his late edition of this Poet; designed not only to correct the said Edition, but to restore the true Reading of Shakespeare in all the Editions ever published'. The title sounds aggressive, but it was not meant to be so, for in his Introduction Theobald wrote 'I have so great an esteem for Mr. Pope . . . that I beg to be excused from the least intention of derogating from his merits.' And again, and even more ingenuously, 'Wherever I have the luck to be right in any observation, I flatter myself Mr. Pope himself will be pleased that Shakespeare receives some benefit.' Others must have been less sure than Theobald that Mr Pope would be pleased by the exposure and correction of his errors.

Shakespeare Restored is the first, and one of the most important books ever to be written on Shakespeare, at least on his text. Here was a scholar who had read not only the other Elizabethan dramatists, but also many of the books that Shakespeare himself had read—Holinshed's *Chronicles* and North's *Plutarch*, for example—and, aided by his collection of early quartos, methodically applying his unique knowledge to the restoration of corrupt passages. Although it was not his object to expose Pope's incompetence, inevitably he did so by his illustration of false and misleading punctuation, the omission of words and lines and subtraction of whole passages. Then he showed that corruptions in the fourth folio, the basis of Rowe's and Pope's text, could often be restored by reference to the early editions, and finally he gave a number of his own conjectural emendations, many of which have been generally accepted. The most famous of these is Mistress Quickly's lament for Falstaff, already quoted: 'his Nose was as sharpe as a Pen, and a Table of greene fields.' Pope had copies of the 'bad' quarto of *Henry V* and Jaggard's reprint, dated 1608, in neither of which is there any mention of 'a table of green fields', so he added the jaunty note, 'This nonsense got into all the [later] editions by a pleasant mistake of the stage editors. . . . A table was here directed to be brought in (it being a tavern scene where they drink at parting), and this direction crept into the text from the margin. Greenfield was the name of the property-man in that time who furnished implements, etc., for the actors.' Perhaps, but how did Pope know? There is no other trace of this hypothetical Greenfield, and after all the words are in the folio, the only good text of the play. Theobald was not satisfied. He had an edition in which 'a gentleman sometime deceas'd' had changed 'table' to 'talked', and this inspired his brilliant improvement: instead of *a' (he) talked* he read *a' babbled of green fields*. It may be wrong—Dr Hotson thinks it is—but it has the authentic Shakespearean ring, and two hundred years ago nobody but Theobald could have produced such a felicity. Pope said no more about Greenfield, but added a note to his second edition: 'Mr. Pope omitted the latter part because no words are to be found in any edition till after the author's death. However, the Restorer has a mind they should be genuine, and since he cannot otherwise make sense of 'em, would have a mere conjecture admitted.' Mere conjecture! Pope's editing was little but conjecture—when it was not mere negligence—though he was not the sort of man who liked the world to be told so.

Pope bided his time, and it was two years before a volume of *Miscellanies* appeared, 'consisting of several copies of verses, to which is prefixed A Discourse on the Profund, or the Art of Sinking in Poetry'. In this discourse, one of the 'Geniuses in the Profund' is a certain L.T., a swallow of an author whose agility is employed to catch flies, an obscure eel of an author who wraps himself up in his own mud, the author of a play called *Double Distress*. As an example of Theobald's Bathos, Profund, or Sinking in Poetry, Pope quoted the line from *Double Falsehood*,

> None but itself can be its parallel.

This, Pope submitted, was profundity itself, 'unless it may seem borrowed from the thought of that master of a show in Smithfield, who writ in large letters over the picture of his elephant, "This is the greatest elephant in the world, except himself."'

But this was mere skirmishing, only a prelude to the assault. Among the verse contributions to *Miscellanies* was a *Fragment of a Satire* in which Theobald, among many others, received honourable mention:

> Should some more sober critics come abroad,
> If wrong, I smile; if right, I kiss the rod.
> Pains, reading, study are their just pretence,
> And all they want is spirit, taste and sense.
> Commas and points they set exactly right,
> And 'twere a sin to rob them of their mite.
> In future ages how their fame will spread
> For routing triplets and restoring *ed*.
> Yet ne'er one sprig of laurel graced these ribalds,
> From sanguine Sew— down to piddling T—s,
> Who thinks he reads when he but scans and spells,
> A word-catcher that lives on syllables.
> Yet even this creature may some notice claim,
> Wrapt round and sanctified with Shakespear's name;
> Pretty, in amber to observe the forms
> Of hairs, or straws, or dirt, or grubs or worms;
> The thing, we know, is neither rich nor rare,
> But wonder how the devil it got there.

If not Pope at his best, it was good, though the gibes at commas and other minutiae of textual criticism were merely a measure of his own inadequacy as an editor of Shakespeare. And the barbed epithet stuck; henceforth Theobald was Piddling Tibbalds.

Pope's object was to provoke an angry retort, to which he had already prepared a counter-riposte. But Theobald contented himself with a spirited and learned defence of 'parallel', a few more restorations, a protest that he never intended to hurt Pope's feelings, and a promise (or was it a threat?) of a further criticism of the second edition of his *Shakespear*. But six months before this was issued Pope launched his real offensive. And offensive is the exact word.

In May, 1728, appeared a small volume with a frontispiece depicting an owl standing on a column of books, the base formed by Cibber's *Plays*, the capital *Shakespeare Restored*. It was *The Dunciad*, a celebration of the Empire of Dulness. 'Book and the man I sing,' Pope began in epic vein. The man was Theobald, the book *Shakespeare Restored*. The satire is not confined to the verse, but, in later editions at least,

Look you, how pale he glares!
My father, in his habit as he lived!

Frontispiece to *Hamlet*, from Rowe's edition of Shakespeare, 1709

What, frighted with false fire!

Frontispiece to *Hamlet*, from Hanmer's edition of Shakespeare, 1744

overflows into the notes, and the fun begins at once. 'It may well be disputed whether *Dunciad* be a right reading: Ought it not rather to be spelled *Dunceiad*, as the etymology evidently demands? That accurate and punctual Man of Letters, the Restorer of Shakespeare, constantly observes the preservation of this very letter *e* in spelling the name of his beloved author, and not like his common careless editors, with the omission of one, nay sometimes of two *ee*'s, as Shakspear, which is utterly unpardonable.' Theobald is described in terms of the Art of Sinking in Poetry:

> Studious he sate, with all his books around,
> Sinking from thought to thought, a vast profound!
> Plung'd for his sense, but found no bottom there:
> Then writ, and flounder'd on, in mere despair.

Among his books were those of Caxton and Wynkyn de Worde, books that Pope had never read, but from which Theobald had been able to supply the meaning of 'the dreadfull Sagittary' in *Troilus and Cressida*. And Pope, quite unaware that his satire is double-edged, makes him outline his critical method to the Goddess of Dulness:

> Here studious I unlucky Moderns save,
> Nor sleeps one error in its father's grave,
> Old puns restore, lost blunders nicely seek,
> And crucify poor Shakespear once a week.
> For thee I dim these eyes and stuff this head
> With all such reading as was never read.

It was reading that Pope was not prepared to undertake, but it was essential reading for the competent editing of Shakespeare. The brilliant ridicule goes on; Theobald is crowned, and '"God save King Tibbald!" Grubstreet alleys roar.'

Pope cannot resist further sport with the line, 'None but itself can be its parallel', and he adds the note: 'A marvellous line of Theobald; unless the play called the *Double Falsehood* be (as he would have it believed) Shakespear's. But whether this line be his or not, he proves Shakespear to have written as bad.' He then professes infinite concern that so many errors have escaped the learned editor of the play, and suggests a few emendations. For example:

> To oaths no more give credit,
> To tears, to vows; false *both*!

E

False grammar I'm sure. *Both* can relate but to *two* things. This I fear is of a piece with *None but itself can be its parallel.* Yet let us vindicate Shakespear where we can and see! how easy a change sets it right:

> To tears, to vows, false *troth*!

In later editions Pope dethroned Theobald in favour of Cibber, with inevitable loss of point, but in its original form *The Dunciad* is the most brilliant piece of writing ever inspired by the squabbles of editors and critics: a strange monument to the cult of Shakespeare.

Although Theobald himself was past restoring, he remained sensibly good-tempered and contented himself with a mild letter which, however, carried a sting in its tail. 'If Mr. Pope is angry with me for attempting to restore Shakespeare, I hope the public are not. Admit my sheets have no other merit, they will at least have this: They will awaken him to some degree of accuracy in his next edition of that poet which we are to have in a few months; and then we shall see whether he owed the errors of the former edition to indiligence or to inexperience in the author. And as my remarks upon the whole of Shakespeare shall closely attend upon the publication of his edition, I'll venture to promise without arrogance that I'll then give above five hundred more fair emendations that shall escape him and all his assistants.'

When, therefore, Pope brought out his second edition of *Shakespear* in November, 1728, his predicament was apparent. He could not very well ignore Theobald's emendations, many of which were obviously correct, yet if he adopted them he would be indebted to his own king of dunces. Some, therefore, he incorporated without acknowledgment, others he inserted in the form of a list at the end of his last volume, where 'it can spoil but a half sheet of paper that chances to be left vacant here' (as a matter of fact he had to sully several pages), and finally he acknowledged that 'we have inserted in this impression as many of 'em as are judged of any the least advantage to the poet; the whole amounting to about twenty-five words'.

It took Theobald only a few days to glance through the text and write a letter to the press pointing out that so far from there being only 'about twenty-five words' there were 'about a hundred' important changes adopted from his restoration. 'If want of industry in collating old copies,' he wrote, 'if want of reading proper authors to ascertain points of history, if want of knowledge of the modern tongues, want of judgment in digesting his author's own text, or want of sagacity in restoring it where it is manifestly defective, can disable any man from a title to be the editor of Shakespeare, I make no scruples to declare that hitherto Mr. Pope appears absolutely unequal to that task.' And he promised a detailed exposure in the volumes of emendations that he was preparing for publication.

Theobald was even better than his word. Instead of further volumes of *Shakespeare Restored* he produced his own edition of Shakespeare's plays. Pope tried hard to prevent publication, but failed, though before it was issued he did succeed in depreciating its value and traducing the editor, partly through the medium of his own paper, *The Grub-street Journal*, partly by way of obedient sycophants who attacked Theobald's piddling industry:

> Thus nicely trifling, accurately dull,
> How one may toil and toil—to be a fool.

But when at length it did appear, at the end of 1733, it was at once recognised by those who knew anything about Shakespeare as infinitely superior to Pope's edition, and petty criticism merely recoiled on itself. Theobald wisely made no attempt to answer scurrility with scurrility, but his notes were full of stinging taunts at the expense of 'the late learned editor' as he called Pope. Thus, in *Richard II* the Queen remarks to her ladies,

> My wretchednesse, vnto a Rowe of Pinnes,
> They'le talke of State.

This is the perfectly comprehensible folio reading, but either Pope failed to understand it, or thought 'pins' too mean a word for a tragic queen, and he substituted the fatuous, 'My wretchedness suits with a row of pines'. 'This', remarked Theobald acidly, 'is merely, I presume, *ex cathedra Popiana*, for I can find no authority for it any more than any sense in it.' Pope replied by incorporating his lines on 'piddling Tibbalds' in his *Epistle to Dr Arbuthnot*, and adding a note to a new edition of the *Dunciad*: 'He since published an edition of Shakespear, with alterations of the text, upon bare conjectures either of his own, or any others who sent them to him.'

Unfortunately, the latter part of the gibe was true. Theobald was too generous in accepting, and acknowledging, suggestions from others, even when he was unconvinced of their propriety. One of these encumbering amateurs was a young Lincolnshire clergyman, William Warburton, who had come to Theobald's aid at the time of the publication of the *Dunciad*, and attacked Pope in a series of anonymous articles. Pope, he wrote, 'having left Shakespear where he found him, returns to his primitive occupation of libelling and bawdy ballad-making'. Yet, not exactly as he found him; was there not that felicitous emendation in *Henry V*, of 'nook-shotten isle of Albion' to 'short nooky isle'? It was excellent, even if securely anonymous, but as the price of his chivalry he pressed on Theobald ten emendations of his own, one of which he persuaded the grateful but embarrassed editor to adopt. Warburton was warming to the work; fascinated by this business of restoring Shakespeare, there was now scarcely a line that failed to inspire his inventive brain with some fanciful improvement. These he communicated to his friend, so that when Theobald published his edition it was liberally larded with notes on Warburton's observations and suggested readings and, unfortunately, more than a hundred of his emendations in his text. Pope was quite right to attack these 'bare conjectures', but it was hard that Johnson should write that 'when Theobald published Shakespear, in opposition to Pope, the best notes were supplied by Warburton'.

The Fates, indeed, conspired against Theobald. First, Warburton changed his allegiance, rallying to the defence of Pope when he was assailed for his *Essay on Man*. It was a politic move, for the grateful poet, unaware of his former anonymous attacks, which Theobald did not divulge, introduced him to his wealthy patron, Ralph Allen of Bath, whose niece he married, thereby acquiring his estate and the bishopric of Gloucester. Then, more disinterestedly, Warburton befriended Johnson, and as Johnson never forgot anybody who helped him at the beginning of his career, he was always prepared to defend the arrogant divine. When, therefore, Warburton began abusing Theobald, Johnson accepted his judgment, and in his *Life of Pope* took the part of the poet and the parson against the scholar, 'a man of heavy diligence, with very slender powers'. What Johnson wrote might almost be said to have been engraved, so that the reputation of poor Theobald, first of all great Shakespeare scholars, sank lower and lower as a succession of editors disparaged while they plundered his work, without acknowledging the source of their riches. Pope, the irresponsible man of genius, had defeated the conscientious man of talent in the first great Shakespeare controversy.

Yet it was only the first round of the controversy, and Pope himself, although a very sick man, had not yet quite done with Shakespeare. At about the time of his quarrel with Cibber, which led to the revision of *The Dunciad* with his new antagonist instead of Theobald as the hero, he heard that another editor was in the field. This was an elderly baronet, Sir Thomas Hanmer, quondam Speaker of the House of Commons, who had retired from politics just as the Pope–Theobald squabble broke out. It was a godsend for the old gentleman, for it supplied him with the perfect hobby, and thenceforth he divided his time between the improvement of his Suffolk garden and the improvement of Shakespeare. Pope was furious, and of course put him into his new *Dunciad*:

> There mov'd Montalto with superior air,
> His stretch'd-out arm display'd a Volume fair . . .
> 'What! no respect', he cry'd, 'for Shakespear's page!'

And he added a note: 'An edition of that author, with his text arbitrarily altered throughout, was at this time printing at the University Press.'

Warburton, too, had a thing to say. *His* edition of Shakespeare was almost ready for the press, and now it was to be anticipated by the expensive nonsense of an ignorant amateur. According to Hanmer, Warburton had invited himself to his house on the pretext of having emendations to show him, but then 'the views of interest began to show themselves', and he conceived the idea of publishing his own edition of Shakespeare. Warburton angrily denied the charge as a falsehood from beginning to end. It was a complete reversal of the truth; Hanmer had approached *him*, invited him to his house, then used his emendations in his edition. The first thing Warburton published after Pope's death was another edition of *The Dunciad*, with an additional note on Montalto: 'An eminent person, who was about to publish a very pompous edition of a great author, *at his own expense.*'

Hanmer's *Shakespear* came out in 1744, a sumptuous production in six quarto volumes 'adorned with sculptures designed and executed by the best hands'. 'What the public is to expect', Hanmer wrote modestly in his Preface, 'is a true and correct edition of Shakespear's works.' Careful not to give a loose to fancy, he selected those readings of his predecessors that he approved of and added his own incomparable conjectures; lightly changing, for example, Hamlet's 'I'll have a suit of sables' to 'I'll have a suit of ermine', so making, in his opinion, better sense. But an even more memorable emendation was his masterly rendering of 'Cassio. . . . A fellow almost damn'd in a fair wife' as 'damn'd in a fair phyz'. This he justified in a note: 'Cassio's beauty is often hinted at, which it is natural enough for other rough soldiers to treat with scorn.' He emphatically approved of Pope's throwing to the bottom of the page those passages that he considered spurious; but Pope was half-hearted in his rejections, and other passages went the same way, the most considerable of which was 'that wretched piece of ribaldry in *Henry V*, put into the mouths of the French princess and an old gentlewoman, improper enough as it is all in French, and not intelligible to an English audience'. Johnson generously conceded that Hanmer had the first requisite to emendatory criticism, 'that intuition by which the poet's intention is immediately discovered'. Unfortunately he worked almost entirely from intuition, and without consulting any edition earlier than Pope's.

Theobald and Pope both died in 1744, and Hanmer two years later. The field was at last clear for Warburton, and in 1747 he brought out his eight volume edition. His Preface is not remarkable for its Christian charity, and he soon dismisses his two immediate predecessors. Hanmer, of course, was absolutely ignorant of the art of criticism, though not absolutely destitute of all *art*, 'for having a number of my conjectures before him, he took as many of them as he saw fit, and by changing them to something similar he made them his own, and so became a critic at a cheap expense'. Theobald, too, was guilty of the same mean trick, but then he was only a piddling bookworm: 'What he read he could transcribe: but, as what he thought, if ever he did think, he could but ill express, so he read on: and by that means got a character of learning.' It is true that by referring to the old editions he sometimes restored the original readings, but when it came to conjectural emendation he was so ignorant of Shakespeare's language that he could not understand what was right; 'nor had he common judgment to see, or critical sagacity to amend, what was manifestly faulty'. Was there ever such impudence and ingratitude! Theobald, who had read everything Elizabethan on which he could lay hand, 'all such reading as was never read', who had refused to betray Warburton's anonymous attacks on Pope, and, in his edition, had honoured his traducer by calling him 'my ingenious friend'. 'In a word,' Warburton concludes, Theobald and Hanmer 'separately possessed those two qualities which, more than any other, have contributed to bring the art of criticism into disrepute, *dulness of apprehension*, and *extravagance of conjecture*.'

After this contemptuous dismissal of his dead rivals, Warburton proceeded to refine on the *art* that he had so high-mindedly condemned, and to appropriate the best things in Theobald as his own. As an example, Theobald had ingeniously altered the folio reading of Sir Toby's reference to Sir Andrew's hair, from 'thou seest it will not coole my nature' to 'curl by nature'. Warburton had to adopt this so patently correct reading, but, without any mention of Theobald, he managed to imply that it was his own. 'We should read,' runs his note, '*it will not curl by nature*. The joke is evident.' It is—as revealed by Theobald, but very doubtful if the pompous priest would ever have discovered it. At least, he did not see how wildly funny some of his own conjectures were.

But Thomas Edwards did, and within a few months his *Supplement to Warburton's Edition* was on sale. The book consists of twenty-one 'Canons of Criticism' (later increased to twenty-four) by which Warburton, Edwards ironically suggests, was guided in his self-styled office of 'Professed Critic'. For example:

I. A Professed Critic has a right to declare, that his author wrote whatever He thinks he ought to have written, with as much positiveness as if he had been at his elbow.

II. He has a right to alter any passage, which He does not understand.

IV. Where He does not like an expression, and yet cannot mend it, He may abuse his author for it.

VI. He may alter any word or phrase, which does not want amendment.

IX. He may interpret his author so, as to make him mean directly contrary to what he says.

XIII. He need not attend to the low accuracy of orthography, or pointing; but may ridicule such trivial criticisms in others.

XIX. He may use the very same reasons for confirming his own observations, which He has disallowed in his adversary.

XXIV. He may dispense with truth, in order to give the world a higher idea of his parts, or the value of his work.

Edwards then gives numerous examples illustrating Warburton's scrupulous adherence to these Canons. Thus:

In 1 *Henry VI*, where the vulgar editions, that is all but his own, have,
> 'tis present death;

He assures us that Shakespear wrote
> i'th' presence 't's death;

a line which seems penned for Cadmus when in the state of a serpent.

Once more. In *Othello*, the common editions read,
> Farewell the neighing steed, and the shrill trump,
> The spirit-stirring drum, th' *ear-piercing* fife.

This epithet of *ear-piercing* a poet would have thought not only an harmonious word, but very properly applied to that martial instrument of music; but Mr. Warburton says he would read,
> th' fear-spersing fife,

which is such a word as no poet, nor indeed any man who had half an ear, would have thought of; for which he gives this reason, which none but a Professed Critic could have thought of, that piercing the ear is not *an effect on the hearers.*

And the second example adduced in support of the last Canon is worth quoting:

The Tempest. 'And like the baseless fabric of *their* vision.' Mr. Theobald, *upon what authority I know not*, changed into '*this* vision.' Warb.

It is strange that Mr. Warburton should not know, that it was upon the authority of the first Folio, which has this reading.

When it is remembered that there is no quarto edition of *The Tempest*, and that for this play—and seventeen others—the first folio is the only text of any authority whatever, it gives some idea of the value of Warburton's edition.

When Warburton, as Pope's literary executor, published a complete edition of his friend's works, he added a note to *The Dunciad* on 'one Mr. Thomas Edwards', a libeller and 'a Grub-street critic run to seed'. A few more shots were exchanged, but it was virtually the end of the Twenty-five Years' War fought over the text of Shakespeare.

Five editions of the plays had been published during the first half of the eighteenth century, and you could take your choice. Discredited Warburtons were going at a substantial discount, and a set could be picked up for eighteen shillings instead of the published price of forty-eight. Hanmers, on the other hand, were at a premium, having risen from three to nine guineas, not, however, because of the baronet's editorial prowess, but because of Francis Hayman's illustrations. Hanmer had set great store by these, and looked upon his edition as 'another small monument designed and dedicated to Shakespear's honour'. The other and larger monument to which he referred was in Westminster Abbey. It was the elegantly pensive statue of the poet designed by Kent, carved by Scheemakers, and erected by public subscription in 1740. The Swan of Avon had at last reappeared upon the banks of Thames.

V

SHAKESPEAR CELEBRATED

As Shakespeare had arrived in London, so London was arriving in Stratford in ever increasing numbers, obligingly credulous and eager for anecdote. There was no shortage of supply. Pilgrims now learned that, as Shakespeare was no scholar, he employed one of those chuckle-pated historians to supply him with the necessary facts, which he would then work into 'all shapes and forms, as his beautiful Thoughts directed'. Then, it was discovered that two large chests of the Great Man's loose papers and manuscripts had perished in the great con-flagration at Warwick, where they had been in the hands of an ignorant baker. Shakespeare's epitaph on John Combe had long been known, and it was the most natural thing in the world that a similar one on his brother Tom should turn up in Stratford, though admittedly a some-what disappointing piece of verse:

> Thin in beard, and thick in purse;
> Never man beloved worse:
> He went to th' grave with many a curse:
> The Devil and he had both one nurse.

Fortunately, too, the first stanza of the bitter ballad that Shakespeare had written against Sir Thomas Lucy was found to have been pre-served in the memory of a very aged gentleman living in the neighbour-hood of Stratford:

> A parliament member, a justice of peace,
> At home a poor scarecrow, at London an ass,
> If lousy is Lucy, as some volke miscall it,
> Then Lucy is lousy, whatever befall it.

And, as Lucy was the original of Justice Shallow, so it was discovered that Falstaff was drawn from a townsman of Stratford who broke a contract or spitefully refused to sell him some land near the town. An even more aged gentleman, apparently a centenarian, was Shakespeare's younger brother, who, after the Restoration, could still faintly remem-ber having seen Will play Adam in *As You Like It*.

But more compelling and endearing were those intimate anecdotes, most of them relating to his human weaknesses, in which the voice of the bard himself was heard. There was the story of how once he went over to Bidford to challenge the merry topers there. 'Where can I find the Bidford drinkers?' he asked a shepherd. 'They are away, but the sippers are at home,' was the reply, 'and no doubt they will be more than a match for you.' They were, and the poet spent the night in a hedge under a crab-tree, which soon became a subsidiary shrine. Again, a drunken Stratford blacksmith once greeted him, as he was leaning over a mercer's door, with,

> 'Now, Mr. Shakespear, tell me if you can,
> The difference between a youth and a young man.'

to which the nimble-witted poet immediately replied,

> 'Thou son of fire, with thy face like a maple,
> The same difference as between a scalded and coddled apple.'

This last anecdote was related to Charles Macklin and young David Garrick one fine day in May, 1742, by Sir Hugh Clopton, the elderly, hospitable and garrulous owner of New Place. Not exactly Shakespeare's New Place, it is true, for the original rambling half-timbered structure had been replaced in Queen Anne's reign by an elegant house of brick. Still, it was Shakespeare's house only at one remove, and it certainly was Shakespeare's garden in which they were sitting, under the very mulberry tree that he had planted with his own hands, as Sir Hugh was at pains to inform them. The two actors listened eagerly to their host's reminiscences: how Shakespeare's granddaughter, Lady Bernard, had carried away many of the poet's papers from New Place after her second marriage, and so on. They were in great spirits; no wonder they had followed Betterton's footsteps and made a jaunt to Stratford, for they had both just leaped into fame from Shakespeare's shoulders: Macklin by rescuing Shylock from the burlesque performances of low comedians and playing him seriously as 'the Jew that Shakespear drew', Garrick by his personation of Richard in Cibber's version of *Richard III*.

For in spite of the restoration of Shakespeare's text by the scholars, the playwrights and players were still intent on the demolition they euphemistically described as reformation or refinement. Indeed, the actors of the old school seemed as unaware of the activities of the restorers as they were ignorant of any text save that supplied by the reformers. Thus, when Garrick revived *Macbeth* in 1744 'as written by Shakespear' (that is, without Davenant's Lady Macduff, though with all the apparatus of his flying witches) his veteran rival, Quin, was genuinely perplexed. 'What does he mean?' he asked, 'Don't I play Macbeth as written by Shakespear?' He did not; he played it as written by Davenant, just as he and others played the Davenant–Dryden *Tempest*, Dryden's *Troilus and Cressida*, Shadwell's *Timon*, Tate's *Lear*, Granville's *Jew of Venice*, Otway's *Caius Marius*, Cibber's *Richard III*. All these, and others, had become stock pieces, and the only unrefined Shakespearean plays in their repertoires were *Hamlet*, *Othello* and *Henry IV*.

Moreover, further onslaughts had been made in the thirty years since Betterton's death, the period of Theobald, who had so lovingly restored the least important of commas to the text. But then Theobald was himself one of the offenders: restorer in the study and reformer on the stage. Not only was there the mysterious *Double Falsehood*, but in 1719 he produced a refinement of *Richard II* in which he admitted that he had made 'some innovations upon History and Shakespeare'. He had. By omitting the first two acts he contrived a desirable unity of action, and by introducing a love story between Lady Percy and Aumerle further 'supported the dignity of the characters', most of whom perished in the final scene. Then there was Aaron Hill's *Henry V*, unified by the omission of all the comic characters and dignified by the insertion of a pathetic little romance in which a distracted Harriet, after attempting to kill her betrayer, the former Prince Hal, kills herself. The histories were particularly popular material for the improvers at a time when the Hanoverians were by no means securely settled on the throne, and there was no saying when a second Jacobite rebellion would occur. Thus, the title of the dreariest of all adaptations, *The Invader of his Country*, John Dennis's recast of *Coriolanus*, speaks for itself, as his Prologue speaks for all the other well-intentioned refiners of Shakespeare,

> In whose Original we may descry
> Where Master-strokes in wild Confusion lye,
> Here brought to as much Order as we can
> Reduce those Beauties upon Shakespear's plan.

Now, however, by 1742, there were signs of a change for the better. After all, the restorers must have had some effect; people were beginning to read the plays as Shakespeare really wrote them, and 'the ladies of the Shakespear Club', whoever they may have been, were pressing the theatre managers to produce them on the stage. Yet it was more than this; the town was tiring of classical tragedy and satirical comedy, partly, it is true, because there was a dearth of star tragedians and good dramatists, but partly because there was a new feeling in the air, an as yet inarticulate desire for something more natural, something, it might almost be said, more romantic. A symptom of the change was an interest in the neglected comedies of Shakespeare, and in 1740–41 the original *Twelfth Night*, *As You Like It* and *Merchant of Venice* were presented for the first time since the closing of the theatres exactly a hundred years before. Macklin had played Malvolio, Touchstone and Shylock—and Garrick was only twenty-five.

After leaving Sir Hugh Clopton at New Place, it would be only natural for the two London celebrities to call on Joseph Greene, headmaster of the grammar school over the way, and for Greene to offer to accompany them to the church to see Shakespeare's monument and grave. Garrick, an amateur of sculpture, must have been astonished at what he saw. Could this shabby bust within its battered niche represent the same man as the thoughtfully genteel figure in Westminster Abbey? It was not his idea of the dramatist at all. Greene was distressed, and went to London to see the rival statue. Then he wrote to the *Gentleman's Magazine*. He allowed that the Abbey figure was in a noble attitude, exciting an awful admiration in the beholder, that the face was venerable and majestic, well expressing that intenseness of serious thought, that depth of contemplation, which the poet, undoubtedly, sometimes had. Yet was it not equally true that the face of the Stratford bust was also somewhat thoughtful, although appearing to arise from a *cheerfulness* of thought, which, it must also be allowed, Shakespeare, at proper times, was no stranger to? However, let it be admitted that the two faces had little, if any, resemblance to each other, what then? So much the worse for London. The admirers of the Westminster monument averred that the Stratford bust differed as much from the likeness of the man as it did from the figure in the Abbey, and tried to depreciate its merit. But there could be not the slightest doubt as to which was the real likeness. Scheemakers had worked from imagination more than a century after the poet's death, whereas the Stratford bust had been erected shortly afterwards by his relations, who might be allowed to have been aware of his appearance. Besides, it resembled the engraving in the folio, which Ben Jonson plainly asserted to be a great likeness.

Still, the loyal schoolmaster, jealous for the honour of Stratford, was not satisfied. The effigy of his most distinguished old boy was in a deplorable condition, calculated to excite the incredulity, risibility even, of London visitors. If only he had the money he would become the Theobald of Stratford, and produce another version of Shakespeare Restored. His chance came a few years later when Mr John Ward, soon to become the grandfather of Sarah Kemble, better known as Mrs Siddons, brought his company of players to Stratford and gave a performance of *Othello* in the old Town Hall. Greene saw to it that they were hospitably received, and even composed an elegant Prologue, which was spoken in an admirable manner by Mr Ward himself, and contributed not a little to the evening's entertainment. His scholarly review of the Attic theatre and Roman stage led cunningly into the main theme:

> But, to great Nature to hold up the glass,
> To show from her herself what is and was,
> To reason deeply as the Fates decree,
> Whether 'tis best *to be, or not to be,*—
> This, *wond'rous* SHAKESPEAR, was reserv'd for THEE!

The peroration was a very pardonable puff for Stratford, and a more subtle depreciation of the claims of London:

> Hail, happy STRATFORD!—envi'd be thy fame!
> What City boasts than thee a greater name?
> 'Here his first infant lays sweet SHAKESPEAR sung;
> Here the last accents falter'd on his tongue!'
> His honours yet, with future time shall grow,
> Like Avon's streams, enlarging as they flow.

Mr Ward was so pleased that he gave most of the receipts from the performance to the fund for the restoration of the monument, and by the beginning of 1749 the chipped and broken stones had been replaced, the gilding renewed and the old colouring revived. Let London laugh at that! And what had London to offer against the Birthplace, the Grave, the Monument, New Place and the Mulberry Tree? All seemed set fair for the prosperity of Stratford. But pride was only the prelude to disaster.

Two years later Sir Hugh Clopton died, and New Place passed into the hands of the Reverend Francis Gastrell, vicar of Frodsham in Cheshire, and canon residentiary of Lichfield, a man who, in the light of later events, the indignant Stratfordians were to stigmatise as one who 'felt no sort of pride or pleasure in this charming retirement, no consciousness of his being possessed of the sacred ground which the Muses had consecrated to the memory of their favourite Poet'. Or perhaps he was a priest of puritanical persuasion, who considered plays the very pomps of the devil, and officiously set out to nip in the bud this nascent idolatry of a playwright. But most probably the poor man was quite ignorant of the Cult when he bought the house, desiring only a charming retirement, and was exasperated to find that his peace was shattered day and night by importunate tourists knocking at his door to beg a fragment of the mulberry tree, and by mischievous boys climbing his wall to rend off whole branches. For two years he put up with these impositions and depredations, but when for the third time the tourist season came round the distracted (or sacrilegious or besotted) priest could bear it no longer, and ordered the tree to be felled and chopped into firewood. 'Ephesian destruction', the outraged Stratfordians called it.

Happily, however, the tree was bought by a far-sighted Mr Thomas Sharpe, who soon began to convert it into small boxes, goblets, punchladles, toothpick-cases, tobacco-stoppers and other desirable knicknacks that were eagerly snapped up by the voracious curio-hunters. Sharpe was only thirty-two when he bought the tree, and for the next forty years turned out the lucrative mementoes until it began to be whispered that the original tree must long ago have been exhausted and replaced by others. Mr Sharpe was very properly shocked, and called in the Mayor and another Justice of the Peace to witness an affidavit that would convince people of the wickedness of their insinuations and reassure them of the proper value of the relics made from the celebrated tree. 'I have often heard', he affirméd, 'Sir Hugh Clopton solemnly declare that the Mulberry-tree which growed in his garden was planted by Shakespear, and he took pride in showing it to, and entertaining persons of distinction, whose curiosity exited them to visit the spot, known as the last residence of the immortal Bard.' Then, when the Rev. F. Gastrell cut it down, he had bought it 'out of a sincere veneration for the memory of its celebrated planter, and worked it into many curious toys and usefull articles. And I do hereby declare,' he concluded, 'and take my solemn oath, upon the four Evangelists, in the presence of Almighty God, that I never worked, sold, or substituted any other wood than what came from, and was part of, the said tree.'

It was deeply sworn, and perhaps it was, after all, a very big mulberry tree.

Mr Gastrell appears to have been the least avaricious of men. Anyone with the least flair for business, with such a relic in his garden, would have anticipated Sharpe and out of it made a comfortable income for life. But no, he ordered it to be cut down for firewood. And he was soon to destroy a far greater source of potential revenue. New Place, like any other property, was subject to monthly assessments for the maintenance of the poor, but as the canon spent some of his time in Lichfield he expected to be relieved of a proportionate part of his Stratford rates. But after the mulberry tree incident the borough council was little inclined to be sympathetic, and insisted on his paying the full amount. Now, apparently, this modern Eratostratus really did lose his temper; he swore that *his* house at least should never again be assessed, and in 1759 razed it to the ground, sold the materials, and left the town amidst the execrations of its inhabitants. Just as the Cult was getting fully under way it was deprived of its most cherished relic and most imposing shrine, and all that remained were foundations and a tree stump. Gastrell was nothing if not thorough, and seldom can a private citizen, within the limits of the law, have inflicted such havoc on a town within the space of a few years. As a final humiliation, at the very time when Gastrell was demolishing New Place, the fashionable sculptor Roubiliac was carving another statue of Shakespeare for London. It had been commissioned by Garrick, and was even more thoughtful than the figure in the Abbey.

Garrick could scarcely do less. He had taken Shakespeare into partnership, and with his assistance made a reputation and a fortune. By 1747, when he became manager of Drury Lane, at least a dozen of the plays—tragedies, comedies and histories alike—were annual fixtures in his repertoire, and moreover, to some of these he restored approximately the original text. To the *Macbeth* that so puzzled Quin he added *Coriolanus, Cymbeline, The Tempest, Antony and Cleopatra* (though people still preferred Dryden's *All for Love*) and *Romeo and Juliet*, for which he wrote an improved version of Otway's final scene when Juliet wakes in the tomb—'Soft—she breathes and stirs!' On the other hand, he courted popularity by making pretty little entertainments out of the most effective scenes in some of the comedies; with appropriate pastoral song and dance *Florizel and Perdita* made a dainty trifle, as did *Catharine and Petruchio* and *The Fairies*, abstracted from

A Midsummer Night's Dream. The operatic *Tempest* was a more serious offence. Shakespeare's verse is merely the chain on which to string the pearls of song by Mr Smith. Thus, charmed by her father's magic, Miranda breaks into the air,

> Come, O sleep, my eyelids close,
> Lull my senses in repose.

And, when the lovers meet, Prospero melodiously expands Shakespeare's 'At the first sight they have changed eyes' into,

> In tender sighs he silence breaks,
>   The fair his flame approves,
> Consenting blushes warm her cheeks,
>   She smiles, she yields, she loves.

There was a certain lack of geniality in Theophilus Cibber's comments on this emasculation and trilling of trios: '*The Midsummer Night's Dream* has been minc'd and fricaseed into an undigested and unconnected Thing; *The Winter's Tale* mammoc'd into a Droll; *The Taming of the Shrew* made a Farce of; and *The Tempest* castrated into an Opera.' Nevertheless, he had to admit that Drury Lane was crowded. Shakespeare, under the expert guidance of Garrick, had scaled fresh pinnacles of fame.

When the year 1764 came round, the bicentenary of Shakespeare's birth, it might have been expected that Stratford, still shaken by Gastrell's Ephesian destruction, would call in Garrick to help restore their prestige by some sort of celebration. Instead, however, they rebuilt the Town Hall in the Tuscan manner, and it was only when it was finished that the idea of approaching the English Roscius occurred to them. Towards the end of 1768, George Steevens, who had just published reprints of twenty Shakespearean quartos, was the guest of honour at a convivial gathering at the White Lion Hotel. The talk turned naturally on the recently finished Town Hall, and the tantalisingly empty niche in the north façade. Steevens mischievously suggested approaching Garrick who, after all, made a hobby of commissioning statues, and readily agreed to get into touch with him. Garrick was flattered, in every sense of the word, by Steevens's advances, and was soon in amicable correspondence with the Stratford Corporation, who lost no time in presenting him with the freedom of the borough, enclosed in a small neat chest, made from the celebrated mulberry tree. This judicious and well-timed compliment elicited a very gracious letter of thanks and hints of favours to follow.

So it came about that in the summer of 1769 Garrick informed his Drury Lane audience that it would see him no more until the opening of the winter season,

> Unless we meet at Shakespear's Jubilee
> On Avon's banks, where flowers eternal blow;
> Like a full stream our gratitude shall flow.
> There let us revel, show our fond regard;
> On that loved spot first breathed our matchless bard.

There was to be a Grand Shakespeare Jubilee at Stratford in September, with Garrick himself as Master of Ceremonies.

Preparations were already well advanced in Stratford, where an octagonal wooden amphitheatre was rising on the Avon's bank. No expense was spared in adorning and rendering commodious this elegant piece of architecture; ceiling and cornice were covered with tasteful and appropriate paintings, and from the dome, supported by columns of the Corinthian order, richly gilt, was suspended a huge chandelier containing eight hundred wax lights. There was room for more than a thousand spectators, and the orchestra would accommodate a hundred performers. On the margin of the river was ranged a battery of artillery, while under the direction of the pyrotechnic genius, Mr Angelo, two waggons arrived from London stuffed with fireworks and variegated lamps for the illuminations.

Advance publicity was not neglected, and the July issue of the *Gentleman's Magazine* contained the first illustration ever to be published of the Birthplace. Unfortunately the correspondent who sent the drawing expressed doubts as to whether the apartment where the incomparable Shakespeare first drew breath could now be ascertained. But Garrick had no such doubts, and on his arrival at once indicated the authentic room. Now that New Place and the mulberry tree were gone, it was important to emphasise the Birthplace, even though it was a dilapidated hovel. 'The Gothic glories of the ancient Church, the modern elegance of the Civic Hall, cease to be regarded, when it is remembered, that the humble shed, in which the immortal bard first drew that breath which gladdened all the isle, is still existing; and all who have a heart to feel, and a mind to admire the truth of nature and splendour of genius, will rush thither to behold it, as a pilgrim would to the shrine of some loved saint; will deem it holy ground, and dwell

F

with sweet though pensive rapture, on the natal habitation of the poet.'

The August number of the *Gentleman's Magazine* was less encouraging. An anonymous article professed to give more detailed information about the impending solemnity than that already published in the papers. The pageantry, the literati were assured, was designed solely to please the million, but a dish of caviare was prepared for intellectual spirits susceptible of more abstracted and refined indulgence. For their entertainment the great Roscius would deliver an eulogium on the Avon bard, demonstrating his triumphs and pointing out those pieces that would have received additional beauty by an adherence to the rules of dramatic writing. On the second day he would analyse the poet's versification, with special reference to the wonderful attention that he gave to the variation of his pauses. 'These observations the great artist will exemplify by reading several passages, in which occasion will offer of pointing out, but with great good nature, the errors of some modern performers in respect to accent, emphasis and rest. Much delightful instruction, it is expected, will be derived from this part of the intellectual feast. Afterwards he will deliver a specimen of a projected edition of the Stratford Swan, which a retreat from the stage may, perhaps, some time or other, enable him to accomplish. The whole will conclude with the apotheosis of Shakespear.' There can be little doubt that this was one of the many squibs directed by Steevens at Garrick's vagary.

By the end of August the nobility and gentry were pouring into Stratford, and a week before the high festival began the neighbouring towns and villages were crammed with visitors paying exorbitant prices for quite inconsiderable accommodation. Even Garrick had to lodge with a grocer. There was plenty to do. They could buy Jubilee Medals, in copper, silver or gold, with a likeness of Shakespeare on one side and 'D.G.' on the other, and suspend them from specially manufactured Jubilee Ribbons that united and blended all the colours of the rainbow, symbol of the bard's universal genius. By the fifth of September all was ready: the poet's bust in the church was loaded with laurel; the Birthplace was covered with a curious emblematical transparency of the sun struggling through the clouds, a figurative representation of the fate and fortune of the much-beloved bard; transparent silk paintings hung in the windows of the Town Hall, the Genius of Shakespeare flanked by Falstaff and Pistol, Caliban and Lear in the act of execration, while on the walls hung the two paintings presented by Garrick. One, by Benjamin Wilson, represented the poet in an attitude of inspiration, his face, after the manner of the ancient painters when they despaired of properly giving the features of their subject, being thrown into deep shade. Opposite was a whole length portrait by Gainsborough, depicting the actor reclining against a pedestal that supported a bust of his favourite author. Some of the natives were not yet quite clear as to what this Jew Bill was all about, though a Banbury man assured them that it was to be the celebration of the resurrection of Shakespeare.

At five o'clock the next morning, Wednesday, September 6th, the town was startled out of its sleep by the roar of cannon. The Jubilee had begun. As the noise died away the most important lady visitors, and there were some very important lady visitors, found themselves serenaded by actors fantastically attired, and singing to the accompaniment of hautboys, flutes, clarinets and guitars:

> Let beauty with the sun arise,
>   To Shakespear tribute pay;
> With heav'nly smiles and speaking eyes,
>   Give lustre to the day.

Nor had Garrick forgotten to write an aubade for the natives:

> Ye Warwickshire lads, and ye lasses,
>   See what at our Jubilee passes;
> Come revel away, rejoice, and be glad,
> For the lad of all lads was a Warwickshire lad,
>   Warwickshire lad,
>   All be glad,
> For the lad of all lads was a Warwickshire lad.

By eight o'clock the Corporation had assembled in their formalities to present Garrick with his insignia of office as Steward: a medal, carved with the bust of the bard, richly set in gold, and a wand, both made from the celebrated mulberry tree. The completion of this ceremony was announced by the ringing of bells, the firing of cannon and a public breakfast in the Town Hall, price a shilling for the holders of guinea festival tickets. Most of the guests, including those of the highest quality of both sexes, wore the Jubilee Ribbon and Medal, and while they drank their tea, coffee or chocolate, a party of drums and fifes gave much satisfaction by playing outside the Hall.

At half past ten the company proceeded in regular order to the church, where Dr Arne conducted his *Judith* oratorio, performed by the most famous artists of the day, a full chorus and the complete Drury Lane orchestra. After the performance, which gave great satisfaction to a very numerous and polite audience, a procession was formed, headed by Garrick and the vocalists singing:

> This is a day, a holiday! a holiday!
> Drive spleen and rancour far away,

but when they reached the emblematical transparency on the Birth-place, mood and measure became more complex:

> Here Nature nurs'd her darling boy,
> From whom all care and sorrow fly,
> Whose harp the Muses strung:
> From heart to heart let joy rebound,
> Now, now we tread enchanted ground,
> Here Shakespear walk'd and sung.

At three there was a sumptuous public ordinary—price half a guinea—in the amphitheatre. Lord Grosvenor proposed a bumper to the Steward, the Steward replied with another to the Bard, the band struck up, and Garrick, flourishing his cup, burst into song:

> Behold this fair goblet, 'Twas carv'd from the tree,
> Which, O my sweet Shakespear, was planted by thee;
> As a relic I kiss it, and bow at the shrine;
> What comes from thy hand must be ever divine.

All joined in the chorus, 'All shall yield to the mulberry tree', and in the other glees and catches, before withdrawing at seven to prepare for the assembly and ball. This began at nine and lasted till three, while, for the benefit of those who could not afford a ticket, the town was illuminated, drums were beaten, immense quantities of fireworks were touched off by Mr Angelo, and a tumult of perfect satisfaction ended the first day's entertainment.

The sleepy revellers were called again at five by cannon, drums, bells and serenaders, somewhat muffled, however, by a Warwickshire drizzle. After another public breakfast in the Hall, about to be dedicated to Shakespear, the company repaired to the amphitheatre to hear the Dedication Ode, with incidental music by Dr Arne. Garrick stood in the centre of the orchestra, mulberry-wand in hand and medal on breast, dwarfed by the elegant lead statue of the bard, cast for the occasion at his own expense. It was a variation on the theme of Schee-

makers, and was subsequently raised to fill the ample niche so provi-
dently prepared by the Corporation. After a short overture and a
respectful bow, Garrick began his Ode with a rhetorical question:

> To what blest genius of the isle
> Shall gratitude her tribute pay,
> Decree the festive day,
> Erect the statue, and devote the pile?

The answer was not unexpected:

> 'Tis he!—'tis he!—that demi-god!
> Who Avon's flow'ry margin trod,
> While sportive fancy round him flew;

and the chorus proclaimed the immortal name, 'Shakespear! Shakespear! Shakespear!' At the end of every recited part of the Ode, Garrick sat down and gave the singers an opportunity to display their
abilities, and it was the chorus who swept all together at the end:

> We will his brows with laurel bind,
> Who charms to virtue human kind:
> Raise the pile, the statue raise,
> Sing immortal Shakespear's praise!

Yet the brows remained unlaurelled. There was to have been a procession composed of all the principal characters in the plays, and a
satyr-drawn triumphal car containing Melpomene, Thalia and the
Graces, who, to the accompaniment of Dr Arne's music, would have
crowned the statue. But a steady drizzle had become a steady down-
pour, and the ceremony was postponed.

Nothing daunted, Garrick rose to deliver a panegyric in prose, concluding with an open challenge to refute what he had said. It was
accepted by the celebrated London comedian, Thomas King, who
attacked Shakespeare as an underbred bully of our passions, making us
laugh and weep at will. Those in the audience who did not know him
thought he was serious and made a move to throw him out, and so
great was the press that benches collapsed and a falling door felled the
Earl of Carlisle. However, Garrick restored order and good humour
by reciting an arch poetical epilogue addressed to the ladies, with an
appropriate allusion to the statue still towering in their midst:

> Untouch'd and sacred be thy shrine,
> Avonian Willy, bard divine,
> In studious posture leaning!

After three o'clock dinner and five o'clock glees, Garrick's 'Sweet Willy O' being a particularly popular item, the town was again illuminated in spite of the rain that had turned Avon's flowery margin into a morass, and the indomitable Mr Angelo once more exhibited his dexterity with the whole machinery of pyrotechny in a grand and beautiful manner. The meanest sort of fancy dress cost four guineas the hiring, so that many had to be admitted with masks only, and others managed to squeeze in—and squeeze it was—without even a mask. There were Merry Wives, Mistress Quicklys, Witches and Slenders, as well as sailors, harlequins, waggoners and jockeys, but most of the literary gentlemen wore dominoes. And many literary gentlemen were there. Young James Boswell was one, though not in a domino. Having just published his account of Corsica and its patriot, Paoli, he created a sensation with his Corsican costume, pistols in belt, musket on back, and in his cap in letters of gold the legend *Corsica Boswell*. But his great friend Johnson was not there. The Doctor was taking the sea air at Brighton with Mr and Mrs Thrale. Yet if any literary gentleman might have been expected to attend that festival of genius it was Johnson. Not only was he the latest editor of Shakespeare, his long-expected edition of the plays having appeared in 1765, but Garrick was his oldest friend and most brilliant pupil. And yet the only trace of Johnson's presence at Stratford was in a shop window where a literary haberdasher displayed Jubilee Ribbons over a quotation from his famous Prologue for the opening of Drury Lane theatre: 'Each change of many-colour'd life he drew.' It was another seven years before Boswell got Johnson on to the classic ground of Shakespeare's native place, and even then the Doctor was disappointingly reticent about the Bard.

By the time the dancing was done and Mr Angelo's last squib had fizzled, the rain had become a deluge. The swirling river threatened to carry away the amphitheatre itself. Horses had to wade through the meadow, knee-deep, to reach it, and the revellers escaped on planks stretched from the entrance to their carriage doors. Such a flood had not been seen there in the memory of man. The postponed pageant was cancelled, as was a second recitation of the Ode, which Garrick had very politely consented to perform, and the brows of the Stratford statue remained for ever uncrowned. Many of the visitors left, but the race for the Jubilee Cup, value fifty guineas, on the sodden Shottery course, specially improved for the occasion, afforded much diversion to lovers of the turf. Five colts ran, and the Cup, engraved with Shakespeare's arms, was won by Mr Pratt, a groom, who loyally declared that, though he knew very little about plays and Master Shakespeare, he would never part with his prize. After this the weather improved, and that evening Mr Angelo was able to show what he really could do with a firework. There was a final grand ball at which Mrs Garrick distinguished herself by her inimitably graceful dancing of a minuet, and by four o'clock on Saturday morning the revels were ended.

It was all rather ridiculous, though it was not the fault of Garrick that the weather had failed them. He had done his best, and carried all before him by his gusto, confidence and irresistible good humour, and in three days done more than all the editors of half a century to make Shakespeare a national institution. Yet there had not been a performance of even a single scene from the plays, but only Garrick on the Bard, in Ode, Oration and a series of songs to Sweet Willy O. There was a certain air of patronage about it all, as though the articles of partnership had been modified, as though the firm was now not Shakespeare and Garrick, but Garrick and Shakespeare.

In Stratford, rain had robbed Garrick of his cherished pageant, but not even floods should deprive him of it in London, and that autumn saw his pageant of *Jubilee* at Drury Lane. A number of scenes depicting the comic Stratford yokels led up to the cancelled procession. First came the most famous characters from the plays, then the Comic Muse, Thalia, in a splendid car drawn by satyrs, then Melpomene attended by Apollo and the other seven Muses, and last a model of the Stratford statue, with emblematical ornaments and a numerous train of attendants. In the final tableau, 'decorated with transparent pictures', the Bard was nightly crowned with laurels, and sometimes Garrick would recite his Ode to the enraptured audience. This extravagant spectacle had the phenomenal run of ninety performances. In one sense at least Garrick fulfilled

> his Wish, his only Plan,
> To lose no Drop of that immortal Man,

but in another sense it was not easy to square this profession with his performance.

Hamlet was almost the only play on which no reformer had dared to lay his improving hand, yet now it was wilting under the irony of M. Voltaire, who called it a work so coarse and barbarous that one would think it the product of a drunken savage. Garrick was impressed and, full of confidence after his Jubilee successes, chivalrously came to the rescue of his countryman, though what exactly he did to the play we do not know, for his version was never published. However, we learn that 'the tedious interruptions of this beautiful tale no longer disgrace it; its absurd digressions are no longer disgusting. . . . This brilliant Creation of the Poet's Fancy is purged from the Vapours and Clouds which obscured it; and like his own Firmament, it appears to be finely fretted with Golden Stars.' Among the absurd digressions were the voyages of Laertes and Hamlet, now providentially prevented by storms, the *grossièretés abominables* of the grave-diggers and Hamlet's equally disgusting jests, by the omission of which the barbarous piece was refined and given a tidy classical unity. It is scarcely necessary to add that Garrick contrived the insertion of a few more speeches for himself.

This was the very year in which George Steevens published his edition of Shakespeare, and the editor-restorer wrote ironically to congratulate the player-reformer: 'I think you need not fear that the better part of your audience (as Othello says) should *yawn at alteration.* You had better throw what remains of the piece into a farce, to appear immediately afterwards. No foreigner would ever believe it was formed out of the loppings and excrescences of the tragedy itself. You may entitle it "The Grave-diggers; with the pleasant humours of Osrick, the Danish Macaroni."' Steevens's irony was justified; the better part of the audience, those who knew no more of neo-classical regulation than the audience for which Shakespeare had written, would have nothing to do with Garrick's version; they wanted their grave-diggers, and within a few years they were back on the stage again for good.

There were no more Jubilees for more than half a century. In the year after the 1769 affair the Stratford Corporation approached Garrick again, but he excused himself; he felt ill, and contented himself with a few words of advice about a projected annual celebration. This, he suggested, should be on the birthday of 'our Immortal Bard'—one of the first uses of the immortal phrase—and should take the form of the junketings that he had inaugurated: balls, bonfires, drums, choruses, mirth and good fellowship. Then, remembering his unhappy experiences in the rains of the previous autumn, he finished with a piece of constructive admonition: 'Let it not be said, for your honour and, I hope, for your interest, that the town which gave birth to the first genius since the creation is the most dirty, unseemly, ill-paved, wretched-looking place in all Britain.'

Garrick was not asked again. He died in 1779, and was buried in Westminster Abbey at the foot of the Scheemakers statue. Charles Lamb was then four years old, but soon after the turn of the century, while taking a stroll in the Abbey he came across an affectedly histrionic figure which proved to be the statue of Garrick. Underneath were the following lines:

> To paint fair nature by divine command,
> Her magic pencil in her glowing hand,
> A Shakespear rose: then, to expand his fame,
> Wide o'er this breathing world, a Garrick came.
> Though sunk in death the forms the Poet drew,
> The actor's genius bade them breathe anew;
> Though, like the bard himself, in night they lay,
> Immortal Garrick call'd them back to day;
> And till Eternity with pow'r sublime
> Shall mark the mortal hour of hoary Time,
> Shakespear and Garrick like twin-stars shall shine,
> And earth irradiate with a beam divine.

'It would be an insult to my readers' understandings', Lamb tartly remarked, 'to attempt anything like a criticism on this farrago of false thoughts and nonsense.'

Of course it is nonsense, yet Garrick had done more than any other man to popularise Shakespeare and establish the Cult, and he did at least revive a number of the plays 'as written by Shakespear'. On the other hand, by extracting episodes and transforming them into tinselly entertainments he set a disastrous example to his successors, who felt justified in trimming the plays in order to squeeze them into their picture-frame stages heavily embarrassed with apparatus.

VI

SHAKSPEARE FABRICATED

GARRICK's mantle fell on the shoulders of John Philip Kemble. At Drury Lane until 1802, and then at Covent Garden for another fifteen years, he and his sister, Mrs Siddons, were mainly responsible for presenting Shakespeare to London audiences. The theatres, however, were growing less and less like those for which Shakespeare had written. In 1782 Covent Garden was enlarged, and a few years later Drury Lane was completely rebuilt with a stage accommodation much larger than that of any other theatre in Europe, the painter and machine contriver having a prodigious space for the exertion of their abilities. The sheer size of stage and auditorium necessitated a reversion to the slow formalised style of acting, which Garrick had replaced by a rapid naturalism, and the slower the pace and more sumptuous the presentation, the less time there was for Shakespeare. And Kemble presented Shakespeare very sumptuously. He ordered stock sets of Gothick scenery, including 'a chapel of the pointed architecture', the Tower of London at the time of Richard III, views of New Palace Yard and the old Palace of Westminster, and numerous wings representing ancient English streets and other scenes 'selected on account of their picturesque beauty'. Properties were on the same grand scale and, according to one dramatic critic, when *Cymbeline* was produced, Imogen's bed was so vast that Iachimo 'stood almost in need of a ladder to take a view of her person'.

Fortunately, the period of classical improvement was almost over, and though Kemble still played many of the old adaptations, such as Tate's *King Lear* and Cibber's *Richard III*, he rarely sinned by presenting a completely new version of a play as a substitute for Shakespeare. His method was different, his approach less frivolous. According to his biographer and friend, James Boaden, when he set himself seriously to prepare a play for presentation, he considered it attentively 'in the author's genuine book', then examined what 'corrections' could be admitted into his text, and finally, 'what could be cut out in the representation, not as disputing the judgment of the author, but as suiting the time of representation to the habits of his audience'. That, at least, is frank. There simply was not time for Shakespeare as well as scenery and spectacle, and if one of the three had to go it must be Shakespeare. Thus, in *Measure for Measure*, Mariana, Mistress Overdone and the Elbow–Pompey–Froth comedy could easily be cut, and 2 *Henry IV* was equally loaded with superfluities that could be purged: the Induction and first scene, for example, the beginning of the third act and Lady Percy, while the King's soliloquy on sleep might well be transferred to the beginning of act four. There, indeed, we have it. Not only was Shakespeare to be cut, but he was to be turned inside out to avoid overmany changes of scene. It was reformation with a difference; the nineteenth century method of shuffling with the scenes; Shakespeare, in short, transposed.

It would be interesting to know what Boaden meant by 'the author's genuine book'. It is doubtful if he meant a quarto or a folio text, or even the text of Rowe, Pope, Theobald, Hanmer or Warburton. Four more editors were in the field. Johnson's edition had appeared in 1765, but as it was based on Warburton's, with little further collation of original editions, it had small claim to be called 'the genuine book'. Indeed, so inadequate was it, apart from its Preface (in which, as Boswell has it, 'the excellencies and defects of that immortal bard are displayed with a masterly hand'), that a certain William Kenrick aspired to emulate Theobald, and published a *Review of Dr. Johnson's new edition of Shakspeare; in which the Ignorance, or Inattention of the Editor is exposed*. His proposals for an edition of his own came to nothing. Johnson, a far greater man than Pope, made no reply, though he allowed himself the luxury of an epigram when Goldsmith confessed that he knew nothing about Kenrick: 'Sir, he is one of the many who have made themselves *publick*, without making themselves *known*.'

The Doctor dismissed an actual, as well as the potential, editor with equal brevity: 'If the man would have come to me, I would have endeavoured to endow his purpose with words, for as it is, he doth gabble monstrously.' The man was Edward Capell, whose edition of Shakespeare followed hard on the heels of Johnson's. Capell had no very high opinion of the work of his predecessors, and Hanmer's editorial labours, 'wantoning in very licence of conjecture', filled him with such astonishment and indignation that he 'resolv'd himself to be the champion . . . and save from further ruin an edifice of this dignity, which England must for ever glory in'. Thereupon he surrounded himself with all the editions on which he could lay hands, including almost all the quartos, and twenty-five years later, having, it is said, transcribed Shakespeare's works ten times, produced his own beautifully printed text. Although it was another ten years before his *Notes* were published, his text was the best that had yet appeared, for Capell was a genuine scholar, versed 'in all such reading as was never read'. Unfortunately he was no stylist, the sentences of his long Introduction sprawling ineffectually over the pages, an easy prey for Johnson's mordant wit.

George Steevens, mischievous instigator and mocker of the Jubilee, was only a few years behind Capell, his edition with notes by Johnson and himself appearing in 1773. As there was little more textual emendation to be done, his main object was to illustrate Shakespeare by the study of writers of his own time, which no doubt accounts for his defence of Theobald as a scholar who deserved a more honourable repository than the Temple of Dulness. His own scholarship, however, roused the fury of Joseph Ritson, an irascible young antiquary, author of *The Stockton Jubilee, or Shakspeare in his Glory*, a squib directed at the principal burgesses of that town, and he soundly castigated Steevens for his indolence, ignorance, temerity and mendacity.

Although undeserving of such abuse as this, Steevens was a legitimate target for satire. In spite of what Boswell called his 'acute discernment and elegant taste', he refused to admit the *Sonnets* into his edition 'because the strongest act of parliament that could be framed would fail to compel readers into their service', and maintained that if Shakespeare had produced no other work than this, he would be no better known to posterity than Thomas Watson, 'an older and much more elegant sonnetteer'. Then, he was plagued by an imp of perversity, which, among other frolics, drove him to write an entirely imaginary account of the upas tree to hoodwink good Erasmus Darwin, and to hoax the Society of Antiquaries with the tombstone of Hardicanute, embellished with an Anglo-Saxon inscription of his own invention. This passion for practical joking he carried into the editorial province. After the death of Capell in 1781, the long delayed *Notes* on his text were published by the Rev. John Collins, a stout defender of his author against the criticisms of Steevens. Steevens replied by coupling Collins with another parson against whom he had a grudge, and ascribing to the two innocent clergymen his own notes on the bawdier passages in Shakespeare. Then, there was the case of the 'Elizabethan'

letter. This, dated 1600, was contributed by an anonymous correspondent to the *Theatrical Review* of 1763:

Friend Marle,
    I must desyre that my Syster hyr watche, and the Cookerie book you
promysed, may be sente bye the man. I never longed for thy company more
than last night: we were all very merrye at the Globe, when Ned Alleyn did
not scruple to affyrme pleasauntely to thy friende Will, that he had stolen his
speeche about the qualityes of an Actors excellencye in Hamlet his Trajedye
from conversations manyfold whych had passed betweene them, and opinyons
given by Alleyn touchinge the subjecte. Shakespeare did not take this talke in
good sorte; but Johnson put an end to the strife with wittylye remarkinge,
'This affaire needeth no contentione; you stole it from Ned, no doubt; do not
marvel: Have you not seen him act tymes out of number?'
Believe me most syncerilie,
Yours, G. Peel.

It is, of course, a patent forgery; Marlowe and Peele were dead long
before 1600, and even if the date were wrong, Jonson was only twenty
when Marlowe was killed in 1593. Who the forger was we do not
know, but the malicious and tricksy Steevens, 'the Puck of commentators', has only himself to blame if there are those who consider him the
most likely culprit.

    Steevens grew more capricious and irritable with age, and the
appearance of a rival editor only added to his spleen. In 1780 two
volumes appeared, each of more than seven hundred pages, entitled
*A Supplement to the Edition of Shakspeare's Plays by Samuel Johnson
and George Steevens*. The first contained observations on the English
drama and theatre, and a reprint of the poems, including the *Sonnets*,
the second a reprint of the seven doubtful plays added to the third folio.
The author was Edmond Malone, an Irish barrister. Malone was all
courtesy and deference to the older man, but ventured to disagree with
him on a number of points, maintaining, for example, that part of
Pericles at least was genuine. Steevens was not too well pleased, and
Malone's ten-volume edition of Shakespeare in 1790 so excited his
jealousy that he reissued his own work in fifteen volumes, with additional and frequently reckless emendations and notes.

    Malone was the last of the great eighteenth-century editors, though
he was less concerned with textual emendation than with the discovery
of new material that would throw light on Shakespeare and his work.
Tireless in his researches, he unearthed a mass of contemporary
records from which to write an invaluable *History of the Stage* and to

expand Rowe's tenuous sketch of Shakespeare's life into a monumental biography of some five hundred pages. His Stratford incursions were not without incident.

In the prospectus for his twenty-volume edition he wrote that his *Life of Shakspeare* would be ornamented with a delineation of the bust at Stratford, of the head of which he possessed a facsimile. Unfortunately, in taking a cast of the effigy in 1793, the colouring so lovingly restored by Joseph Greene fifty years before had been damaged; but this, said Malone, was of no consequence; let the barbaric colours be covered with a coat of white paint, in accordance with the chaster taste of the present age. The young vicar, James Davenport, was easily over-awed and acquiesced, much to the delight of the tourists who soon covered this ideal writing surface with their pencilled autographs. Stratford opinion however, was divided. Some said that that grub Malone should have repaired his mischief, that the paint was merely a pretext for parsimony, and scurrilous verses appeared at the tomb:

> Traveller, to whom this monument is shewn,
> Invoke the poet's curses on Malone,
> Whose meddling zeal a barbarous taste displays,
> Daubing his tombstone, as he marr'd his plays.

Davenport had the satisfaction of presenting the imperturbable biographer to an octogenarian alderman who, as a boy, had eaten surreptitiously of the fruit of the celebrated mulberry tree, branches of which hung invitingly over his father's wall next door to New Place, before Mr Gastrell cut it down. The scene so moved Malone that he broke into poetical rhapsody, an amiable foible of his in moments of stress:

> In this retreat our Shakspeare's godlike mind
> With matchless skill surveyed all human kind;
> Here let each sweet that blest Arabia knows,
> 'Flowers of all hues, and without thorn the rose,'
> To latest times their balmy odours fling,
> And Nature here display eternal spring.

Then, returning to his prosaic researches, he discovered evidence that the destruction of the mulberry tree was not entirely Mr Gastrell's doing. A friend told him of a charitable Lichfield lady who had recently been turned out of the house that she rented by the owner, 'little more than a fiend', on the ground that the poor should not derive any benefit from any inhabitant of *that* property. The ultimatum has a familiar ring. The owner was Mrs Gastrell. No wonder it was common knowledge in Lichfield that it was Mrs Gastrell and not her husband who had cut down the mulberry tree. Malone was too cautious to swallow the whole of the Lichfield story, and by way of compromise concluded that it was a case of divided delinquency. He was not always equally cautious.

The Garrick Jubilee had fertilised the imaginations of the Stratfordians and stimulated the growth of a new crop of legends. It had also produced a new poet. This was John Jordan, a self-educated wheelwright with a taste for the antique. His first literary production had been a poetical address to Garrick on the occasion of the Jubilee, the success of which encouraged him to write a romantic-archaeological poem on his, and Shakespeare's, native countryside:

> On Welcombe Hills I tune my willing verse,
> Point out their beauties, and their fame rehearse.

He is as good as his word, and after a dissertation on the Dark Ages returns to his own, concluding with the beauty of the prospect from the summit:

> Hence eastward, Warwick's tow'rs attract the sight;
> And westward, Stratford's domes no less delight,
> Chiefly that ancient solemn pile, whose stones
> Have long enclos'd the much-lov'd Shakspeare's bones.

Poetry and prehistory, however, proved unrewarding, and the opportune arrival of a biographer in search of an author led to a slight change of emphasis in his researches, so that soon he was unofficial guide to Stratford with a highly vendable commodity, an original collection of Shakespeareana that he was prepared to retail to any sympathetic, and preferably affluent, inquirer. 'Alas,' he complained to Malone, 'I am unnoticed by the world, oppressed with affliction, and wrecked with despair; the anchor of hope has totally forsook me; I am dashed by the waves of a boundless sea of trouble, sorrow and misery, which brings to my mind an expression of Shakspeare, that

> Misery trodden on by many,
> Being low is not relieved by any.'

Malone was sympathetic, generous, and all ears. He heard an embroidered version of the crabtree story, finishing with Shakespeare's extempore verses on

Piping Pebworth, Dancing Marston,
Haunted Hillborough, Hungry Grafton,
Dadgeing Exhall, Papist Wicksford,
Beggarly Broom, and Drunken Bidford.

Jordan supplied a similarly embellished account of how Shakespeare fanned up his verses on John Combe and his brother Tom, and he actually produced the manuscript of the ballad on Sir Thomas Lucy, 'A parliement member, a justice of peace'. This had been found in a chest of drawers that formerly belonged to Mrs Dorothy Tyler of Shottery, who died in 1778 at the age of eighty. Malone was sceptical; the style was as modern as the handwriting, and though he included it in his new edition it was with the note that 'one part of this ballad is just as genuine as the other; that is, the whole is a forgery'. The age of fabrication had begun.

It was unfortunate for those seized with the new romantic passion for antiquity, and plagued with the Shakespeare mania, that now, apparently, nothing remained to be done. The plays had been edited and re-edited, annotated and re-annotated; Pope and Johnson had pronounced finally on the merits and demerits of the dramatist; Richard Farmer had written learnedly about his learning, Maurice Morgan about his characters, and now Malone had gleaned all information about his life. Stratford offered a fair field for the exploitation of her immortal bard, but for the more ambitious the only Shakespearean path to celebrity lay in the discovery of sensational new material, real or fictitious. Since the Jubilee, Mrs Hart, wife of the descendant of the poet's sister Joan, had been doing a brisk trade in relics at the Birthplace. In 1777 Horace Walpole had been shown the chair in which the bard used to sit in the chimney-corner. In 1785 the Hon. John Byng bought a slice of it 'the size of a tobacco-stopper', and after some bargaining carried off the lower cross-bar as well. By the time he returned some years later the last chip had gone. But Sharpe's mulberry shop still displayed its questionable wares, and there was a bookseller who claimed to have bought the New Place library. In the spring of 1793 Malone called on Jordan, ordered the monument to be painted white, and later in the year Samuel Ireland, accompanied by his seventeen-year-old son William-Henry, arrived in Stratford to draw his *Picturesque Views on the Warwickshire Avon*.

Samuel Ireland was the kindest and most ingenuous of men, and the most incompetent of artists. His real passion was for antiquities of every

Sketch of Stratford Jubilee Booth or Amphitheatre.

Immortality of Garrick, by George Carter, *c.* 1780

:speare, accompanied by Comedy and Tragedy, awaits Garrick's arrival
'arnassus

'The Bard, sitting in an antique chair, in an attitude of inspiration.

After the painting by Benjamin Wilson, presented by Garrick, 1769,
and formerly in the Town Hall, Stratford

kind, but particularly for old books, and of all writers of books Shake-speare was the supreme master. He never tired of extolling his genius, and in the evening frequently read his plays aloud, dwelling with enthusiasm on passages that particularly pleased him, and declaring that a single vestige of the poet's handwriting would be a pearl beyond all price, far dearer to him than his whole collection. To this atmosphere of antiquities, old books and Shakespeare in which his son William-Henry was brought up, was added another influence, the theatre. Samuel was friendly with Sheridan, the proprietor of Drury Lane, so that William had the free run of the playhouse, even behind the scenes, and one of his favourite pursuits was making pasteboard theatres. After a protracted visit to France, William returned to London to be articled to a solicitor, and to follow his father's hobby of collecting old books. Collecting led naturally to reading, and in this way he discovered Chaucer, Percy's *Reliques of Ancient Poetry* and Grose's *Treatise on Ancient Armour*, so that his bedroom became a regular armoury, which by moonlight appeared to him like some scene from *The Castle of Otranto*. Then he discovered Chatterton, the marvellous boy who had written the poems that he ascribed to a fifteenth-century monk, Thomas Rowley, and committed suicide when he was starving after the discovery of his fraud. William used frequently to envy his fate, and desired nothing so ardently as to perish in a similar way for a similar cause.

These, then, were the innocents who entered the atmosphere of chicanery that enveloped Stratford in the summer of 1793, the credulous antiquarian Shakespeare worshipper and his morbidly romance-saturated son. Fate could not have delivered a more promising prey into the hands of John Jordan.

Fortunately William-Henry, in his *Confessions*, has left us an account of this visit to Stratford and its consequences. As soon as they arrived Samuel plunged extravagantly into every research that might throw light on the history of the dramatic bard, accompanied of course by the plausible Jordan, who had fastened on them at once. He had a new anecdote for them. It was in Fulbrook park, not Charlecote park, that Shakespeare had poached Lucy's deer, and he showed the enchanted Irelands the keeper's lodge where the poet was confined until the charge was brought against him. Samuel added the building to his portfolio of picturesque views. But this is to anticipate; the very first place that Jordan took them to was Sharpe's mulberry shop, where

G

Samuel bought a number of the precious relics, including a goblet, for which he paid what he admitted to be an adequate price. And so to the church. 'It would', wrote William, 'be impossible for me to describe the thrill which then took possession of my soul.' No doubt Samuel was equally overcome by the proximity of 'the ashes of our immortal bard', but he soon recovered sufficiently to draw, cursing the while the folly of colouring the natural stone of the monument. The white paint had not yet been applied, the colour was damaged, and he wildly thought of following Malone's example and making a plaster cast of the bust. While his father was sketching, William strolled about the church until he was drawn, like a water diviner to water, towards a door which he pushed open, revealing to his horrified delight a pile of human bones. Samuel quoted *Hamlet*, and observed that this undoubtedly accounted for the verse on Shakespeare's gravestone: 'Curst be he that moves my bones.' That night, and every night of their week's stay, the talk was all of Shakespeare, the immortal and divine Shakespeare.

When they visited the site of New Place, and stood reverently in the garden imagining the mulberry tree as it had flourished forty years before, Jordan told them that on the destruction of the house all the furniture and papers had been removed to Clopton House on the outskirts of the town. This was the kind of news that Samuel had dreamed of, and within a few minutes they were at Clopton, where they found to their consternation that the owner was a wealthy farmer, ominously devoid of every refinement. Samuel's forebodings were justified. The rooms were dark and damp, full of mouldering old furniture, and when he asked if there were any ancient deeds or manuscripts in the house, the man replied: 'By God, I wish you had arrived a little sooner! Why, it isn't a fortnight since I destroyed several baskets-full of letters and papers, in order to clear a small chamber for some young partridges which I wish to bring up alive: and as to Shakspeare, why there were many bundles with his name wrote upon them. Why, it was in this very fireplace I made a roaring bonfire of them.' 'My God,' cried Samuel, leaping from his chair and clasping his hands, 'Sir, you are not aware of the loss which the world has sustained. Would to heaven I had arrived sooner!' It was only too true; the small chamber was full of partridges, but of Shakespeare's manuscripts not a line was to be found.

The catastrophic knowledge that they had missed this Shakespearean treasure by only a fortnight made their visit to the 'lowly mansion which had given birth to our immortal dramatist' something of an anticlimax. Mrs Hart was gone, and with her, or rather before her, the last chip of the bardic chair. But old Thomas Hart the butcher was still living, and he told them how, when a boy, he and his friends used to dress up in the poet's clothes. He had no objection to Samuel's making a drawing of the kitchen where the great man must frequently have sat, and of a little parlour adjoining. It was in the tiling of this house, Jordan observed, that the 'spiritual will' of Shakespeare's father, apparently a devout Catholic, had been discovered some years before. William, a devout Protestant, shuddered, yet wished with all his soul that he was the owner of the humble tenement.

Still under the guidance of the indefatigable Stratford Poet, they visited the cottage whence our bard had married Anne Hathaway. It was eminently picturesque, and swarming with impoverished descendants of her family, who, when Samuel had finished his sketch, showed him the very bugle purse that our poet had given to the object of his choice, and the old oak chair on which he used to sit during his courtship, with Anne upon his knee. Samuel added them both to his collection. There remained the crab tree, and Jordan gave them his latest version of the toping episode as they rambled from Shottery to Bidford, where Samuel made a very correct drawing of the town and another of the tree. His portfolio was now full, the tour was over, and he and William returned to London with their mulberry relics, sliver of crab, bugle purse and old oak chair, but, alas, no Shakespearean manuscripts.

The atmosphere of bardolatry became even more oppressive in the Norfolk Street house; the beauties of Shakespeare were the daily theme of Samuel's after-dinner conversation, and in the evening William and his sister were allotted parts in the play selected for reading aloud. But Samuel never ceased to lament the loss of the treasure that had so nearly been his at Clopton House, and to repeat that the possession of even a signature of the bard would make him the happiest of human beings. William—he was barely eighteen—determined to make him so, though maybe his altruism was not quite as unalloyed as he would have us think. A moody and frustrated romantic, he was a late developer and considered stupid. Here was a golden opportunity to increase his importance and his own happiness as well as his father's. But first, to prepare the way.

At the beginning of December, 1794, William mentioned to his father that he had recently met a wealthy young gentleman who, finding him interested in ancient documents, had invited him to look through a chest of family papers. He had done so, and soon made an astonishing discovery. The gentleman had recognised its importance, but insisted that he should have the document, though only on condition that his name should never be divulged. He was, William added, a very diffident and retiring young gentleman indeed. Samuel was all agog to see the promised find; but it was not yet quite ready.

As William was frequently left alone in the office of his employer, a conveyancer, he manufactured some ink that dried an antique brown, cut off a piece of parchment from an old rent-roll, placed a Jacobean deed on his desk and, imitating the writing as best he could, drew up a mortgage, dated 1610, between 'William Shakespeare of Stratford on Avon Gent of thone Pte and Michael Fraser and Elizabeth hys Wife of the othere Pte'. Shakespeare's signature he copied from a facsimile in Steevens's edition, wrote Fraser's with his left hand, and with some difficulty affixed an old seal bearing the impression of a quintain.

One evening, shortly before Christmas, he drew the deed from his bosom and presented it dramatically to his father. 'There, sir, what do you think of that?' Samuel's excitement froze him into a state of false equanimity as he examined the document, folded it again and returned it, saying, 'I certainly believe it to be a genuine deed of the time.' Then followed a remarkable exchange of civilities: 'If you think it so, I beg your acceptance of it.'—'It is impossible for me to express the pleasure you have given me by the presentation of this deed; there are the keys of my book-case; go and take from it whatsoever you please; I shall refuse you nothing.'—'I thank you, sir, but I shall accept of nothing.' But Samuel insisted and, taking a book from his shelves, pressed it on his son. It was Stokes's *Vaulting Master*. Mr Ireland was, for the moment, the happiest of human beings.

The next day a stream of antiquaries began to pour into the Norfolk Street house to inspect the document. All seemed to be convinced that it was genuine, and that the impression of the quintain—a post for tilting at with a spear—was the peculiar and appropriate seal of the monarch of the drama. But where, they asked, had the deed been found? William repeated his story about the generous and retiring gentleman, but virtuously refused to reveal his name. Yet he did not escape thus easily. The antiquaries pointed out to Samuel that wherever the deed had been found, there, no doubt, were all the Shakespeare papers that had so long and vainly been sought by the scholars. Samuel then appealed to his son, pleaded with him, cajoled him, ordered him to resume his search, even taunted him for being such a fool as to allow so rare an opportunity to escape him. William succumbed, and found another document.

This was Shakespeare's note of hand, promising to pay his colleague, John Heminge, the sum of five pounds five shillings in return for 'hys greate trouble in settling and doinge much for me at the Globe Theatre as also for hys trouble in going downe for me to stratford'. Heminge's signed receipt on the very day that payment was due was another and very satisfactory proof of Shakespeare's uprightness of dealing and punctiliousness in matters of business.

William was gaining confidence, and became more venturesome. He knew Davenant's story, recorded by Rowe, that the Earl of Southampton had once given Shakespeare a thousand pounds 'to go through with a purchase that he had a mind to', and confirmation of this princely gift was not long in forthcoming. Not only had Shakespeare thoughtfully made a copy of his letter of gratitude, 'a Budde which Bllossommes Bllooms butte never dyes', but Southampton had replied to his 'Deare William', gently chiding him for accepting only half of the sum he had offered. The spelling was becoming more choicely antique, and Shakespeare's style was applauded beyond measure. The only disappointment in the correspondence was the failure to mention the exact sum and the purchase that the poet had a mind to.

If Samuel and his fellow antiquaries were so hot for certainties in Shakespeare's life, they should have them; and now began that curious reconstruction of the poet after William's own sentimentally romantic image. He remembered the spiritual will of John Shakespeare, which Jordan had told him of, and determined that there should be no misunderstanding about his son's religion, but that the bard should prove of the like persuasion as himself, a zealous Protestant, devoid of superstition and bigotry. So he wrote a long profession of faith, signed 'Wm Shakspeare', taking care to use the letters contained in the signature as much as possible: '. . . O cheryshe usse like the sweete Chickenne thatte under the coverte offe herre spreadynge Wings Receyves herre lyttle Broode ande hoverynge overre themme keepes themme harmlesse and in safetye.' William himself was so affected by the sublimity of this effusion that, as he told Samuel, he made it his morning and evening prayer, and all agreed that such genuine feeling breathed throughout the whole that it must be from the pen of the great dramatist, and that the idea of his having been a Catholic was now satisfactorily disposed of. The pompous and Reverend Dr Samuel Parr, Johnson's self-appointed successor, even went so far as to pronounce, 'Sir, we have very fine passages in our church service, and our litany abounds with beauties; but here, sir, is a man who has distanced us all!' William could scarcely believe his ears; he had never doubted his genius, but hardly dared to hope that it was on the same plane as Shakespeare's. He retired to the dining-room where, in spite of cooling his forehead against the window-pane, he completely surrendered himself to vanity and ambition.

Full of his new importance and self-importance, William began to boast of the treasures he had seen at the gentleman's mansion, including a splendid full-length portrait of the poet, two or three manuscript plays, and hundreds of annotated books that must have come from New Place library. Moreover, his friend, Mr H. as he began to call him, had made a deed of gift, which of course he kept himself, making over to William all the Shakespearean material that he might discover. This was more than Samuel's curiosity could bear, and he wrote an affable letter to Mr H., hinting at a speedy delivery of the portrait and manuscript plays; but the gentleman was evasive, and his reply was devoted mainly to congratulating Samuel on being the father of such a son.

William had overreached himself about the portrait, and when he produced an amateurish pen and ink sketch resembling the folio engraving, in earnest of what was to come, it was not well received. However, Samuel was somewhat mollified by William's discovery the next day of Shakespeare's accompanying letter to the actor Cowley, explaining that it was a 'whymsycalle conceyte' that he would at once understand. Its meaning, however, quite escaped the Norfolk Street antiquaries. William was piqued, and tried another drawing.

As he was walking along Butcher Row, he saw an old coloured print for sale, framed between two pieces of glass, one side having the figure of an old Dutchman, the other a young man in early seventeenth-century costume. Seeing that it would be useful in his Shakespearean employment, he bought it, drew a pair of scales and a knife for the Dutchman, and touched up the young man's face to make it look something like the folio portrait. He also added the Shakespeare arms, the initials W.S. and the titles of some of the plays. The two figures on this remarkable pastiche were at once interpreted by the connoisseurs

as representations of Shylock and of Shakespeare himself in the character of Bassanio, and Samuel found good reason to believe that the print
used to hang in the greenroom of the Globe.

The appetite of Samuel and his cronies grew by what it fed on, but
they rationalised their pardonable cupidity by persuading themselves,
and William, that the more papers were found the more probable would
their authenticity appear. This was where the New Place library came
in useful, and dozens of old books and pamphlets arrived, all with
Shakespeare's name on their title-pages and with marginal notes in his
hand. Those in a first edition of the *Faerie Queene* were so elegant that
a gentleman immediately offered Samuel sixty pounds for the volume,
and the very feeling note in a tract describing the execution of Guy
Fawkes was welcomed as further proof of the poet's philanthropy: 'Hee
hadd beene intreated bye hys freynde John Hemynges to attende sayde
executyonne butte he lykedde notte toe beholde syghtes of thatte
kynde.' William's one regret was that he failed to find a copy of
Holinshed's *Chronicles* with pages big enough to take his invaluable
marginalia. Not, of course, that he was interested in making any profit
out of his fabrications, although it was true that his father had agreed
to put any receipts into a trust fund until he came of age.

Another device for speeding bulk production was the fabrication of
playhouse receipts, tied up in bundles with pieces of worsted unravelled
from an old tapestry in the House of Lords. In this he almost came to
disaster. One of the most curious of the receipts was considered to be:

> Inne the Yeare o Chryste
> Forre oure Trouble inne goynge
> toe Playe before the Lorde Leycesterre
> ats house and oure greate
> Expenneces thereuponne 19 poundes
> Receyvedde ofs Grace the Summe
> o 50 Poundes
>   Wm Shakspeare

Originally, the Yeare o Chryste was given as 1590, but just in time
William discovered that Leicester had then been dead two years, and
he tore off the corner containing the date. He was as economical as he
was ignorant and extravagantly careless.

Yet of one thing he was very careful: not to be discovered at his
Shakespearean labours. He had a friend, Montague Talbot, like himself employed in a conveyancer's office, but with his heart in the

theatre, and he used to twit William about his passion for old manuscripts. When, therefore, he heard of the Norfolk Street papers his suspicions were roused, and he laughingly accused his friend of having forged them. William denied the charge, and moved his desk closer to the window that every visitor had to pass on his way into the office. One day, however, Talbot surprised him by bending double and creeping close to the wall beneath the window, then darting into the office and seizing his arm while he was working on one of the documents. Fortunately, Talbot thought it a splendid joke and readily agreed to hold his tongue, though, when the forgeries began to pay a handsome dividend, he did make a half-hearted attempt at blackmail. As Samuel was the treasurer, Talbot got nothing, but being an easy-going fellow with no wish to get involved in anything unpleasant, he kept the secret, though the knowledge that he could have exposed him at any moment was a perpetual source of worry to William.

It was at about this time, early in 1795, that one of the most interesting of the Shakespeare papers came to light, a letter from Queen Elizabeth herself to 'Master William Shakspeare atte the Globe bye Thames':

Wee didde receive youre prettye Verses goode Masterre William through the hands off oure Lorde Chamberlayne ande wee doe Complemente thee onne theyre great excellence Wee shalle departe fromme Londonne toe Hamptowne forre the holydayes where wee Shalle expecte thee withe thye beste Actorres thatte thou mayste playe before ourselfe toe amuse usse bee notte slowe butte comme toe usse bye Tuesdaye nexte asse the lord Leiscesterre wille bee withe usse

As the Globe was built ten years after Leicester's death, some of the more knowledgeable Elizabethan scholars may have been not entirely convinced. Perhaps they also wondered at the royal prodigality of the spelling, with its flourish of final *e*'s and double consonants. Then, what a shame the pretty verses were missing. There was no satisfying the antiquaries. Yet within a few days some original verse was discovered, five stanzas of it, with a lock of the bard's own hair, dark, straight and wiry, tied with a piece of knotted silk, in a love-letter addressed to Anna Hatherrewaye:

Deareste Anna
      As thou haste alwaye founde mee toe mye Worde moste trewe soe thou shalt see I have stryctlye kepte mye promyse I praye you perfume thys mye poore Locke withe thye balmye Kysses forre thenne indeede shalle

Kynges themmselves bowe ande paye homage toe itte I doe assure thee no
rude hande hathe knottedde itte thy Willys alone hathe done the worke
Neytherre the gyldedde bawble thatte envyronnes the heade of Majestye noe
norre honourres moste weyghtye wulde give mee halfe the joye as didde thysse
mye lyttle worke forre thee The feelinge thatte dydde neareste approache
untoe itte was thatte whiche commethe nygheste untoe God meeke ande
Gentle Charytye forre thatte Virrtue O Anna doe I love doe I cheryshe thee
inne mye hearte forre thou arte ass a talle Cedarre stretchynge forthe its
branches ande succourynge the smallere Plants fromme nyppynge Winneterre
orr the boysterouse Wyndes Farewelle toe Morrowe bye tymes I wille see thee
tille thenne Adewe sweete Love

Thyne everre

Wm Shakspeare

The verses to the siren of Shottery, courted on the very chair now in
Samuel's study, began,

> Is there inne heavenne aught more rare
> Thanne thou sweete Nymphe of Avon fayre
> Is there onne Earthe a Manne more trewe
> Than Willy Shakspeare is toe you

There was the same lamentable lack of punctuation in verse as in
prose, as, indeed, in the prose of the Queen herself and all her subjects.
They might almost be scriveners in a conveyancer's office. No wonder
Theobald had insisted on the proper pointing of the plays.

Acquisitive antiquary as Samuel was, he was no miser gloating privately over his literary treasure, but eager, only too eager, to let the
world share his rapture. Number 8, Norfolk Street, was now one of
the most famous addresses in London, and celebrities flocked to see the
Shakespeare Papers. On February 20th Boswell came. He was impressed, nay, by internal as well as by external evidence, he was convinced of the validity of the manuscripts. Then, having drunk a tum-
bler of warm brandy and water, he redoubled his praises and, sinking
on his knees, he said, 'I now kiss the invaluable relics of our bard: and
thanks to God that I have lived to see them!' Rising, he continued, 'I
shall now die contented, since I have lived to witness the present day.'
It was just as well, for he died three months later.

On the same day, May 19th, 1795, Ritson wrote to a friend, 'The
Shakspeare papers, of which you have heard so much, are, I can assure
you, a parcel of forgeries, studiously and ably calculated to deceive the
public.' William was quite right. Ritson's piercing eye, silent scrutiny

and laconic questions had filled him with dread, and when he left the house without giving any opinion, he was convinced that he knew the papers were spurious. Nor, with equal reason, had he any more faith in the gullibility of old George Steevens when he visited the house. Malone, a barrister as well as a scholar who knew more about Shakespeare than any man living, was too shrewd to go to Norfolk Street where he would not be able to examine the papers in detail, and asked to see them on neutral ground, but not unnaturally Samuel refused to let them out of his hands. Malone had sniffed forgery at once, particularly when he heard of the scorched appearance of the papers, the result of William's having to hold them to the fire to give his ink its antique appearance. The objection had been raised before, but Samuel blandly assured such chicken-hearted sceptics that the scorching was only another proof of authenticity. It was well known that John Warburton's famous collection of old plays and manuscripts had been unluckily burned or used as pie-bottoms some forty years before. Ecce signum! But Malone was not impressed by the story of the bakings of Betsy, and wrote to tell his friend, Lord Charlemont, that he was sure the documents were forgeries.

Others were less violent in their incredulity, and contented themselves with parodying the worst excesses of Shakespeare's orthography. Thus, a correspondent to one newspaper contributed his own literary discovery:

Tooo Missteerree Beenjaammiinnee Joohnnssonn
Deeree Sirree
     Wille youe doee meee theee favvourree too dinnee wythee meee onnn Friddaye nextte attt twoo off theee clockee too eatee sommee muttonne choppes andd somme poottaattooeesse
                 I amm deerree sirree
                 Yourre goodde friennde
                 Williame Shaekspare

On the whole, however, people were prepared to accept the manuscripts as genuine, but Samuel was so distressed that anybody should doubt their authenticity that, a few days after Boswell's visit, Dr Parr persuaded a number of convinced adherents to sign a Certificate of Belief. In addition to himself and Boswell, there were Samuel's friends, the Hon. John Byng (owner of two chips of Shakespeare's chair) and Francis Webb, as well as Garter King-of-Arms, Poet Laureate Henry James Pye, and a dozen others. Samuel had little doubt that the next additions to his collection would convince all disbelievers.

These were the manuscript plays that William had told him about early in January, though it was the end of February before Mr H. could be induced to part with the original *King Lear*. William had been in a dilemma, for though he had a copy of the first folio, its text was eyed with much suspicion by the editors of the day; he wanted an early quarto of the play, which he naturally assumed would be closer to the original. Then he found a copy of the first, the 1608, quarto in his father's library, and secretly carried it off to his office where he made a transcript in his version of Shakespeare's hand. He could not know that the folio *King Lear* was a much better text, and the quarto probably a pirated edition printed from shorthand notes made at a performance. However, this was not very important; his mission was to produce the Shakespeare that he and the late eighteenth century expected. It was generally admitted to be extraordinary that the plays were so very unequal, abounding in ribaldry and quite unworthy lines, so that by cutting these he would be performing the entirely laudable act of proving them to be the players' interpolations, just as by making such other alterations as he considered appropriate he would prove Shakespeare an even better writer than had ever been suspected.

The manuscript was prefaced by the interesting apologetic note:

TRAGEDYE OF KYNGE LEARE

Isse fromme Masterre Hollinneshedde I have
inne somme lyttle deparretedde fromme
hymme butte thatte Libbertye wille notte
I truste be blamedde bye mye gentle
Readerres

Wm Shakspeare

All the Fool's bawdiness goes, of course, with much of Kent's anni-
hilating vituperative assault on Oswald, and the more unseemly passages of Edgar's madness. By his lofty additions and deft abstractions William immensely improved the final scene:

Cordelya staye O staye yette a lyttle
Whatte ist thou sayst her voyce was everre softe
And lowe sweete musyck oere the ryplynge Streame . . .

Then, Kent's last words,

I have a journey, sir, shortly to go;
My master calls me, I must not say no,

seeming to him a jingle quite inadequate for the occasion, he composed a little speech that he was, even ten years later, 'so arrogant as to believe would not injure the reputation of Shakspeare':

> Thanks Sir butte I goe toe thatte unknowne Land
> That Chaynes each Pilgrim faste within its Soyle
> Bye livynge menne mouste shunnd mouste dreadedde
> Stille mye goode masterre thys same Journey tooke
> He calls mee I amme contente ande strayght obeye
> Thenne farewelle Worlde the busye sceane is done
> Kente livd mouste true Kente dyes mouste lyke a Manne

The critics went even further than William, and pronounced that the manuscript proved beyond doubt that Shakespeare was a much more finished writer than had ever before been imagined.

Samuel was in ecstasies, though just a little dashed when he heard that one of the other manuscript plays that William had found was merely a fragment. The drudgery of editing and transcribing *Lear* had so wearied William that he produced only a few tantalising pages of *Hamblette*, sufficient, however, to show that Shakespeare was in no way responsible for Hamblette's indecencies; here was no talk of lying between maids' legs, and even the prince's prose was found to be no more than a player's paraphrase of the original verse:

> A great Mans memorye maye outelive hys life
> Bye halfe a yeare butte thenne by youre Ladye
> Hee muste builde Churches else looke you
> Hee shalle sufferre notte thynkynge ont
> Ande thenne withe Dobyne and the hobbye horse
> Hee shalle goe goe

Altogether, William's variations confirmed the growing opinion as to Shakespeare's correctness as a writer, and, as Samuel put it, 'The small fragment of Hamlet will constrain us the more sincerely to regret the loss of the rest of these simple, yet impressive, effusions of his natural and easy vein.' However, an even more impressive effusion was now in his hands, or virtually so.

One of the Shakespearean manuscripts that William had so recklessly described as being in the possession of Mr H. was a hitherto unknown play of *Vortigern and Rowena*. It was a happy coincidence, for it was the very subject of a large drawing in Samuel's study, depicting Rowena offering wine to Vortigern, a copy of a picture by John

Hamilton Mortimer, made by Samuel himself. When he recklessly announced his discovery William had not even thought of a subject, but this drawing had inspired him to look up the story in his father's Holinshed and try his prentice hand at Shakespearean blank verse. To save time he wrote it in his own hand, pretending that he had copied it from the original, and delivered it to his impatient father a few sheets at a time. By the end of February it was almost complete, and this was the effusion on which Samuel mainly relied to convince unbelievers of the authenticity of the Shakspeare Papers as a whole.

The time had come to take preliminary measures for their publication. They would, he thought, give infinite satisfaction to the public, and incidentally prove a source of benefit to his family. William, however, was alarmed; the affair was growing quite beyond his control, but when he protested that Mr H. would never agree to the papers being made public, his father asked him why on earth his friend should oppose a scheme that might well bring him a fortune. 'But suppose they should not be really manuscripts of Shakspeare?' the unhappy boy objected. 'If all the men of abilities living', Samuel replied, 'were now to come forward and severally attest that each had undertaken his particular part to produce those papers, I would not believe them.' How, then, could William ever convince him that he, a rather stupid boy of eighteen, had produced them? He had to submit, 'But', he added, 'if you are determined on publishing them, remember, I deliver this message from the gentleman, "You do it at your own risk"; as he will have no concern in the business, or ever give up his name to the world.' 'On those terms', replied Samuel, 'I very willingly accept his acquiescence.'

And so, on March 4th, 1795, Samuel drew up the prospectus for his literary treasure. It was to consist of a variety of authentic documents representing the private and public life of our divine bard, a copy of *King Lear* differing materially from any other extant edition, and a number of facsimiles and engravings. No expense was to be spared in the production of this sumptuous folio, the price of which would be four guineas. Samuel added a postscript: the newly discovered play of *Vortigern* would not be published until the eve of its appearance on the stage. Subscriptions were invited and tickets printed, admitting potential subscribers to view the Papers at Number 8, Norfolk Street, Strand, between the hours of twelve and three.

The nobility and gentry rallied to the cause, and among the hundred and twenty-two subscribers were Boswell, George Chalmers, Glasgow College, Mrs Jordan, New College, Oxford, Henry James Pye, Rev. Dr Samuel Parr and Richard Brinsley Sheridan. And there was Charles Macklin, who half a century before had sat with Garrick under the celebrated mulberry tree in New Place garden, and afterwards delivered the first course of lectures on Shakespeare. He should have had a rare nose for authenticity, for he himself had once possessed a Jacobean pamphlet of anecdotes about Shakespeare and Ben Jonson, lost, unfortunately, on its passage from Ireland. But then his judgment was passed its meridian, for he was nearing his century.

As a friend of Samuel's and a subscriber to the Papers, Sheridan naturally expected to have the right of producing *Vortigern*. He read as much of the play as was already in Samuel's possession, and agreed to produce it at Drury Lane sometime before the publication of the Papers in December. This was all very well, but Samuel wanted a contract. Naturally this had to wait until Sheridan had read the complete manuscript, though when he had done so he wondered if he had been wise. There were, he admitted, some bold ideas, but they were singularly crude and undigested; Shakespeare, he thought, must have been a very young man when he wrote the play. However, he had given his word, but it was September before the contract was signed. The terms were not generous, but Samuel looked forward to a long and successful run.

Meanwhile, an interesting point had been raised by one of the subscribers. Suppose a descendant of Shakespeare should be found? Would not the Papers legally be his? It was a staggering suggestion. Samuel and William remembered the old butcher of the Birthplace; but it was not long before William's inventive brain had devised a means of safeguarding what was, after all, his own property. After a decent interval he discovered a fascinating piece of biographical information.

It was already known that in 1604 the tenant of the Blackfriars house bought by Shakespeare in 1613 was one William Ireland, but it was not known that there was any closer relationship between the two. What was the excitement then, when William discovered tributary lines from Shakespeare to Ireland, whose second name, by the strangest coincidence in the world, proved to be Henry. Beneath the linked arms of Ireland and Shakespeare (reversed) the poet had written:

Inne life wee
wille live togetherre
Deathe
shalle forre a lyttelle
parte usse butte
Shakspeares Soule restelesse
inne the Grave shalle uppe
Agayne ande meete hys freynde hys
IRELANDE
Inne the bleste Courte of Heavenne

He added a postscript: 'Keepe thys forre mee ande shoud the Worlde prove sowerre rememberre oune lives thatte loves the stylle'.

This was merely an antiquarian's appetiser. There followed a deede of guyftte from Shakespeare to Ireland, dated 25 October 1604:

. . . Onne or abowte the thyrde daye of the laste monethe beyng the monethe of Auguste havynge withe mye goode freynde Masterre William Henrye Irelande ande otherres taene boate neare untowe myne house afowresayde wee dydd purpose goynge uppe Thames butte those thatte were soe toe connducte us beynge muche toe merrye throughe Lyquorre theye didde upsette oure fowresayde bayrge alle butte myeselfe savedd themselves bye swimmyng for though the Waterre was deepe yette owre beynge close nygh toe shore made itte lyttel dyffyculte for themm knowinge the fowresayde Arte Master William henrye Irelande notte seeynge mee dydd aske for mee butte oune of the Companye dydd answerre thatte I was drownynge onn the whyche he pulledd off hys Jerkynne and jumpedd inn afterre mee withe muche paynes he draggedd mee forthe I beynge then nearelye deade and soe he dydd save mye life and for the whyche Service I doe herebye give hym as folowithe!!! fyrste mye writtenn Playe of Henrye fowrthe Henrye fyfthe Kyng John Kyng Leare as allsoe mye written Playe neverr yett impryntedd whych I have named Kyng henrye thyrde of Englande alle the profytts of the whych are whollye toe bee for sayde Ireland and atte hys deathe thenne toe hys fyrste Sonne namedd alsoe William henrye . . .

and so on. William had an additional piece of news for his father: Mr H. himself had discovered evidence among his family papers, proving that he, William-Henry, was the direct descendant of the William Henry Ireland of the deed of gift, so that he no longer regarded William's possession of the manuscripts as a favour, but as his by right of descent. So much for the old butcher of Stratford.

Although William's claim to the Papers was now satisfactorily established, there were some who thought the coincidence of the names William Henry too strange to be true; and how many Elizabethan commoners, Malone caustically asked, had two Christian names? In

July, Ritson was writing again about his visit to Norfolk Street: 'It would be a very easy matter to demonstrate, as well by intrinsic as by external evidence, every article to be a recent and palpable forgery. It appeared to me, at the time, that Ireland himself was the dupe of this imposture, but whether he is still ignorant of its real nature and design, I cannot be quite so positive.'

No wonder Samuel was getting worried. Then Sheridan was still shying at the *Vortigern* contract, the Papers had already gone to press, and subscribers were wanting to know more about the mysterious Mr H. If only he could discover who he was his Preface to the Papers would carry much more conviction. All manner of inquiries were set afoot, and William was constantly shadowed in the reasonable belief that he must sooner or later lead his pursuers to the house of his wealthy friend. Nobody thought of spying what he was up to in his office, or of picking the lock of the window-seat that contained his simple apparatus. At last Samuel appealed to Mr H. himself, but all he received in return was a panegyric on William. The young man despised the unromantic drudgery of law, and though he was generally regarded as a dullard, he was in reality a genius, 'a second Shakspeare'. As proof of this Mr H. enclosed a speech from a play that William himself had written, not a transcript from a new discovery, but from an original work in the Shakespearean manner on the subject of William the Conqueror. Samuel was delighted to hear that his son was brother in genius to Shakespeare, but the knowledge did not relieve his anxiety; perhaps it only increased it.

William's labours in the first two or three months of the year had been prodigious. Not only had he forged innumerable minor documents, but he had also transcribed *King Lear* with improvements, written *Vortigern*, and somehow contrived to satisfy his employer that he was not entirely inefficient as a conveyancer's clerk. Now, completely carried away by vanity, he was preparing to appear as an original dramatist, and proposed to write a series of history plays dealing with all the reigns not already covered by Shakespeare, from William I to Elizabeth. It was a dangerous move at this critical stage. Even William saw this, and decided that it would be better to find another Shakespeare play, say *Henry II*. At the same time he would do his best for his father, whose anxiety was becoming painful, and discover another document that would help to account for Mr H.'s strange behaviour. He would do something for Shakespeare as well.

'Shakspeare as Bassanio'
from Samuel Ireland's *Shakspeare Papers*, 1796

Is there onne Earth a Manne more trewe
Than Willy Shakspeare is to you

Shakspeare's letter to Anna Hatherrewaye, with a lock of his hair, from Samuel Ireland's *Shakspeare Papers*, 1796

The poet's recently discovered will was an unsatisfactory document. There was that unfortunate bequest of his second best bed to his wife, and equally distressing, there was no mention of literary matters, of plays or books or even of theatres. The discovery, therefore, was another deed of gift, anticipating and supplementing the will. First, his deare Wife was to have £180, his suyte of greye Vellvett and his lyttlle Cedarr Trunke with its contents. Then followed legacies to his deare Daughterr (presumably Susanna) and to his fellow actors at the Globe, among whom he distributed most of his plays. A particularly pleasing item was the gift of 15 shyllyngs to little Jonas Greggs for ye troble he hathe hadd inn goynge often tymes withe letterrs toe ye Globe. Finally, a Chylde who muste nott be named here was to have three hundred pounds, three houses and the remaining eight plays, one of which was *Kynge Vorrtygerne*. Shakespeare's trustee was his old and tried friend John Heminge, who, in return for seeing the deed rightly executed, received twenty pounds and four plays, including *Henry VII*.

It was easy enough to reconstruct what had happened. Presumably Ireland had stood godfather to the unmentionable child, and, when Heminge had defaulted and embezzled the property, adopted young William-Henry Shakespeare as William-Henry Ireland. Mr H. was undoubtedly a Heminge, a descendant of Shakespeare's faithless friend, and having discovered his ancestor's infamy, was anxious to restore the manuscripts to their rightful owner. Naturally, he was equally anxious to remain unknown.

The document was William's masterpiece, but over-ingenious for Samuel's purpose, as a prefatory explanation of how the papers had come into his hands. However, as publication day approached, he received encouragement from the very highest quarters. One of the staunchest believers was the actress Mrs Jordan, and it was she who brought Samuel and William to the attention of her royal lover, the Duke of Clarence, whom she had recently presented with an addition to their rapidly expanding family. Courteously received at St James's Palace one November day, Samuel was able to answer satisfactorily all the Duke's queries and objections, and to dispel any doubts that arose in the simple mariner's mind.

St James's Palace led inevitably to Carlton House and a visit to the Prince of Wales. But a few days before this, on Christmas Eve, the *Miscellaneous Papers of Shakspeare* had been published. Samuel was unable to tell his readers anything about the 'gentleman of considerable

H

property' who had given the manuscripts to his son, but what of that? The Papers spoke for themselves, and any disinterested critic or antiquarian could see that they were 'no other than the production of Shakspeare'. His Preface is as dignified as it is pathetic. 'Next to the crime of attempting to impose on others,' he wrote, 'and inviting them to countenance the imposition, is the cruel and unmanly charge of taxing another with so unworthy a design. To the Editor that charge has been imputed: and to this he can with truth reply, that no consideration should, under such circumstances, have induced him to practise such a fraud, had the quality of the thing pretended been ever so excellent; and that, had even the possibility of forging these papers been in his estimation within the reach of art, they never should have met the public eye.' Poor gullible Samuel; the situation was becoming as tragic as it was ludicrous.

On the morning of December 28th, as Samuel was preparing to leave for Carlton House, his friend Albany Wallis arrived breathless with the news that he had something in his pocket that would completely 'knock up the Shakspeare Papers'. It was a signature of John Heminge that he had just discovered, and placing the neat autograph beside William's scrawled forgery he asked what Samuel was going to do. Samuel had no idea; no sooner had the Papers been published than they were, apparently, proved to be spurious, and it was with this knowledge that he went to Carlton House to persuade the Prince of Wales of their authenticity.

When William returned from the office that afternoon, Samuel told him the dreadful news. He was terrorstruck, but kept his head, and at once went to see Wallis, who showed him the genuine signature. After studying it with the greatest concentration he left, but an hour later returned with another receipt signed by Heminge, in a hand indistinguishable from that on Wallis's document, and with a remarkable story. He had explained what had happened to Mr H., who, seeing his distress, smiled as he took from a drawer the receipt that William now held in his hand, saying, 'Take that to Mr Wallis, and see if it does not correspond with the handwriting to his deed.' Then Mr H. explained that there had been two John Heminges, the one Shakespeare's friend and colleague at the Globe, the other connected with the Curtain, known familiarly as the tall and the short John Heminge respectively. This, of course, quite simply accounted for the two different signatures. Wallis was convinced; there could be no question of forgery in such a short space of time. He reckoned without William's extreme dexterity —and sinisterity—his photographic memory, inventiveness and reckless effrontery. He was so convinced, indeed, that he signed a second Certificate of Belief drawn up by Samuel. There was urgent need to rally the forces of faith, 'the ingenuous, intelligent and disinterested believers' as Samuel called them.

The publication of the Papers had been the signal for a more vicious and concentrated attack. Boaden, originally an ardent supporter, went over to the other camp, and in *A Letter to George Steevens* assailed the Papers as exquisite nonsense, dismissing the once so much admired Profession of Faith as 'nothing but the puerile quaintness and idiomatic poverty of a methodist rhapsody'. Dr Parr was shaken and ignored Samuel's appeal to write a reply, but Francis Webb put up a spirited and rhapsodical defence, declaring that the Papers not only had the signature of Shakspeare's hand, but also the stamp of his soul; 'If these are not his,' he asked, 'to whom do they belong?' Only William and Montague Talbot knew the answer to that, but there was no lack of those who knew they were not Shakespeare's. Most formidable of these was Malone, who now saw the Papers, or rather their facsimiles, for the first time, and rapidly began to pen his deadly *Inquiry into the Authenticity*.

William had just discovered *Henry II*, which had taken him ten weeks to write. He considered it a more finished piece than *Vortigern*, as indeed it was, and wished that this rather than the other could be the play for production at Drury Lane. But it was too late. So, for that matter, was *Vortigern*. Sheridan had promised that it should be produced in December, before the publication of the Papers, but it was January, 1796, before rehearsals began. By this time everybody knew that the two greatest Shakespeare scholars of the day thought the Papers forgeries, and eagerly expected the issue of Malone's *Inquiry*, which, however, was growing to a portentous length. Boaden's *Letter to Steevens* appeared at the beginning of February, and Boaden was the friend of Kemble, who, cast for the part of Vortigern, smiled grimly as he prepared the play, according to his custom, 'from the author's genuine book'. His sister, Mrs Siddons, discovered that she was too indisposed to undertake the part of Edmunda, and Henry James Pye, after two half-hearted attempts to write a Prologue, and an interview with Kemble, resigned the task to one of the disinterested baronets, Sir James Bland Burgess. The date for the first performance remained to be fixed. Kemble suggested April 1st. The decision was overruled only after Samuel's strenuous protests to Sheridan; it should be the day after All Fool's Day. Nevertheless, Kemble got his way in the matter of an afterpiece, and the playbill stated that 'a play called Vortigern' would be followed by a neat little farce called *My Grandmother*. Two days before, on March 31st, Malone published his *Inquiry*.

Samuel was in a state of frenzy, but quickly drew up a reply to this 'malevolent and impotent attack' on the eve of presentation, and appealed to the public to hear the play 'with the candour that has ever distinguished a British audience'. He had this protest printed as a handbill, and on the evening of the performance, Saturday, April 2nd, 1796, the excited crowds that jostled in the streets leading to Drury Lane were further inflamed by the sheets thrust into their hands.

The great theatre was crammed, and so fierce was the rush that people paid box prices to get a seat in the pit. Samuel and his friends sat conspicuously in a central box, but William, weak with fright, retired behind the scenes where he spent most of the time drawing courage from Mrs Jordan, who played the part of Vortigern's daughter, Flavia. The wretched youth had every reason to be frightened. The first night of a play is gruelling enough for a mature and experienced author, and William was not only appallingly inexperienced and ignorant, but facing one of the most difficult audiences in the history of the theatre, prepared, eager perhaps, to find the whole affair a hoax. Worst of all, he was overcome with a feeling of guilt and shame, knowing, as he himself put it, that he 'did not stand upon the basis of truth'. Yet, for a boy of eighteen writing in the eighteenth century, *Vortigern* is a remarkable achievement, even though by any literary standard it is nothing, and if we laugh to-day it is not at the youthful author, but at the men who fatuously believed this inflated nonsense to be genuine Shakespeare.

The Prologue was not calculated to dispel William's alarm:

> If hope of fame some modern bards has led
> To try the path where Shakspeare wont to tread;
> If, with presumptuous wing, they dar'd aspire
> To catch some portion of his sacred fire,
> Your critic pow'rs the vain attempt repell'd,
> The flimsy vapour, by your breath dispell'd,
> Expos'd the trembling culprit to your sight,
> While Shakspeare's radiance shone with doubled light.

From deep oblivion snatch'd this play appears:
It claims respect, since Shakspeare's name it bears;
That name, the source of wonder and delight,
To a fair hearing has at least a right.
We ask no more—with you the judgment lies;
No forgeries escape your piercing eyes.

The curtain rose, revealing a large Gothick hall, the British king Constantius, his trusted general Vortigern, and Vortigern's son Pascentius.

Vortigern has the classical simplicity of any refined version of Shakespeare; its complexity lies in the baffling echoes from other plays, notably *Macbeth*, *Lear*, *Hamlet* and *As You Like It*, and, as they listened, the annotators and commentators in the audience must have itched for a printed copy. In his first speech Constantius resigns half his power to Vortigern, who loses no time in telling the audience that he must unmannerly push the good king from his seat, and with him his two sons. 'Now woe indeed hath made its masterpiece', exclaims the already rejected Edmunda when she hears of her husband's promotion. The murderers are suborned, and Vortigern awaits their news:

So now, good king, prepare thee for the worst;
And, ere the thick and noisome air of night
Shall with damn'd Hecate's baneful spells be fill'd,
Thou must from hence to the cold bed of death,
To whom the peasant and the king are slaves.
Come, then, black night, and hood the world in darkness;
Seal close the hearts of those I have suborn'd,
That pity may not turn them from their purpose.

The rightful king is now the eldest son of Constantius, Aurelius, whom Flavia loves, and when Vortigern orders her to marry another, disguised as a boy she runs away accompanied by Pascentius and the faithful Fool, who cheers them with his merry song, 'Lack, lack, and a well a day!' Aurelius and his brother, in Rome, hear that the usurper Vortigern is really their father's murderer, and hasten to join the Scots whom he has accused of the crime.

So far so good. The play had survived two acts and, as the curtain fell, Samuel smiled happily, and Mrs Jordan congratulated William on the success of the piece. But William was haunted by a presentiment that it would never be acted twice. He was right. The fun began after a few lines of act three, when a patriotic baron called for war against the Scots. 'Sound yon brazen trump,' he cried. It sounded, but not long enough for a second baron, who called for more: 'Nay, stop not there, but let them bellow on!' Unfortunately, the part was played by Dignum, the comedian, and his well-known voice sent the whole house into convulsive peals of laughter. The tension was broken, and the audience slipping out of control. However, the remainder of the act passed off pretty well. Mrs Jordan sat her down and courted sweet music's aid:

> She sang, while from her eye ran down
> The silv'ry drop of sorrow.

This was received with unbounded applause, but as Edmunda was no singer, her mad song, 'Last Whitsunday, they brought me roses,' had to be rendered by one of her maids, which was not quite so effective, though she talked very prettily about little birds, and raged in lines that were certainly suggestive of Shakespeare:

> O, you great gods! why pelt ye thus my brain,
> And with your thunders loud, cause such dire outrage
> Within this little ball, this O, this nothing? . . .
> And have I need of these vile rags? off! off! . . .
> There is my gage, farewell; good night, sweet! good night!

These affecting scenes, however, were prelude merely to further disaster. Vortigern calls in the Saxons, Hengist and Horsus, to help him against the Scots. Horsus is confronted by Pascentius; they fight, and Horsus falls, feeling death's cold and heavy hand like ice upon his parting soul. The drop-curtain also fell, but on the prostrate Saxon, played by the comic-nosed Phillimore, whose legs were left on the wrong side of the next scene, a wood. The roller that struck his stomach was heavy; he groaned and, having recovered his wind, scrambled out, assisted by a sympathetic Member of Parliament in one of the stage boxes.

The audience was now enjoying itself hugely, and quite out of control, though somewhat sobered by the affecting scene at the beginning of act five, in which Edmunda, despite the disability of her sex, continues to play Lear, being restored to her senses by soft music and the ministrations of her daughter, Flavia:

> 'Tis long, long since I was thus kindly treated:
> Your pardon, but I fear you scoff at me . . .
> Bring here my glasses, stand before me here!
> Now, now, I'll judge thee well; I'll see this straight.

The climax of stirring scenes when, laughing siege to scorn Vortigern plays Macbeth, was even more to the audience's liking:

> *Vor.* Then fight, I say.
> Go, get you hence.
> No, no; thou must stay here: thou'rt my sole prop.
> I sicken fast, and 'gin again to flag.
> Pour forth, I pray thee now, some flatt'ring words,
> For I am weary, and my lamp of life
> Doth sadly linger, and would fain go out;
> For, look you, my poor soul is sore diseas'd . . .
>   *Enter an Officer*
> *Off.* My lord! my lord!
> *Vor.* Wherefore dost tremble thus, paper-fac'd knave?
> What news should make thee break thus rudely in?
> *Off.* Your newly married Queen—
> *Vor.* Speak, what of her?
> *Off.* My lord, she hath ta'en poison, and is dead . . .
> *Vor.* If it be so, then will I out and die.

Final disaster came in the great apostrophe to Death:

> O! then thou dost ope wide thy boney jaws,
> And, with rude laughter and fantastic tricks,
> Thou clapp'st thy rattling fingers to thy sides:
> And when this solemn mockery is o'er—

Kemble delivered the last line in his most sepulchral voice, and paused. Perhaps it was the prearranged signal for the Malone faction, but in any event 'the most discordant howl echoed from the pit that ever assailed the organs of hearing'. It was ten minutes before Kemble could resume, and then, instead of beginning at the next line, he repeated in the same funereal voice, 'And when this solemn mockery is o'er'. From that moment the uproar was so deafening that not another word was audible. William was right; there was to be no second performance. He went home and slept more soundly than he had done for months.

When Kemble tried to stage *Vortigern* on the following Monday he was howled down and had to put on *The School for Scandal* instead. *Vortigern* was dead. Even before its production it was staggering from the impact of the *Inquiry*, and when people had time to read Malone's four hundred pages at leisure it went down with the *Shakspeare Papers* in the general ruin. Malone, a barrister it will be remembered, as well as a Shakespeare scholar, had no difficulty in demolishing William's amateurish fabrications, but perhaps he would not have written with such malicious ferocity and gusto had he known that his victims were a half-crazy boy and an infatuated elderly man. He reproduced genuine signatures of Queen Elizabeth, Southampton and Heminge, and set them beside William's crude forgeries; he demonstrated that the orthography of the Papers was not only not the orthography of that time, but the orthography of no period whatsoever; that the language was not the language of the Elizabethans, but the language of more than a century later; that the dates and almost all the facts were refuted by indisputable documents, and that the law of the legal instruments was as false as the spelling and phraseology were absurd and senseless. 'I trust', he concluded, 'that I have vindicated Shakspeare from all this imputed trash, and rescued him from the hands of a bungling impostor, by proving all these Manuscripts to be the true and genuine offspring of consummate ignorance and unparalleled audacity.'

Although Malone had mentioned no names, Samuel was inevitably branded as the impostor, for nobody credited his apparently stupid son with the talent to deceive a body of distinguished antiquaries and even the College of Arms. They, at least, refused to believe that they had been hoodwinked by a mere boy, though Samuel, after seeing his extract from *William the Conqueror*, must have had an uneasy suspicion of the truth. The wretched father appealed to his son to produce the diffident gentleman, and at last William promised to do so—and also to produce further fantastic treasures in the possession of his friend, including the manuscripts of most of Shakespeare's plays. He also announced that Harris had offered him a contract to write for Covent Garden, and that he was engaged to be married to a beautiful young lady of fortune. By the beginning of May he had become more rational, and agreed to confide in Wallis as the representative of Samuel and his friends. On the fateful Sunday Samuel watched from a window opposite Wallis's house. He saw William arrive and enter, but never a sign of Mr H. When William left, Samuel rushed across the road, but Wallis was evasive. Although William had confessed everything, he had advised him to keep his secret, while he himself would report that Mr H. would not be 'exactly safe in committing his name to the public'.

Samuel was as much in the dark as ever; the malicious attacks continued, the demand for his work declined disastrously, and his health was broken. In June he went for a holiday in the country, whence he wrote a final appeal to William: 'I do assure you my state is truly wretched . . . I have no rest either night or day. . . . It is universally allowed that no obligation should lead a parent into ruin.' Before the letter arrived in London, William had left home for good.

A few days later he wrote to his father confessing that he had written the Papers. There was no apology, only a resentful reproach that 'for the language you think me incapable, and there it is I am wronged. . . . If the writer of the Papers shows any spark of Genius and deserves Honour, I, Sir, your son, am that person.' Samuel replied bitterly: 'I have not words to express the high indignation I feel at yr. unnatural conduct. You have left me with a load of misery and have, I fear, about you a load of infamy that you will find perhaps more difficulty than I shall in getting rid of.' On second thoughts he added, 'Your character, if you insist on this, will be blasted. Therefore, do not suffer yourself from vanity or any other motive to adhere to any such confession.' He preferred to take the obloquy upon himself rather than ruin his son's career, and he continued rigidly to defend the authenticity of the Papers. This, however, was not William's idea of how affairs should be conducted; the Genius and Honour were his, and in December he published *An Authentic Account of the Shakspearian Manuscripts*, confessing, or rather boasting, of his forgery of the Papers, and sneering at the credulity and incompetence of those he had so easily deceived. Samuel replied with a *Vindication of his Conduct*, defending the Papers and attempting to invalidate Malone's *Inquiry*. Few people believed either father or son, though Ritson did: 'You may depend upon it for a truth, that all the plays, deeds, letters, and papers of every description which have been produced by Ireland, owe their existence solely to his son William-Henry, a boy of nineteen, in whom no talents of any kind were ever before discovered, even by the father himself, who has, in fact, been the completest of all possible dupes to the astonishing artifices of this second Chatterton.'

William's hopes of fame and fortune quickly faded; nobody would accept his plays, and he was reduced to selling copies of his forgeries to those who would pay a few shillings for such curiosities. At the beginning of 1797 he wrote a moderately apologetic letter to his father asking him for help in finding employment that would keep him from starvation. In March they met at Wallis's house, but when William insolently insisted on his authorship of the Papers, Samuel flatly told him that he did not believe him. They never saw one another again.

The final humiliation of Samuel came later in the year, when Gillray published a brutal print entitled 'Notorious Characters, No. 1', depicting him with 'Ireland's Shakspeare' half-hidden under his cloak, and beneath a quotation supplied by Steevens: 'Such cursed assurance is past all endurance.' Samuel sought an action for libel, but was helpless without evidence from William, and had to content himself with writing a pathetically ineffective *Investigation into Mr Malone's Claim to the Character of a Scholar*. Two years later he published *Vortigern* and *Henry II* with Introductions describing the mean and paltry artifice that had been employed to prejudice the public, and 'the mass of dulness and conceit' displayed in Malone's *Inquiry*. He died in the following year, July 1800, maintaining to the last his own innocence and his belief in the authenticity of the Papers.

Interest in the forgeries was now beginning to wane, for these were the years of the rise of Napoleon and the threat of a French invasion. The final stages of the controversy did, however, inspire two interesting books in defence of those who had been so ignominiously deceived by William. These were *An Apology for the Believers in the Shakspeare-Papers* and *A Supplemental Apology*, in which Chalmers ingeniously argued that, though the Papers were undoubtedly forgeries, they might well have been genuine, almost, indeed, ought to have been genuine, and incidentally made valuable contributions to the history of the stage and the study of Shakespeare's punctuation.

William had ruined his own career as well as his father's. If only he had been less vain and had not succumbed to the temptation to achieve early recognition at all costs, he might have made an honourable name for himself as a contemporary of Coleridge and the other romantic writers, for he had undoubted talent. There are some good things in *Vortigern*, and better ones in *Henry II*, and that he could turn a pleasing lyric is shown by his *Acrostic on Shakspeare*, with its echo of *The Phoenix and Turtle*.

> Softly gliding down the stream,
>   Hear the dying swan divine,
> Avon's bard, Apollo's beam,
>   Kindred of the muses nine . . .

But it is scarcely to be wondered at that nobody took an impostor seriously as a writer, and he was driven to turning out second-rate novels and stories under various assumed names. His best book is his *Confessions*, a very readable though idealised account of the forgeries and himself, marred only by his gibes at those whom he deceived and those who exposed him. He died in 1835, aged sixty.

VII

SHAKSPEARE ILLUSTRATED

SAMUEL IRELAND was not the only artist interested in the illustration of Shakespeare. In the late eighteenth century a visitor to the Royal Academy would expect to find at least a dozen fanciful reconstructions of the more popular scenes from the plays. In 1790, for example, the very first painting he would see was Joseph Wright's 'Romeo and Juliet', and the fifth J. Graham's 'Macbeth's Last Stake'. Wright also contributed 'Perdita and the Flowers', and Francis Wheatley a melancholy 'Jaques and the Stag'. Then there were 'Arthur and Hubert', 'Orlando and Adam', 'Hermia and Helena', and 'Whitfield as Williams in *Henry V*'. Two of the miniatures were scenes from *The Tempest* and *Romeo and Juliet*, and among the smaller pictures in the ante-room were 'The Twins' from *The Comedy of Errors*, 'Lady Macbeth prevented from stabbing the king by his resemblance to her father as he sleeps', and even a drawing of Herne's Oak, immortalised in *The Merry Wives*.

Although the illustration of Shakespeare was essentially an eighteenth-century phenomenon, there were two earlier examples. The first, indeed, could scarcely have been earlier, for it was made, apparently by Henry Peacham, about 1595, when Shakespeare was just beginning his career. It is a drawing of a production of *Titus Andronicus*, depicting Tamora pleading with Titus, and a coal-black Aaron standing with drawn sword above her kneeling sons. This picture, however, was not intended for publication, and the first book illustration is the title page of the 1655 edition of *The Rape of Lucrece*. Here Lucrece is sheathing in her harmless breast a harmful, and particularly unhandy, knife, while Collatine stands stone-still, astonished with the deadly deed. Above, quite unastonished, Shakespeare gazes from a cartouche. The portrait is William Faithorne's reversal of the folio engraving.

There were no illustrations of the plays in the quartos or folios, and Shakespearean illustration really begins with Jacob Tonson's publication of Rowe's edition in 1709. Tonson, influenced by French models —he produced an illustrated *Racine*—was a pioneer in the new art, and to each of the plays in Rowe's six volumes he supplied a frontispiece. As, however, he employed a Flemish engraver, Michael Vandergucht, and the Frenchman, Louis du Guernier, he can scarcely be said to have captured the essential quality of Shakespeare, though the plates generally seem to represent scenes from contemporary performances. For example, the first suggests the Davenant–Dryden–Shadwell version of the shipwreck in *The Tempest*, a sensational picture of the ship splitting amid showers of fire, lightning and horrid shapes flying down among the sailors. The Witches produce their Show of Eight Kings to a Macbeth who looks like the victor of Blenheim, and a periwigged Betterton-Hamlet, apparently in a box set, knocks over a Queen Anne chair on the appearance of the Ghost. In a second edition of 1714, revised by du Guernier, we catch a dramatic glimpse of the incestuous bed, which no doubt accounts for the agitation of the portrait of Hamlet's father, which positively leans out of its frame on the wall. The plates were still further frenchified when Tonson had them re-engraved by Foudrinier for Pope's fourth edition of Shakespeare, but by this time a more important French artist was working in England. This was Hubert François Gravelot, who designed plates for Theobald's second edition of 1740, and was then engaged by Sir Thomas Hanmer to beautify his sumptuous volumes 'with the ornaments of sculpture'. But Gravelot was merely the engraver of the drawings of an English artist, Francis Hayman.

Hayman was originally a scene painter, at this time decorating the Prince of Wales's Pavilion at Vauxhall with four episodes from Shakespeare, and his drawings for Hanmer's edition of 1744 reflect both his scenic art and the French influence of Gravelot, modified, however, by the native tradition and the work of Hogarth. There is little attempt at historical accuracy; King John dies in a rococo chair placed in front of a drop-scene of a conventional Swinstead, Lady Macbeth somnambulates in a Georgian drawing-room, and the gothic gates of Troy are defended by portcullises. Horace Walpole complained of the large noses and shambling legs of Hayman's figures, but there was good reason for Hanmer's boast; Shakespeare was at last worthily produced, visually at least, and Hayman's plates created such a demand that the old baronet's whimsical text was soon sold out.

Hayman's success naturally encouraged imitators, and in the early seventies John Bell's popular edition of Shakespeare was embellished with cheap and simple cuts by a number of undistinguished artists. But the influence of Hayman extended beyond book illustration. It was he who popularised the painting, as distinct from the drawing, of scenes from Shakespeare. His pictures were not concerned with particular actors, but when Garrick leaped into fame in 1741 he saw the possibilities of such a medium for publicity, and so we get Benjamin Wilson's 'Garrick as Hamlet', 'Garrick as King Lear', 'Garrick and Mrs Bellamy in (Garrick's) *Romeo and Juliet*', and Zoffany's 'Garrick and Mrs Pritchard in *Macbeth*'. Then, by way of variation, there was Gainsborough's portrait of Garrick embracing the bust of the bard, for presentation to Stratford, and the inspiring perpetuation by his friend, Robert Edge Pine, of the splendid moment of his recitation of his Ode.

The year of the Stratford Jubilee, 1769, was also the year of the first exhibition of the newly founded Royal Academy, under the patronage of George III and the presidency of Sir Joshua Reynolds. It was Reynolds's firm belief, proclaimed in his *Discourses*, that 'history' painting was the highest form of art, by which he meant classical history in the sublime style, or, if the history really must be more recent and prosaic, at least in decent classical garb. But breaches were soon made in this doctrine by painters who now had a chance of exhibiting their wares in public; after all, not every painter was capable of rising to the sublime, and others began daringly to introduce historical, or what they imagined to be historical, costume into their extensive canvases. The crisis came as early as 1771, when Reynolds heard that King George's 'monstrous favourite', Benjamin West, was painting 'The Death of Wolfe' as it really happened, or might have happened, instead of as a scene from Roman history. 'I foresee,' said Reynolds, 'that this picture will not only become one of the most popular, but occasion a revolution in the art.' He was quite right. It prepared the way for a broader interpretation of the 'history' picture, which included not only contemporary events, but illustrations from literature, particularly from Shakespeare. And it was certainly popular. John Boydell made £15,000 out of the sale of its engraving.

Alderman Boydell was himself an engraver, but a far better man of business. In 1751 he had set up on his own as a printseller and publisher, and by commissioning engravings of the paintings of Reynolds, Wilson and West, had turned the balance of trade with France in works of art from import to export. By 1790, when he became Lord Mayor of London, the foreign trade in exported engravings was worth

£200,000 a year. The new vogue in illustration had inspired him with
another idea: 'to establish an English School of Historical Painting'. In
the middle eighties he began commissioning paintings of scenes from
Shakespeare for exhibition in the Shakespeare Gallery which he built in
Pall Mall, the pediment crowned with an allegorical group of the
Bard between the Dramatic Muse and the Genius of Painting. The
sculptor was Thomas Banks. Boydell employed only one other sculptor, the Hon. Mrs Damer, a lady of high birth and accomplishment,
who contributed two bas-reliefs.

The opening of the Gallery in 1789 was celebrated in a drawing by
Francis Wheatley, depicting Boydell receiving the Dukes of York and
Clarence, the Duchess of Devonshire chatting with Reynolds, and
Lady Jersey looking at the pictures, one of which is Reynolds's 'Mac-
beth and the Witches'. At the Academy banquet that year the health
of 'the commercial Maecenas of England' was proposed by Burke, and
drunk by the assembled guests, among whom was the Prince of Wales.
'No single school in Europe', said Reynolds enthusiastically, 'could
produce so many good pictures, and if they did they would have a
monotonous sameness. Here, as an emblem of the Freedom of the
Country, every artist has taken a different road.' A few weeks later the
Bastille fell; another country could boast of its freedom, and Boydell's
export trade was soon in ruins.

John Wolcot, the Devonshire doctor, better known as Peter Pindar,
did not entirely agree with Reynolds. On his arrival in London a few
years before he had set up as an art critic and vigorously vented his
opinions in a series of Lyric Odes to the Royal Academicians. The
chief object of his satire was West, with his canvases 'broad as the
mainsail of a man-of-war'. 'O West, what *hath* thy pencil done?' he
asked, and then, when West was elected President of the Royal Academy on the death of Reynolds in 1792,

> What! after Reynolds, to take up with West!
> The antipodes thou seekest, I protest,
>   From Jove's grand thunder, to an infant's drum.

West, of course, was one of the artists commissioned by Boydell, and
so was young John Opie, whom Wolcot had discovered in Cornwall
and brought to London with him. There were thirty-one others, and
by the end of the century a hundred and sixty pictures.

'Boydell', wrote John Northcote, who was very satisfactorily represented, 'did more for the advancement of the arts in England than the whole mass of nobility put together.' Robert Smirke probably did as well as anyone. He had twenty-six paintings, most of them comic scenes, and his representation of Falstaff established the traditional conception of his appearance. Matthew Peters also did well. A student of Rubens and Titian, he specialised in plump and lightly draped young ladies, which Boydell found made exceedingly popular engravings. But his popularity waned when, in 1781, he was ordained and took to painting 'An Angel carrying the Spirit of a Child to Paradise', 'The Resurrection of a Pious Family on the Last Day', and kindred subjects. However, when Boydell began collecting for his Gallery, Peters realised that there was 'no more harm in a priest's painting Shakspeare than for Bishop Warburton to comment him', and supplied five large canvases in his unregenerate secular style. His favourite theme was *The Merry Wives of Windsor*.

Boydell paid according to the reputation of his artists. Angelica Kauffmann received two hundred guineas for each of her two paintings, but West and Reynolds got a thousand guineas apiece for theirs. This led to some trouble with Romney, who was paid only six hundred for his *Tempest* shipwreck and his allegory of Shakespeare as a very solid Teutonic babe flanked by Comedy, Tragedy, Love, Envy, Fear and other personifications. Joseph Wright of Derby was assessed at only half of Romney's rate, and after painting two pictures quarrelled with Boydell and left. He was more interested in the Sistine Chapel, Vesuvius and the Industrial Revolution than in Shakespeare.

The best painting in the Gallery was adjudged to be 'The Death of Cardinal Beaufort', Reynolds's last picture—the Histories, including the three parts of *Henry VI*, were naturally very popular with the Historical School—but James Barry's 'King Lear and Cordelia' is perhaps the only picture that transcends the limits of illustration. Apart, that is, from the work of Fuseli. But then Fuseli's grotesque Bosch-like creations have nothing to do with the English School of Historical Painting.

The Shakespeare Gallery proved such a paying proposition that W. Bowyer set up a rival Historic Gallery, and the versatile nonagenarian Macklin a Poets' Gallery. Not only were there the receipts from admission tickets, but profits from the sale of engravings were most satisfactory. Boydell intended leaving his Gallery to the nation, but the outbreak of the war with 'Vandalick' revolutionary France cut

off his foreign trade, and by 1804 the old alderman was driven to appeal
to Parliament for permission to dispose of his stock by lottery. 'I have',
he said, 'laid out with my brethren, in promoting the commerce of the
fine arts in this country, above £350,000.' The lottery brought in
£45,000. The Gallery was taken over by the British Institution, and,
when sold by auction, the pictures and the two bas-reliefs by the Hon.
Mrs Damer realised £6,000. Banks's 'Apotheosis of Shakespeare' was
reserved for a monument over the remains of Boydell, who died shortly
before the lottery was drawn, but, proving somewhat excessive for St
Olave's church, it was removed to Stratford, where it is now in the
garden of New Place. It was only fifteen years since *The Companion to
the Shakspeare Gallery* had so confidently declared that 'what the
Gallery of Florence is now, shall be a few years hence the Shakspeare
Gallery'. Charles Lamb wrote its epitaph: 'What injury did not Boydell's Shakspeare Gallery do me with Shakspeare! To have Opie's
Shakspeare, Northcote's Shakspeare, light-headed Fuseli's Shakspeare,
wooden-headed West's Shakspeare, deaf-headed Reynolds's Shakspeare, instead of my own and everybody's Shakspeare. To be tied
down to an authentic face of Juliet! To have Imogen's portrait!
To confine the illimitable!' It is one with his famous dictum,
'The Lear of Shakspeare cannot be acted', another facet of his
plea for the imagination and the fine abstraction of reading, not seeing, the plays: 'It is difficult for a frequent playgoer to disembarrass
the idea of Hamlet from the person and voice of Mr Kemble. We
speak of Lady Macbeth, while we are in reality thinking of Mrs
Siddons.'

Lamb, the romantic, died in 1834, Sir John Soane, last of the classical school of architects, in 1837, just five months before the accession
of Queen Victoria. More fortunate than Boydell, he was able to leave
his house in Lincoln's Inn Fields to the nation as a museum to be kept
as nearly as possible in the state in which he left it, and it is not uninteresting to note the Shakespeareana collected by a distinguished
amateur in the course of a long life. Sir John liked tall, good-looking
books, and his library contains finely bound copies of all four folios as
well as most of the standard, and at the same time handsome, works of
the eighteenth century, from the editions of Pope and Hanmer to the
twenty-one volumes of the Third Variorum. He was also exceedingly
credulous, and quite persuaded that a sixteenth-century German beer-
jug in his dining-room was the kind of chopine referred to in *Hamlet*;

I

'an excellent elucidation of the passage,' he noted, '"Your ladyship is nearer to heaven . . . by the altitude of a chopine".' On the fireplace in his breakfast parlour are two plaques by Flaxman, modelled for a vase presented to J. P. Kemble on his retirement from the stage in 1817. One represents 'Kemble crowned by Melpomene', the other 'Kemble inspired by the Genius of Shakspeare'. In the same room is an oil painting by Henry Howard, R.A., an Academy picture of 1832 entitled 'The Contention of Oberon and Titania', now, thanks to the bituminous pigment, resembling an aerial view of the Trinidad Pitch Lake. Then there is Westall's little picture from the 1790 Academy, of the apocryphal scene of 'Lady Macbeth prevented from stabbing the king by his resemblance to her father as he sleeps', the dagger dropping from her nerveless hand. Larger paintings are a 'Trial of Queen Katharine' from *Henry VIII*, by Frank Howard, 'The Landing of Richard II at Milford Haven', by William Hamilton, picked up at Christie's for £7, and Mrs C. M. Pope's 'Flowers of Shakspeare', a large watercolour bouquet said to contain all the flowers mentioned in his works, flanked by his bust in pallid plaster. The original bust may still be seen in a niche on the staircase.

The staircase is the place reserved for the principal Shakespearean treasures. Passing a large painting by James Durno of 'Falstaff in disguise led out by Mrs Page', bought for nine guineas at the Shakspeare Gallery sale, we come to the Shakspeare Recess, a sort of shrine below a similar Tivoli Recess on the next floor. On the left wall are engravings of Shakespearean characters by J. H. Mortimer, and two more oil paintings by Henry Howard, an artist much favoured by Soane. One is a 'Lear and Cordelia', the other, painted in 1830, 'The Vision of Shakspeare'. According to Soane it 'represents the bard resting on the lap of Fancy, contemplating the "visions of glory" which she invokes, while Lyrical Poetry, rising from the earth, invites him to ascend the brightest heaven of invention. Tragedy and Comedy are calling before him the shadowy forms of his principal dramatic characters: near him, Titania, watched by Oberon, is sleeping in her bower, and a train of fairies are sporting about him. On one side, the stars are shooting from their spheres "to hear the sea maid's music"; on the other side is the Tempest, the enchanted isle, and its inhabitants; above is Hecate riding on a cloud, and Genii, the offspring of Fancy, are hovering near her sweetest child.' Howard wasted no room on his canvases. In the right-hand wall of the Recess there was once a stained glass window, and at the far end, one almost writes automatically 'at the east end', is a cast of the Stratford bust, made by George Bullock in 1814.

On the whole, the eighteenth century—apart from the inhabitants of Stratford—had a poor opinion of the monumental bust in the church. It preferred the fine, though suitably restrained, frenzy of Scheemakers's and Roubiliac's interpretations of the bard. Nor was it altogether satisfied with the Droeshout engraving in the folio; Gainsborough protested that he had never seen a stupider face, and another genuine likeness began to gain in favour. This was the so-called Chandos portrait, said to have been painted by Richard Burbage, who gave it to the actor Joseph Taylor, who gave it to Davenant. It represents a swarthy, heavily bearded, Italian-looking man with earrings, a quite surprising product of Warwickshire, yet Malone set the seal of authenticity upon it by adopting it as his frontispiece. It followed that Steevens had to find a still more genuine likeness. Fortunately, a Mr Samuel Felton discovered one in 1792, a portrait on a panel, inscribed 'Gul. Shakespear 1597 R.B.' 'The canvas Chandois picture', Steevens pronounced contemptuously, 'has no claim to authenticity.' That was *said* to have been painted by Burbage, this was *signed* by him. The Felton portrait was soon in Boydell's Gallery, and figured as the frontispiece of both of Steevens's Variorum editions. It has the egg-like forehead of the folio print and a similar pose, so that dealers found it exceedingly profitable to make engravings of the Felton head in the Droeshout costume, and sell them as prints of the original portrait from which the folio engraving was made.

Malone's literary executor, the younger Boswell, replied to Steevens's little sally with yet another likeness. This was a miniature by the great Elizabethan limner, Nicholas Hilliard, sent to Boswell by Samuel Ireland's friend, Sir James Bland Burgess, who assured him that it had been painted for Sir William Somerville, who 'lived in habits of intimacy with Shakspeare, particularly after his retirement from the stage'. It is a genuine Hilliard, though nothing could be more unlike the Chandos portrait than this spruce, flaxen-haired, beady-eyed dandy. However, Sir James found 'a general resemblance to the best busts of Shakspeare', Sir Thomas Lawrence agreed that it was an excellent life-portrait of the poet, and Boswell reproduced it in the second volume of the Variorum as an alternative for those who preferred fair Shakespeares to dark. It was all very confusing, and even more confusing when another miniature, the 'Auriol', was found, a dark-haired, hook-nosed Shakespeare 'Aet 33'.

It now became customary to claim any portrait of an unknown man with a lofty brow, painted by a sixteenth- or seventeenth-century artist, as a portrait of Shakespeare. There was, for example, a particularly fine painting by Cornelius Janssen, and any number of Zuccaros: the 'Bath', the 'Cosway', and above all the 'Boston' Zuccaro, said to have been found in the 'Globe Tavern', apparently much frequented by Shakespeare and his cronies. But as Zuccaro was in England only for a few months when Shakespeare was a boy of ten, its authenticity was open to doubt. In this atmosphere of uncertainty imposture flourished, but only the most gullible were deceived by the portrait 'paynted by mee R. Burbage'. This was the product of William Ireland's contemporary, Paul Francis Zincke, who specialised in the portrayal of long-dead literary celebrities. On the back of his painting were lines 'by Ben Jonson', and on another piece of paper: 'Henry Spelman Esq. the gyfte of John Selden Esq. the 4th daye of May 1640.'

Burbage, Hilliard, Janssen and Zuccaro having been exhausted, there was a run on anonymous artists, and the early years of Queen Victoria proved characteristically prolific. The search was now for the 'Droeshout original', that is, for the portrait from which, as the experts explained, young Martin Droeshout must have made his engraving for the folio. The 'Lumley' was a discreet combination of features from the Droeshout, Chandos, and Auriol portraits, the 'Ely Palace', discovered in a pawnbroker's shop, had a right eyebrow that was the image of the one in the folio, and the 'Flower', inscribed 'Willm Shakespeare 1609', might well have been the long lost original, had there not been good reason to think that the painting was made from the engraving, and not the other way round. The 'Hunt' and 'Kesselstadt' were originals of a different kind. The first was a portrait discovered beneath another painting, and after restoration revealed the original from which the Stratford bust was made—painted, apparently, at about the time of the Garrick Jubilee. The other was a death-mask, found in a German rag shop in 1849, and claimed as the genuine death-mask of Shakespeare on the strength of its handsome appearance and the date, 1616. Innumerable other authentic likenesses turned up: the 'Ashbourne', 'Charlecote', 'Dunford', 'Stace', and so on, and even a 'Betrothal Picture' depicting a Dutch couple weighing money, with Shakespeare and Anne Hathaway holding hands in the background.

Amidst all this confused and conflicting evidence it was little wonder that ardent searchers for the truth should agitate for the exhumation of Shakespeare's remains. In the fifties, the gentle American, Delia Bacon, would have liked to explore the grave, but failed through irresolution occasioned by fear of disappointment at what she might find. Her countryman, J. Parker Norris, had no such scruples, and called robustly for the opening of the grave. What would we not give, he asked, for a photograph of Shakespeare's skull, a counterfeit presentment for all time? That was the least we might expect, but there was every reason to believe, he argued seductively, that much more would be found. It was well known that the features and clothing of bodies long buried were frequently preserved. Why not Shakespeare's? Although all would crumble away in a few minutes, only a few seconds were needed by a man with a camera. 'Think of it! A photograph of Shakespeare in his habit as he lived!' True, there was the unfortunate line on the gravestone, 'Curst be he that moves my bones'; but Mr Sam Timmins ingeniously suggested circumventing the execration by employing a woman. The Shakespeare Gesellschaft supported the movement, and so did Dr C. M. Ingleby, who wrote a book on the subject, *Shakespeare's Bones*, published in 1883. 'Only over my prostrate body,' was the Vicar of Stratford's grim reply, and outraged England was behind him. Perhaps it was best to accept the Stratford bust and the Droeshout engraving as reasonable likenesses of the poet. After all, Mrs Shakespeare and Ben Jonson seemed to think them so.

VIII

SHAKSPEARE EVISCERATED

OLD Thomas Hart had died at the Birthplace soon after the visit of Samuel and William Ireland. The property was inherited by his son, John Shakespeare Hart, but as he was a Tewkesbury chairmaker he let the house to his cousin, Thomas Hornby and his wife Mary. When, however, John Shakespeare Hart died, his impoverished widow sold the whole property, the Birthplace as well as the Swan and Maidenhead inn which formed the eastern half, to Thomas Court. This was in 1806. Thus, the direct Shakespeare connection with the Birthplace was now severed; Mr and Mrs Court owned the whole property and lived in the inn, while the Hornbys occupied the Birthplace as their tenants.

This year of change of ownership saw the publication of the first Stratford guidebook, the work of Robert Bell Wheler, a young man laudably desirous of publicising his native town. Although John Jordan was still alive, he had retired from his role of cicerone, so that in the year after Trafalgar we may take a stroll through Stratford with his youthful successor of the romantic school. As we walk down Church Street we learn that there are 2,500 inhabitants, 510 houses and 550 families; but the church, approached by its avenue of interlacing limes, now attracts our attention. 'It is universally acknowledged to be in a very romantic situation, and in the midst of its spacious cemetery, and embosomed in its encircling lofty elms, presents to the view a pile at once venerable and grand. A recollection that it covers the ashes of our admired Bard, contributes, in some degree, to the reverence this sacred mausoleum inspires; and, by the enthusiastic native in particular, some extraordinary adoration, even with a religious zeal, may justly be offered to the manes of his immortal townsman.' We pass through the nave into the chancel, but the adjacent charnel-house 'in the un-ornamented Saxon Gothic style' has disappeared; in 1800 it was pulled down, and the bones carefully buried. To the left of the altar is the effigy of John Combe, celebrated by Shakespeare in his witty extempore verses, and only a few feet away on the north wall is the figure of the poet in the attitude of inspiration. Formerly he was writing his lines about the cloud-capped towers, but now he appears to be writing the name of Arthur Wellesley, future Duke of Wellington.

From the church we pass the site of the old College, pulled down in 1799, and pause to meditate on the spot where once stood New Place and the celebrated mulberry tree, and, remembering Mr Gastrell, experience 'those emotions which naturally arise in the breast of the generous enthusiast'. A few yards further up the street is the new Town Hall, with the statue presented by Garrick in its niche in the north wall. 'The bard is represented in a graceful attitude, resting upon some volumes, placed on a pedestal. Upon a scroll, to which he points, are lines judiciously selected from his own Midsummer Night's Dream:

> The poet's eye, in a fine frenzy rolling,
> Doth glance from heaven to earth, from earth to heaven . . .'

And here, curiously enough, our young guide leaves us. The Birthplace is only a quarter of a mile away, yet, although it is the subject of one of the eight engravings with which his book is embellished, Wheler has nothing to say about it, save that the house where the pride of nature and paragon of poets was born is still standing. But then Mrs Hornby, unlike Jordan, was not one of his subscribers.

That lady, now a widow, had found a line of business even more lucrative than that pursued by the recently deceased Thomas Sharpe. The most celebrated mulberry tree will one day be exhausted if quarried for curios, but Mrs Hornby's relics, like those of Chaucer's Pardoner, were virtually imperishable. What they were we learn from the account of a visit by one of the first and most endearing of American writers. In the spring of 1815, shortly before the battle of Waterloo, Washington Irving put up at the Red Horse, armed himself with Wheler's Guide and walked along Henley Street to the mean-looking edifice of wood and plaster that was the Birthplace. The door was opened by Mrs Hornby, 'a garrulous old lady, in a frosty red face, lighted up by a cold blue anxious eye and garnished with artificial locks of flaxen hair, curling from under an exceedingly dirty cap'. She conducted him round the squalid rooms, already covered with names and inscriptions in every language; she showed him, too, the very matchlock with which Shakespeare shot the deer, his tobacco-box, the sword with which he played Hamlet, and the identical lantern with which Friar Laurence discovered Romeo and Juliet at the tomb. There was mulberry tree galore, and most astonishing of all, the oak chair on which the bard used to sit in an attitude of inspiration. Mrs Hornby assured him that so many visitors sat in it that the seat had to be renewed every three years. The marvel was that the original chair, or what remained of it, had been carried off by a Polish princess twenty-five years before.

Irving went thoughtfully from the Birthplace to the church, where he met the old sexton, William Edmonds, and his crony, John Ange, one of the fellers of the mulberry tree. Both men had been employed as carpenters at the time of the Jubilee, and remembered Garrick as 'a short punch man, very lively and bustling'. Mrs Hornby and her relics they regarded with contempt, but then there were vested interests at stake; the Birthplace and the church were rival establishments, and the widow's wonders attracted far more visitors than the whitewashed monument. Yet Irving was inclined to agree with them. The lady had insisted that she was a lineal descendant of the poet, but when she thrust into his hands a play of her own composition his faith in her consanguinity was shaken, and the only relic that he took from Stratford was a slip from one of the yew trees in the churchyard. After all the feverish, inflated and affected nonsense written about Shakespeare at the time of the Ireland forgeries, the sane simplicity and humour of Washington Irving are a breath of fresh air.

The following year was the bicentenary of Shakespeare's death. London honoured the occasion with a revival of Garrick's *Jubilee* at Drury Lane, and Wheler tried to organise appropriate ceremonies in Stratford. But the Corporation was unhelpful, the only theatre was a barn, and he had to be content with arranging a series of meals, speeches and a ball. He also wrote an account of the Birthplace, by no means flattering to Mrs Hornby and her relics. The widow still plied her dubious trade, though under the jaundiced eye of her landlady next door. Mrs Court, also a widow by now, had already raised her tenant's rent from £10 to £20 and, determined to charge what the traffic would bear, was threatening to double it again. This was the situation when Widow Hornby was visited by the sympathetic Miss Hawkins in 1819. She showed the Lady 'the little Shakspeares' as she called her children, her visitors' book inscribed by the Prince Regent, Duke of Wellington, and various refugees from revolutionary France, and of course her relics. These had been considerably augmented in the four years since Irving's visit. There were now the poet's christening-bowl, baby

THIS ALTO RELIEVO
...AKESPEARE SEATED BETWEEN THE DRAMATIC MUSE AND THE GENIUS OF ...
...RMERLY IN THE FRONT OF THE SHAKESPEARE GALLERY, PALL MALL, LONDON)
WAS PRESENTED TO THIS TOWN BY
CHARLES HOLTE BRACEBRIDGE ESQ.,
ATHERSTONE HALL.
1871.

The Shakspeare Gallery
The Apotheosis of Shakspeare by Thomas Banks

The Shakspeare Gallery
A Midsummer Night's Dream, by J. H. Fuseli

The Shakspeare Gallery. *Hamlet*, by Benjamin West

'O West, what hath thy pencil done?'

The Shakspeare Gallery
The Merry Wives of Windsor, by the Rev M. W. Peters

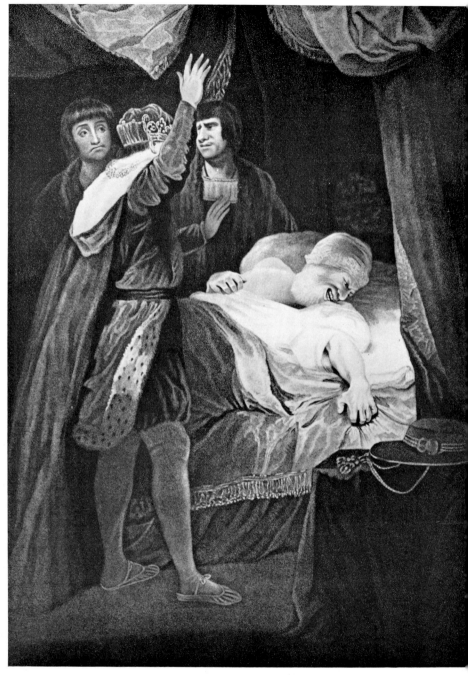

The Shakspeare Gallery

The Death of Cardinal Beaufort, from *2 Henry VI*, by Sir Joshua Reynolds

chair, easy chair, walking-stick, reading-glass, pencil case, the bench and table where he wrote, his bed, the glass from which he drank while lying there in his last illness, an embroidered cloth given him by Queen Elizabeth, and his wife's shoe. Miss Hawkins found the widow a very decent nurse-like woman in appearance, and very voluble, especially about her own literary performances, which she spoke of with great approbation.

One of her latest plays was *The Tragedy of the Battle of Waterloo*, composed from newspaper reports with a fine disregard for chronological sequence, Napoleon's triumphant entry into Paris being followed by his escape from Elba. It was, as she quaintly put it in her Preface, 'Written in the same room which gave birth to my great Predecessor, the immortal Shakspeare'. And, although written in, or at least printed as, prose, there is undoubtedly a family resemblance, as when in the British Camp at Waterloo the Duke addresses his troops: 'My noble friends! My gallant countrymen! Now summon quick your wonted courage up, and show to all th' admiring nations round, that you are men of the true English blood.' It would be interesting to know if Hardy read this tragedy before writing the final scenes of *The Dynasts*. Mrs Hornby had also written some beautiful verses on the Comet, but, not being entirely satisfied with them, had turned them into a play, with Shakespeare as the Comet. She often altered her work, which, she admitted, was much admired by her visitors.

Perhaps the Comet theme was inspired by a line in one of the innumerable verses scribbled on the walls of the room in which the poet first drew breath: 'A Comet streaming through the depth of night.' Ceiling as well as walls was covered with verses and signatures, exhibiting all the worth, rank and genius of the age. There you might see the autographs of half the members of both Houses of Parliament, of the players Kean and Kemble, the poets Moore and Scott, of Russian and Austrian princes, of Lucien Bonaparte, the Duke of Clarence and George IV himself. But Widow Hornby's days amid all this symbolic splendour were numbered. In 1820 she was evicted by Widow Court. She moved only as far as the other side of the road, from which point of vantage she was able to abuse her rival, who replied with a genteel printed card for distribution among the nobility and gentry, inviting them 'to gratify their own laudable curiosity and honour her by inspecting the house in which the Immortal Poet of Nature was born'. But if Widow Court now had the Birthplace, Widow Hornby had the relics, and these proved every bit as popular as the poet's natal dwelling. Mrs Court, however, was in the stronger position. She could assure her visitors that the relics across the way were no more than so much lumber, whereas Mrs Hornby could scarcely deny the authenticity of the Birthplace. She applied, therefore, to the father-in-law of the late Thomas Hart, who signed a certificate that to the best of his belief the relics were genuine, and had been in the possession of the Hart family ever since the death of the poet's sister. To this declaration Mrs Hornby added a footnote: 'The reliques alluded to in the above Certificate, are shewn by Mrs Hornby, at her house, opposite Shakspeare's birth-place, in Henley Street, Stratford.'

Mrs Court replied by displaying a statement from William Shakespeare Hart of Tewkesbury, certifying that when the property was sold in 1806 there was no relic of the great poet remaining. Moreover, he added, 'I further certify my positive belief, that anything advertized or shown there, or in the neighbourhood, at present, as such, must be spurious and deceptive.' The prompting hand of Mrs Court is plain enough. It was a blow to Mrs Hornby, but she was not yet beaten. She called on the only surviving daughter of Thomas Hart for her testimony. This certified that when the Hornbys rented the house, twenty years before its sale to the Courts, they bought all the articles which, from time immemorial, had been shown as relics of the great poet. Her nephew, William Shakespeare Hart, was then a little boy living in Tewkesbury, and knew nothing at all about the matter. Mrs Hornby had won, but it was only a paper victory. The value of the relics slumped, and in 1823 she packed them up and moved to another part of the town, leaving her rival in possession of the Henley Street field.

By this time the great Shakespeare scholars of the eighteenth century had long been dead. Steevens died in 1800, leaving his projected twenty-one-volume edition for his friend, Isaac Reed, to complete. It appeared in 1803. The first three volumes, each of some five hundred pages, were devoted to introductory matter, mainly reprints of the most important critical essays since the time of Rowe; the remainder contained the plays, 'with the Corrections and Illustrations of Various Commentators' and the Notes of Johnson and Steevens. Malone was still working on his own definitive twenty-one-volume edition when he died in 1812, and it was another nine years before James Boswell, the younger, saw it through the press. Similar to, but even more monumental than Steevens, the introductory matter ran to almost eighteen hundred pages; the Poems, which Steevens would have nothing to do with, were included, and again the plays were illuminated by the corrections and illustrations of various commentators. These variorum editions of 1803 (reprinted in 1813) and 1821 summarise the work of eighteenth-century scholars and critics, and are magnificent memorials of their labours.

The age of reason had done its best for Shakespeare, and yet it was not entirely at ease with him. It recognised his supreme genius, it had piously restored his text, yet it did not act the plays it printed and it mistrusted his judgment and his craftsmanship. Johnson epitomised the opinion of his age. As Shakespeare's power was merely the power of nature, his genius was often obscured, sometimes indeed overwhelmed, by his want of art, his inability to construct a perfect whole. 'He has scenes of undoubted and perpetual excellence; but, perhaps, not one play, which, if it were now exhibited as the work of a contemporary writer, would be heard to the conclusion.' Although he was the father of the English drama, 'it must be at last confessed, that as we owe everything to him, he owes something to us.' The last five words reveal the spirit of the eighteenth century as clearly as any others ever written. It was not complacency, but a genuine conviction that, speaking generally, civilisation had at last reached perfection, a Christian society as elegant as Greece, more enlightened and efficient than Rome, and that the future would be little more than variations on the now established theme. It is an astonishing spectacle, this of a so confident society of men, surrounded by the nature that they had subdued, and without the slightest idea of how they had come to be there. The French Revolution had somewhat shaken their faith, but Johnson wrote before that cataclysmic event, and it took more than a political revolution to dislodge Johnson's opinions from men's minds. 'He owes something to us.' No wonder that Johnson defended Tate's *King Lear*, and that Cibber's *Richard III*, Garrick's *Romeo and Juliet* and a dozen other refined versions held the stage, played, of course, in the costume of the eighteenth century.

But the French Revolution, followed by a European war of twenty years, overthrew more than a political tyranny, it overthrew the tyranny of reason that had for so long cabined the imagination and shackled the emotions. Men now began to turn for inspiration to the Middle Ages, that gothick and romantic era, dim and mysterious, before neo-classical pedants had formulated their rules and regulated the arts. Shakespeare became a symbol and a rallying-point for the young writers of Europe. The very characteristics that Voltaire condemned, his lawlessness and irregularity, were seized upon as virtues by the Germans, who hailed him as 'a pure virgin genius, ignorant of rules and limits, a force as irresistible as those of nature'. In France, Victor Hugo proclaimed that art has nothing to do with leading-strings, with handcuffs and gags; let the poet go where he will and do what he pleases, like the god of the theatre, Shakespeare.

In England the Romantic Movement took a less violent course, and even as late as 1815 Wordsworth was asking how much longer his countrymen would accept Johnson's opinion of Shakespeare as a wild irregular genius, in whom great faults are compensated by great beauties. Not much longer, as it happened. It was perhaps the greatest achievement of Coleridge that, by his lectures and critical writings, he convincingly showed that Shakespeare's judgment was equal to his genius, indeed, that his genius revealed itself in his judgment in its most exalted form. The true ground of the mistake that Shakespeare wanted art, the power to create a perfect whole, he explained, lay in confusing mechanical regularity with organic form. His plays were not shaped by any mechanical force impressed from without, but like the forms of nature herself, were shaped as they developed by the vital principle within. Johnson's dictum that 'he owes something to us' was exposed for the nonsense that it was, though in another sense Shakespeare owed more to Coleridge than to any other man. The misconception that had been generally held for a hundred and fifty years, from the Restoration to Waterloo, of the plays as a disorderly heap of treasure, to be plundered and refashioned according to academic canons, was shattered, and there was no longer any excuse for producing in the theatre anything but the work that Shakespeare had written. There were no more refined versions, but the old ones died hard, and every year the difficulty was becoming more acute of presenting more than half the text in theatres where precious hours were wasted changing pasteboard scenery behind perpetually falling curtains. There was, for example, Edmund Kean's revival of *King Lear* in 1820.

This was not Shakespeare's but Tate's *King Lear*. Brand-new scenery by Messrs. Marinari, Andrews, Hollagan and Dixon represented an antechamber in Lear's palace, a room of state, a court before Albany's palace, the gates of Gloster Castle, a forest, a gallery in Gloster Castle, a view near Dover, a chamber in Lear's palace, a valley near the field of battle, Albany's tent, and a prison. The great Land Storm was reproduced after the manner of Loutherbourg's *Eidophusicon*, an antiquated contraption for simulating the more spectacular displays of nature. The scenic trees were made of separate boughs that threshed in the tempest, each pendent leaf contributing its rustle to the uproar. Unfortunately the hurricane was overdone; Kean was almost blown into the wings, his words were inaudible amidst the hubbub of cataracts and thunderbolts, and the queer combination of colours thrown on his face by the new gas-lighting added to the confusion. 'The machinery', wrote *The Times*, 'may be transferred to the next pantomime.' And Lamb: 'The contemptible machinery by which they mimic the storm is not more inadequate to represent the horrors of the real elements, than any actor can be to represent Lear . . . Tate has put his hook in the nostrils of this Leviathan, for Garrick and his followers, the showmen of the scene, to draw the mighty beast about more easily. A happy ending! . . .' Three years later Kean restored the tragic ending, though he retained Tate's other imbecilities. The mixture was not a success, but it was a move in the right direction; the romantics were restoring Shakespeare to the stage. They were also beginning to present him more eruditely.

John Philip Kemble died in 1823 and was succeeded at Covent Garden by his brother Charles, who celebrated the occasion with a completely new production of *King John*. John Philip had at length abolished the traditional bag-wig of Brutus and gold-laced coat of Macbeth, but all the English histories, including *Lear*, were still played in costumes vaguely Elizabethan. There was to be no more of this; romanticism was to be taken seriously in the theatre; after all, the Middle Ages covered some five hundred years, and antiquarianism could no longer tolerate this confusion of the centuries. So *King John* was presented with an attention to detail never before equalled on the English stage. Every character appeared in the precise Habit of the Period; dresses and decorations were executed from indisputable authorities, such as seals and illuminated manuscripts, and the costumes of the principal characters were taken from their monumental effigies in Worcester and Salisbury Cathedrals, the Temple Church, and even the Abbey of Fontevrault. It was a splendid success, and Charles never exceeded his personation of the bastard Faulconbridge. Presumably his text was not taken from the recently published *Family Shakspeare*. If it was, he robbed himself of more than fifty of his most effective lines.

This edition of Shakespeare came out in 1818, three years before Malone's Variorum. Its editor was Thomas Bowdler, a retired doctor. Many years before he had been friendly with the late Mrs Elizabeth Montague, the eccentric literary lady who bound up Mr Gibbon's *History* without the last two offensive chapters, and wrote a celebrated *Essay on the Writings and Genius of Shakspeare*, completely vindicating the British poet from the misrepresentations and censures of Voltaire. Though Johnson did not read it all, he assured Garrick—it was Jubilee year—that there was no real criticism in it; none showing the beauty of thought, as formed on the workings of the human heart. 'Sir,' he added, 'when Shakspeare has Mrs Montague for his defender, he is in a poor state indeed.' Bowdler, however, was an ardent admirer of Mrs Montague, a fellow philanthropist as well as philodramatist— and yet, after all, there was something in what that fellow Voltaire had said. There could be no denying that there were *grossièretés abomin- ables* and *folies dégoûtantes* in the plays of Shakespeare, and it would be doing a service to our poet as well as to our national honour to cleanse his work of these indecencies. Like Samuel Ireland, Bowdler could think of no more pleasing occupation for a winter's evening than read- ing one of Shakespeare's plays to the family circle. But only too often he had stumbled unawares among words and expressions that raised a blush on the cheek of modesty, and made it necessary for him to pause and examine the sequel before proceeding with his entertainment. If only, in his old age, he could free from a similar embarrassment the fathers of future generations, if he could present to the public an edition of the plays which the parent, the guardian and the instructor of youth might place, without fear, in the hands of the pupil, his object would be achieved. And he set to work to transcribe, with certain modifica- tions, the last edition of the late Mr Steevens.

Having finished his reformation, he composed his apologia. To tam- per with the Belvedere Apollo, he admitted, would be an act of scarcely conceivable vandalism, but to try to add to Shakespeare's fame by modifying his work could do no harm, for, even if the attempt should fail, the original would continue unimpaired in thousands of printed copies. That some modification was desirable would be admitted even by his warmest admirers. The language of our immortal bard is not always faultless. Although the vicious taste of the age for which he wrote was largely to blame, nothing can excuse profaneness and ob- scenity. It was the object of his publication, therefore, to exclude anything unfit to be read aloud by a gentleman to a company of ladies. It was lamentable that so many erasures had been necessary, but he hastened to assure his readers that not a single line had been added to the text, never more than two or three connecting particles, in no way affecting the meaning or the story. Sometimes, however, a word that was less objectionable was substituted for a synonymous word that was downright improper.

Happily, there are relatively few examples of profanity, for the writings of our author are, for the most part, favourable to religion and morality. But Bowdler's standards were severe, and there are allusions that call imperiously for their erasement. Such a one occurs in the interlude of the Nine Worthies in *Love's Labour's Lost*, where a reference 'is made (very improperly) to one of the most serious and awful passages in the New Testament'. And so poor Holofernes is put out of countenance without any jests about the kiss of Judas. Then, 'the most Sacred Word in our language is omitted in several instances, in which it appeared as a mere expletive; and it is changed into the word Heaven, in a still greater number, where the occasion of using it did not appear sufficiently serious to justify its employment'. Here, had he known it, he was only completing the work of Jacobean expurgators who, in a desultory manner, had set about purging 'the Holy Name of God' from plays, at least as spoken on the stage.

In his exposition of obscenity Bowdler laboured under the almost insuperable difficulty of being unable to quote the passages that he had omitted. Yet he could give one reference, which, without offending the eye or the ear of modesty, proved that a whole scene could be omitted with manifest advantage to a play. This was the wretched piece of ribaldry in *Henry V*, already discarded by Hanmer, the scene in which Alice teaches Katherine of France a few words of English. Clearly, it was written to raise a laugh by introducing, through the medium of imperfect pronunciation, the two most indecent words in the French language. It has no dramatic significance, nor, added Bowdler severely, is it to be defended on the ground that it introduces to our acquaintance the princess. The excuse is too trifling to be admitted. All the other plays were as easily dealt with as *Henry V*, all, that is, save three, which contained peculiar difficulties. These were *Measure for Measure*, *Henry IV* and *Othello*. In the first of these, Bowdler felt that he had succeeded tolerably well, but he had to confess that he was not entirely satisfied with his treatment of the wantonness of Falstaff and the passions of the Moor. There might still be words that would give pain to the chastest of his readers.

The great defect of *Measure for Measure* is its plot. It is impossible completely to conceal from the reader that Claudio gets Juliet with child, that Angelo tries to seduce Isabella, and that Mariana spends a night in bed with him. Abstract any of these three interwoven themes and there simply is no play. The best that Bowdler could do was to disguise them; to muffle Shakespeare's outrageous frankness, and reduce plain words to hints and ambiguities, even at the risk of a certain loss of clarity. Thus, a chastely ingenuous reader might well be puzzled as to the reason for Claudio's arrest; 'For getting Madam Julietta with child,' says Shakespeare's Mistress Overdone; 'On account of Madam Julietta,' says Bowdler's. Yet somehow Isabella must be told, though even here the impact may be softened by a judicious use of the passive for the active voice: 'His friend's with child by him', instead of 'He hath got his friend with child.' Similarly, the abstract is more delicate than the concrete. It is not the yielding up of Isabella's body that Angelo demands; she has no body, but a person; and when Isabella herself accuses Angelo before the Duke, she modestly transforms Shakespeare's,

> He would not, but by gift of my chaste body
> To his concupiscible intemperate lust,
> Release my brother,

into,

> He would not, but by gift of my chaste person,
> Release my brother.

Isabella is altogether too direct for Bowdler. She is not allowed to call her wavering brother a beast, or to pray,

> Heaven shield my mother play'd my father fair!
> For such a warped slip of wilderness
> Ne'er issued from his blood.

Probably this is both profane and obscene, but one would have thought this innocent enough:

> Even for our kitchens
> We kill the fowl of season: shall we serve heaven
> With less respect than we do minister
> To our gross selves?

It looks almost as though Bowdler was exceeding his terms of reference and using his blue pencil to elevate his author, the culinary image being altogether too trivial for such a sombre context.

The low comedy was easily dismissed. Froth is as superfluous as he is foolish, and with him goes the magnificent comedy of II. ii, in which Pompey Bum defends him against the charges of Constable Elbow, when brought up before Escalus:

Good Master Froth, look upon his honour; 'tis for a good purpose. Doth your honour mark his face? . . . Nay, I beseech you, mark it well . . . Doth your honour see any harm in his face? . . . I'll be supposed upon a book, his face is the worst thing about him. Good then; if his face be the worst thing about him, how could Master Froth do the constable's wife any harm?

Escalus is convinced, and when Elbow assures him that Pompey and all his associates are 'respected' characters, Pompey suggests that the constable's wife is a more respected person than any, respected indeed with Elbow before he married her. Then Elbow:

O thou caitiff! O thou varlet! O thou wicked Hannibal! I respected with her before I was married to her! If ever I was respected with her, or she with me, let not your worship think me the poor duke's officer.—Prove this, thou wicked Hannibal, or I'll have mine action of battery on thee.

Perhaps the loss of these two hundred lines does not greatly affect the action of the play, but the abstraction of Lucio's uncomplimentary remarks to the disguised Duke is the forfeit of an essential ingredient. The fantastic Lucio is the Thersites of *Measure for Measure*, the chorus commenting on the action and characters, and his reflections, however wide of the mark, on the duke of dark corners and his ungenitured agent, are a release for the audience's emotions.

'If my readers should think', Bowdler concluded with satisfaction, 'that "Measure for Measure", as I have now corrected it, is not yet an unobjectionable play, I would request them to peruse it attentively in its original form.' *Corrected* is good.

The problem of *Othello* is much the same as that of *Measure for Measure*. The subject is little suited to family reading; the arguments that are urged, and the facts that are adduced as proofs of adultery, simply cannot be expressed in terms of perfect delicacy. However, Bowdler does his best, allowing himself a little more latitude so as not to injure materially a most invaluable exertion of the genius of Shakespeare, and comforting himself with the thought that the play is

K

calculated to produce an excellent effect on the human mind, by exhibiting a most impressive warning against the admission of that baneful passion, which is the inevitable destroyer of conjugal happiness.

The obscenities of Iago in his conversations with Roderigo are easily purged, even though the process entails a serious modification of his character, and the loss of the central irony that Othello, once ensnared, speaks with the coarse ferocity of his antagonist. This, for example, is what the *Family Shakspeare* makes of Iago's report of Cassio's alleged confession. Bowdler's omissions are printed in parentheses:

Othello.   What hath he said?
Iago. Faith, that he did—I know not what he did.
Oth. What? what?
(*Iago.* Lie—)
(*Oth.*   With her?)
(*Iago.*   With her, on her; what you will).
Oth. (Lie with her! Lie on her!—We say lie on her, when they belie her.— Lie with her! 'Zounds, that's fulsome! Handkerchief—) confessions—handkerchief!—(To confess, and be hanged for his labour; first, to be hanged, and then to confess.) I tremble at it. Nature would not invest herself in such shadowing passion without some instruction. It is not words that shakes me thus. (Pish! Noses, ears and lips.) Is't possible?

The chaste reader might well wonder why Othello should be so moved as to fall into an epileptic fit.

Euphemisms abound; like Isabella, Desdemona has not a body, but a beauty; 'in my bed' is more delicate, because slightly less explicit, than ''twixt my sheets'; 'guilt' or 'love' may be used for 'lust' at discretion; and apparently 'drab' and 'pimp' are preferable to 'bawd' and 'whore'. Even the scene of Desdemona's going to bed is robbed of much of its pathos by the omission of the last verse of the Willow song, and Emilia's ingenuous defence of a small vice.

Until this time *Othello* had suffered less at the hands of the improvers than any of the other great tragedies, and its emasculation, therefore, was Bowdler's most original contribution to the Shakespearean cult. Yet even in Shakespeare it is a near thing, this persuasion of the audience and the reader that Iago could so convince Othello of Desdemona's guilt, and it is perhaps the greatest triumph of his art that we are thus persuaded. Abstract even a little and our faith begins to falter; abstract all that Bowdler does and it crumbles; Othello becomes what Emilia calls him, a gull, a dolt, and tragedy becomes a travesty. Bowdler himself was quite unaware of the outrage. He would have liked to do more. 'If, after all that I have omitted,' he wrote, 'it shall still be thought that this inimitable tragedy is not sufficiently correct for family reading, I would advise the transferring of it from the parlour to the cabinet, where the perusal will not only delight the poetic taste, but convey useful and important instruction both to the heart and the understanding of the reader.'

Of the historical plays, the two parts of *Henry IV* proved much the most difficult to correct for family reading. The main culprit, of course, is Falstaff, of whom Mrs Montague had made a particular study, and Bowdler quotes her findings with approval: 'Every approach to obscenity is an offence for which wit cannot atone. . . . Every scene in which Doll Tearsheet appears is indecent, and therefore not only indefensible, but inexcusable.' After this we are not surprised to hear that the name of 'the last mentioned person' is not to be found in the *Family Shakspeare*. The two scenes in which Doll appears, some four hundred lines in all, are cut clean out.

After this drastic operation the other excisions seem almost trivial, though their sum probably amounts to almost as many lines again. Bowdler was aware that in purging Falstaff of his indecencies and indelicacies he ran the risk of purging him of his wit as well, but he made no concessions, and the old knight is trimmed into a harmless practical-joker, whom Prince Hall has no excuse for treating so shabbily when he becomes king. First, his profanity goes, 'Zounds', 'By the Lord' and the rest of his oaths, and even such apparently innocuous remarks as: 'O, thou hast damnable iteration, and art indeed able to corrupt a saint.' Although Falstaff has forgotten what the inside of a church is made of, he knows more about the Bible than any other character in the plays, yet these picturesque allusions are flung out with the rest of the profanities: 'I never see thy face but I think upon hell-fire, and Dives that lived in purple,' 'You would think I had a hundred and fifty tattered prodigals lately come from swine-keeping,' and though 'Lazarus in the painted cloth' will pass, the sequel, 'where the glutton's dogs licked his sores', is disallowed. This, however, is on account of its vulgarity or indelicacy. And vulgarity or indelicacy is not difficult to find in Falstaff's speech: 'Hang ye, gorbellied knaves,' 'I pray God my girdle break', 'I'll tickle your catastrophe.' Certain parts of the body are not to be named, notably belly, guts and midriff, the more intimate articles of clothing, such as shirts and petticoats, are over-suggestive, and there is the usual juggling with words: 'lady' for 'leman', and 'wench' becomes 'girl', even in the famous line, 'And is not my hostess of the tavern a most sweet wench?' Can we, by any stretch of the imagination, conceive of Falstaff calling that old baggage, Widow Quickly, 'a sweet girl'?

The reception of the *Family Shakspeare* was most satisfactory, and it ran through four editions—and very beautiful editions they were—in little more than as many years. Yet it did not escape censure. The *British Critic* was severe: 'See what a rent envious Pope has made, and here the well beloved Bowdler stabbed,' and Bowdler preferred the more comfortable words of the *Edinburgh Review*, which he quoted with approval in his Preface to the third edition: 'The offensive expressions of our great poet turn out, not to be so much cankers in the flowers, as weeds that have sprung up by their side, and, so far from being missed on their removal, the work generally appears more natural and harmonious without them.' This was the kind of acknowledgment he had hoped for. His professed object had been to purify Shakespeare for the children, but his secret hope was that he had purified him for the fathers as well, and that his edition of our immortal bard would supplant all others. He said as much when he let slip this lofty aim of his prudery in his Preface: 'I have attempted to do for the *library* what the manager does for the stage.' He was too modest; he had succeeded. Shakespeare was tamed and emasculated, made safe for the nursery; no longer would he raise a blush on the cheek of innocence, or plant a pang in the heart of a devout Christian. Not a single letter arrived to tell him of any indecent expression that had escaped his detection. It was most gratifying. He turned to the completion of his edition of 'Gibbon's History of the Decline and Fall of the Roman Empire, reprinted from the original text with the careful omissions of all passages of an irreligious or immoral tendency'.

IX

SHAKESPEARE INCORPORATED

I n the year of Mrs Hornby's expulsion from the Birthplace, or, to be more precise, on December 19th, 1820, a general meeting of the inhabitants of Stratford and neighbourhood was held at the Town Hall to consider the erection of a National Memorial, in the form of a theatre, to the Immortal Memory of Shakespeare. Mr Mathews observed, at considerable length, that the town had no token of national respect and gratitude to its immortal genius, and pledged himself to do all that he could in aid of this important undertaking, even to lay the scheme at the foot of the Throne. It should, he concluded, be the proud boast of every man to say in after times when passing this monument, 'Aye, I had a hand in that.' Mr Bunn then rose in some excitement to report that the very spot on which the immortal poet breathed his last had just come into the market, and, search the whole globe, there could not be found any other site so appropriate. It was true enough, and a committee was formed to raise funds for the purchase of New Place garden and the erection there of a Shakespeare Theatre. But it was more than six years before the foundation stone was laid, and even then it was mainly due to the efforts of the Shakespeare Club.

This was formed in 1824 at a convivial gathering at the Falcon Inn, with the object of organising an annual celebration on the poet's birthday, which every third year was to expand into a Jubilee. The first of these Triennial Commemoration Festivals was duly held in 1827, when, on St George's Day, the pageant projected by Garrick nearly sixty years before paraded the town. Headed by the Mayor and St George, on horseback, the procession of tragic, comic and historical characters, with their appropriate Muses, did homage at the Birthplace, to the great content and profit of Widow Court, before proceeding to New Place, where the foundation stone of the National Monument was solemnly laid. A vocal performance of the music from *Macbeth* followed the ceremony on the spot. In the following year the Birthday was celebrated by a performance of *The Merry Wives of Windsor* in the newly opened theatre.

The Triennial Festival of 1830 was an even more glorious affair, for George IV himself had graciously consented to countenance the undertaking. As in 1827, the Festival headquarters were a temporary amphitheatre in the Rother Market, well away from the river that had so disastrously flooded the approaches to Garrick's arena. It was just as well, for on the morning of April 23rd the rain came down in torrents. However, early in the afternoon the sky cleared and the procession began, again headed by the Mayor and St George on horseback, the former wearing a Jubilee Scarf and a medal suspended by the rainbow-tinted Jubilee Ribbon. St George was personated by Charles Kean, a boy of nineteen. 'Upwards of seventy-five of the more prominent characters of Shakespeare', wrote an enthusiastic eyewitness, 'burst upon the sight at one view, with a vividness and splendour really astonishing.' The junketings lasted four days, with dinners and balls and fireworks and performances in the theatre, at which Mr Kean appeared. The only disappointment was the indisposition that prevented the appearance of the royal debauchee. It was his last indisposition, and he died a few weeks later. 'A small band of men', the anonymous panegyrist concluded, 'have raised up a spirit in their native town, which will perhaps never be destroyed.' Yet, although the Shakespeare Club continued to celebrate the Birthday, it was the last of the Triennial Commemoration Festivals.

In the early years of Queen Victoria there were more important Shakespearean doings than the annual frolics in Stratford. The great eighteenth-century editors had been succeeded by the great Romantic critics, but Coleridge, Hazlitt and Lamb were all dead by 1834, and were in turn succeeded by a new generation of Shakespeare scholars. The first of these was John Payne Collier, a barrister and journalist who devoted his leisure to the study of Shakespeare and the early English drama. The first fruit of this was his *History of English Dramatic Poetry and Annals of the Stage*, which appeared in 1831. It contained an account of an important discovery in the Public Records Office. It was already known that in 1596 the inhabitants of Blackfriars sent a petition to the Privy Council asking them to prevent the Chamberlain's Men, the company with which Shakespeare performed, building a private theatre in their neighbourhood. Now Collier had unearthed the counter-petition of the actors, 'Thomas Pope, Richard Burbadge, John Hemings, Augustine Phillips, Willm Shakespeare, Willm Kempe, Willm Slye, Nicholas Tooley and others', who protested that they had 'no other meanes whereby to maintaine their wiues and fami-

lies but by the exercise of their qualitie', and that though in the summer
they could 'playe at their newe built house on the Bankside callde the
Globe, in the winter they are compelled to come to the Blackfriers'. It
was the earliest official list of the Chamberlain's company, in which, by
1603, Shakespeare had risen to be the leading member. The discovery
earned Collier the post of librarian to the Duke of Devonshire, with
access to the Earl of Ellesmere's library at Bridgewater House, containing the papers of Thomas Egerton, first Lord Ellesmere, the Elizabethan statesman.

The Egerton Papers exceeded Collier's most sanguine expectations.
Large bundles, ranging in date from 1581 to 1616, remained un-
explored, many of them apparently unopened since the day Lord Ellesmere, perhaps with his own hands, tied them together. Among these,
in a most unpromising heap, chiefly of legal documents, Collier found
a bundle containing theatrical records, including records of Shakespeare
himself.

There was, for example, a certificate showing that he was one of the
sharers, or part-owners, in the 'blacke Fryers playehouse' as early as
1589. Another document, apparently some twenty years later, was a
valuation of the shares in the theatre: 'W. Shakspeare asketh for the
wardrobe and properties of the same playhouse 500^{li} and for his 4
shares the same as his fellowes Burbidge and Fletcher 933^{li} 6^{s}. 8^{d}.'
This came to more than £1,400, an astonishing amount, equal to about
£40,000 to-day.

In 1604, shortly after the Chamberlain's had become the King's
company, Samuel Daniel had been appointed licenser for the Queen's
Revels, a company of boy actors, and we find him writing to congratulate Egerton on his choice, and on overlooking the rival claims of one
'which is the authour of playes now daylie presented on the publick
stages of London and the possessor of no small gaines and moreover
himself an actor in the kinges companie of Commedians, who could
not with reason pretend to be m^{r} of the Queenes Maties Reuelles for
asmuchas he wold sometimes be asked to approue and allowe of his
owne writings'. It was a little unfair on Shakespeare, and less generous
than we should expect from the chivalrous Daniel, who was himself a
dramatist, and in the following year licensed one of his own plays,
which, incidentally, got him into trouble for its alleged political im-
plications. However, in 1610, Shakespeare was one of those appointed
by royal warrant 'to bring vpp a conuenient nomber of children and

them to instruct and exercise in the qualitie of playing Tragedies Comedies &c by the name of the children of the reuelles'.

But the most exciting discovery of all was a letter of 1608 from the Earl of Southampton, asking Egerton to support 'the poore players of the blacke Fryers' against the puritanical London Corporation, and in particular the two bearers of his letter, one of whom was Richard Burbage, the other 'a man no whitt lesse deseruing fauor and my especial friende, till of late an actor of good account in the companie, now a sharer in the same, and writer of some of our best english playes. . . . This other hath to name, William Shakespeare.'

As soon as Collier had read these documents he took them to their owner, the Earl of Ellesmere, with whom he left them. The next day, as he was returning to Bridgewater House, he met the Earl, who told him that a publisher had offered £50 for them if they were edited with an Introduction. Collier indignantly refused to make money out of another man's property, but Lord Ellesmere laughed at his squeamishness, protesting that the documents belonged to the one as much as the other, for though they were found in his house, but for Collier, they might never have been discovered. So, in 1835, Collier published his *New Facts Regarding the Life of Shakespeare*. They made the biggest haul of biographical material in the history of Shakespearean research.

The Egerton Papers were not yet exhausted, and in the course of the thirties Collins published *New Particulars* and *Further Particulars Regarding Shakespeare and his Works*. One of the most important new discoveries was an account of payment for a performance of *Othello*, the first on record, when Queen Elizabeth stayed with Sir Thomas Egerton at Harefield Place in 1602: 'x^{li} to Burbidges players for Othello.' Another was a ballad called *The Inchanted Island*, with a plot so like *The Tempest* that it seemed more than probable that Shakespeare used it as a source for his play.

Even more important was the discovery of manuscript notes in the first folio in the Bridgewater library. The Bridgewater Folio of 1623 was well known as one of the finest copies in existence, but it was Collier who first noticed certain corrections in the margin. They were, he wrote, 'probably as old as the reign of Charles I. Whether they were merely conjectural, or made from original manuscripts of the plays, it is perhaps not possible to ascertain.' There were only thirty-two of these corrections, confined to the comedies in the first part of the volume, but they were interesting; moreover they were the only known manuscript authority for the emendation of Shakespeare's text. This, with his former discoveries, encouraged Collier to publish his 'Reasons for a New Edition of Shakespeare's Works, containing notices of the defects of former impressions, and pointing out the lately acquired means of illustrating the Plays, Poems, and Biography of the Poet'. And in the course of 1841–44 he produced his own eight-volume edition of Shakespeare, incorporating his new material.

By 1841, Collier, then aged fifty-two, was acknowledged as the leading authority on Shakespeare and the early drama, and in that year he founded the Shakespeare Society, with a council that included J. O. Halliwell, a young man of twenty. In place of the anarchic rivalry and vituperative individualism of the eighteenth-century scholars, a period of harmonious co-operation in the study of Shakespeare was inaugurated. In addition to its official *Papers*, the Society published numerous old documents and plays, one of which was an edition of *Sir Thomas More*, the manuscript play, three pages of which are thought to be in Shakespeare's hand. Collier himself contributed his *Memoirs of Edward Alleyn* and *The Alleyn Papers*.

The Papers of Edward Alleyn, the great Elizabethan actor, are preserved in the library of Dulwich College, which he founded, and in these Collier was fortunate enough to unearth a few more particulars concerning Shakespeare. There was a list of the King's Men in 1604, beginning 'Burbidge, Shaksp^{re}, Fletcher . . .', a reference to 'Willes newe playe' in some verses addressed to Alleyn, and another allusion to Shakespeare in a mutilated letter written to him in 1603 by his admirable wife, Joan, stepdaughter of Philip Henslowe: 'About a weeke a goe there came a youthe who said he was Mr Frauncis Chaloner who would have borrowed x^{li} to have bought things for . . . and said he was known unto you, and Mr Shakespeare of the Globe, who came . . . said he knewe hym not, onely he herde of hym that he was a roge . . . so he was glade we did not lend him the monney.' It was interesting to know that Shakespeare was on good terms with Alleyn and his family.

Collier was indefatigable in his researches, and *The Diary of Philip Henslowe* was followed by *Memoirs of the Principal Actors in the Plays of Shakespeare* and *Extracts from the Registers of the Stationers' Company*. In 1850 he retired from London to Maidenhead, and this removal was the occasion of the greatest discovery of all. In the previous spring he had picked up a second (1632) folio of Shakespeare for thirty shillings. He already had an imperfect copy of the book, but when he got home he found his new purchase to be in even poorer condition, cropped, stained and lacking several pages, and he threw it on one side without examining it any further. On the cover of the greasy calf binding was inscribed, 'Tho. Perkins his booke'. While arranging his library for removal he noticed some marks in the margin of the folio, but it was some time after he had settled at Maidenhead before he looked at it again. He wondered idly if Thomas Perkins was any relation of Richard Perkins, the early seventeenth-century actor, and then he saw, to his surprise, that there was scarcely a page without numerous emendations of the punctuation or the text, all in the handwriting of the period.

Collier announced his discovery in the *Athenæum* for January, 1852. 'Some of the alterations', he wrote, 'may have been purely arbitrary or conjectural; but others seem to have been justified either by occasional resort to better manuscripts than those employed by the old player-editors, or as is not improbable, by the recital of the text at one of our old theatres when the corrector of my folio of 1632 was present, and of which recital he afterwards availed himself.' As an example of an alteration that seemed to be beyond conjectural ingenuity and probably, therefore, derived from a better manuscript, he quoted the lines from *Coriolanus* (III. i), where the hero refers contemptuously to the Roman people:

> How shall this Bosome-multiplied, digest
> The Senates Courtesie?

This 'the old corrector' of the Perkins Folio had changed to 'bisson [*i.e.* blind] multitude'. It certainly made a good reading, though not necessarily better than that of the folio, 'bosom multiplied'. On the other hand, Collier could not help thinking that the alteration of Iago's line in *Othello* (I. i) was merely speculative. The original folio reading is:

> Others there are
> Who trym'd in Formes, and visages of Dutie,
> Keepe yet their hearts attending on themselues.

The Perkins Folio changed this into:

> Who learn'd in forms and usages of duty.

If, Collier submitted, the corrector had worked from a manuscript, he would have seen that Shakespeare wrote 'train'd' and not 'learn'd', for the line undoubtedly should read,

Who train'd in forms and usages of duty.

This combination of Collier and the old corrector was a formidable one, and their joint emendation decidedly violent. Still, it was more easily comprehensible than the original line.

In January, 1853, Collier published his 'Notes and Emendations to the text of Shakespeare's Plays, from early manuscript corrections in a copy of the folio, 1632, in the possession of J. Payne Collier, Esq. F.S.A. forming a supplemental volume to the Works of Shakespeare by the same editor, in eight volumes, octavo. Printed for the Shakespeare Society'. This was not quite accurate. It was issued by the publishers of Collier's edition of Shakespeare, who supplied the Society's subscribers with copies at cost price. If the Society had published the book, Collier would have received nothing for his labours. As it was, he was paid £120.

In April, Collier learned that a Mr Francis Parry had once possessed a Shakespeare folio with marginal manuscript notes. He had lost the book many years before, but now, after reading *Notes and Emendations*, he felt sure that the Perkins Folio must be the copy that had once been his. Collier called on him and, in the Preface to the second edition of his *Notes*, wrote that his folio of 1632, with its elaborate corrections, had been given to Parry about fifty years before by a relative who lived near Ufton Court, the seat of the Perkins family, whence he might well have obtained it when the library was dispersed. 'Upon the foundations of strong probability,' Collier concluded, 'I am able to carry the folio back almost to the period when it was published.'

In the same year, 1853, appeared the first volume of Halliwell's folio edition of Shakespeare. The review in the *Athenæum* was unfavourable, one mischievous misrepresentation among many others being that the introductory Life of Shakespeare was virtually a reprint of that already published by Halliwell in 1848. In a pamphlet called *Curiosities of Modern Shakespearian Criticism* Halliwell replied that, so far from this being true, the biography had been almost entirely rewritten; that he had been at great pains to examine all documents that he had previously taken on trust, and thus, he added, saved himself from the error of again quoting the Bridgewater papers as genuine. In the volume under review, he had written that some of Collier's finds among the Egerton Papers unquestionably appeared to be modern forgeries, while others were of such a suspicious character that they ought to be submitted to the experts of the British Museum for examination. He also reproduced a facsimile of Joan Alleyn's letter to her husband, which showed quite clearly that, even if the Shakespearean allusion had perished owing to the rottenness of the paper, Collier's interpretation could not be correct, as it was irreconcilable with the position of words that were clearly decipherable in the remaining fragment. Halliwell had been all courtesy towards the Director of the Shakespeare Society; Collier had made an error, and he had been deceived; as the Dulwich letter was merely a misinterpretation, so the suspected documents among the Egerton Papers had doubtless been inserted by a fabricator, and Collier, thinking that they had never been previously examined, naturally assumed that they were genuine.

But the anonymous *Athenæum* reviewer resented this slur on Collier's scholarship, and retorted with a sneaping reference to facsimiles in Halliwell's folio: 'A gentleman, who is very sharp on the blunders of other people, should be a little more accurate himself. Mistakes which Mr Halliwell sets down as evidences of the ignorance of the scrivener, are shown by these facsimiles to be mere misreadings by himself.' Small wonder that in his *Curiosities* Halliwell was more outspoken: 'If I am correct in thinking that the whole of the Shakespearian MSS. in the possession of the Earl of Ellesmere are modern forgeries—that an important letter, discovered at Dulwich College, has been misinterpreted, or that some remarkable ballads are compositions of comparatively recent date—it is unnecessary to say that the chief of the far-famed Shakespearian discoveries of Mr Collier are of small value indeed; and Mr Collier is generally understood to be one of the *Athenæum* reviewers!'

So began the great Shakespeare controversy of the fifties; in the main Collier and the *Athenæum* against the other scholars of the period. Halliwell followed up his *Curiosities* with 'Observations on the Shakespearian Forgeries at Bridgewater House', and in 'The Text of Shakespeare vindicated from the interpolations and corruptions advocated by J. P. Collier', S. W. Singer lustily opened the attack on the genuineness of the Perkins notes themselves. In spite of this Collier published his one-volume 'Plays of Shakespeare: the text regulated by the recently discovered folio of 1632'. It was assailed by the American critic, R. Grant White, and an anonymous opponent contributed a pamphlet with the insulting title, *Literary Cookery*. Collier prosecuted the publishers, but failed. It was the end of the period of harmonious co-operation so happily begun in 1841. The Director of the Shakespeare Society was suspected by the members of his Council of being a fabricator, and the Society came to an inglorious end in 1853.

The dispute, however, continued unabated, though nothing positive could be proved against Collier from internal evidence alone. The critics might argue that some of the words among the emendations to the Perkins Folio could not have been written two hundred years before, as they were no older than the nineteenth century, but Collier shrugged his shoulders and answered mildly that, as the old corrector had used them, the critics must be mistaken. Conclusive proof of forgery could be obtained only from external evidence: not from *what* was written, but from *how* it was written, with what sort of ink, in what sort of hand. This was a matter for the experts of the British Museum. But so long as the folio was in the hands of Collier such a palaeographic test was impossible, and even after he had presented it to the Duke of Devonshire there were difficulties. Dr C. M. Ingleby spent a year in trying to get a view of the book, but the Duke's librarian refused to show it, and the Duke himself did not know where it was. At last, in 1858, Ingleby approached Sir Frederic Madden, Keeper of the Manuscripts in the British Museum, who wrote courteously to Collier, asking if he could procure him a sight of the book. There was no reply. In the following year Sir Frederic applied to the Duke, and on the evening of May 26th the folio was in his hands. It did not take him long to decide that the notes were a modern fabrication.

On July 2nd, a letter from his assistant, Nicholas Hamilton, appeared in *The Times*. After stating that the corrections in the folio could not have been written before it was rebound, about 1750, and that there had been an attempt to obliterate a vast number of them, he came to the most astonishing of his discoveries:

On a close examination of the margins they are found to be covered with an infinite number of faint pencil marks and corrections, in obedience to which the supposed old corrector has made his emendations. These pencil corrections have not even the pretence of antiquity in character or spelling, but are written in a bold hand of the present century. A remarkable instance occurs in Richard III, where the stage direction, 'with the body', is written in pencil in a clear modern hand, while over this the ink corrector writes in the antique and smaller character, 'with the dead bodie', the word 'dead' being seemingly inserted to cover over the entire space occupied by the larger pencil writing, and 'bodie' instead of 'body' to give the requisite appearance of antiquity.

There could be no doubt that both pencil marks and ink corrections were written by the same hand, and that this hand was of the nineteenth century.

This, of course, did not prove that the hand was Collier's, and in August the *New York Daily Tribune* breezily summed up the position:

Thus falls to the ground a literary imposture which, from the fame of the author to whose works it related, and the distinguished position of its first and most eminent dupe and innocent apostle, Mr Collier, has excited a more general interest in the reading world than any other upon record. Its author, who must be a very clever and dexterous fellow, may be yet alive, and chuckling, like his prototype Ireland, over the credulity of his victims.

Although America was on the verge of civil war, the editor could not resist a humorous thrust at his slow-witted cousins:

But how characteristic it is of dear old England that he should have been obliged to wait so long to be found out! Who believes that, had that old folio been brought forward in New-York instead of London, five long years would have elapsed before the array of internal evidence against the authority and antiquity of its corrections produced by the American critic, Mr R. Grant White, would have been sustained by the tests of the microscope and the laboratory?

Neither Ingleby in his *Shakspeare Fabrications*, nor Hamilton in his *Inquiry into the Genuineness of the Manuscript Corrections*, accused Collier of forgery, but in 1860 he issued a *Reply* in defence of the Old Corrector. It was not very convincing, and he even insinuated that Sir Frederic Madden had inserted the pencil markings in order to discredit his discovery. He made a still more damaging insinuation. In a letter to *The Times* of July 7th, 1859, he had written: 'I have shown and sworn that this very book was in the possession of a gentleman named Parry about half a century ago. Mr Parry recognized it instantly, annotated as it is now.' On the 13th Parry went to the British Museum, but when Sir Frederic showed him the Perkins Folio he felt perfectly sure that he had never seen the book before. It was not the folio that had once been his, nor had Collier on any of his visits brought it to him for identification. In his *Reply* Collier suggested that the old man had been deliberately confused by Sir Frederic and his associates passing and repassing folio Shakespeares in front of his eyes, and thus 'cajoled him out of his own conviction'. Parry had no hesitation in flatly contradicting the accusation.

Meanwhile Madden and Hamilton had examined the Bridgewater Folio of 1623, and again discovered pencil marks under the inked-in corrections. Moreover, they concluded that the ink-writing was not in a genuine, but in a simulated seventeenth-century hand that belonged to the nineteenth century. All the other suspected documents—the Players' Petition on behalf of the Blackfriars theatre, and the Egerton and Dulwich Papers—were examined, and proved to be forgeries in the hand of the Old Corrector.

Like Malone, Ingleby was a lawyer, and in 1861 he summed up the case against Collier:

1. One man discovered two folios corrected in manuscript, and (to put the case mildly, say) *three* documents bearing on the life of Shakspere.
2. All the annotations and documents so discovered are forgeries.
3. All the annotations of both folios, and all the documents, appear to be in one handwriting, (or in other words one man forged them all).
4. Lying underneath or alongside the ink-corrections of one of the folios, are found pencil instructions for those corrections in one man's handwriting.
5. The man of section one is the man of section four.
6. The man in question occupied the foremost place as editor of Shakspere, and commentator on Shaksperian literature.

And yet, Ingleby asked, 'Can it be believed that a man of Mr Collier's moral character could have done this?' Well, we *know* that he falsified Joan Alleyn's letter by adding an allusion to Shakespeare.

'This then', he submitted, 'is the case against Mr Collier. It is on this evidence that he stands charged with being himself the corrector of the Perkins Folio, and the concoctor and prime instigator, if not the fabricator, of various documents, all bearing on the life of Shakspere.'

His peroration is a strange mixture of pride in his native literature and mid-Victorian contempt for foreigners and their lingoes. For him, the fabrication of the Perkins notes was much the worst of Collier's offences; the other fabrications merely vitiate our Elizabethan history, these corrupt our language. 'Shame to the perpetrator of that foul libel on the pure genius of Shakspere! The texts of Shakspere and of the English Bible have been justly regarded as the two river-heads of our vernacular English. Gallicisms are constantly percolating into it, as our *social* changes demand the admixture (for no other changes can render the use of French words necessary, much less expedient), and its purity is being constantly violated by the importation of native and (still worse) American slang. To the texts of Shakspere and of our Bible we must cleave, if we would save our language from deterioration. Yet it is one of these texts that a tasteless and incompetent peddler has attempted to corrupt throughout its wide and fertile extent.'

Collier did not reply, and the case was never definitely proved against him. He was by no means altogether an impostor. A genuine scholar who did an immense amount of valuable work, he was at the same time a kind, genial and honourable man, but for one fatal flaw. He could not resist the temptation that the magic name of Shakespeare offered him of gaining an easy celebrity. The result was that everything he touched he tainted; even to-day there are Elizabethan records whose authenticity is suspect, and any new Shakespearean discovery must first be cleared of having come within his scope. He died in 1883, aged ninety-four. When his library was sold a transcript from Alleyn's *Diary* was discovered. It was written in his own hand, with the same interlineations as those forged in the original diary.

X

SHAKESPEARE COMMEMORATED

T H E decade of the great Collier controversy coincided with the heyday of Charles Kean's Shakespearean productions at the Princess's Theatre. His ideal was a strange confusion of the pedantic and the popular, of the scrupulous antiquarianism begun by Kemble and an inflated spectacle, two elements that certainly never occurred to Shakespeare when writing or producing his plays at the Globe or Blackfriars. Perhaps Kean's greatest triumph was his production of *The Winter's Tale* in 1856, greatest because it was the most difficult of all plays to fit into his scheme. As he himself complained, Shakespeare was abominably careless both in his topography and chronology, though such embarrassingly eccentric allusions as those to the Emperor of Russia and Julio Romano in the same breath as to the Delphic Oracle could be eliminated by judicious cutting, while classical Sicily could be reconciled with the sea coast of Bohemia by accepting Hanmer's ingenious substitution of Bithynia. This afforded a most welcome opportunity of reproducing a classical era, and edifying the spectators with *tableaux vivants* of the private and public life of the ancient Greeks. It also afforded an opportunity of introducing a Pyrrhic dance in the first scene, a Dionysiac Festival of three hundred revellers instead of the dance of twelve rustics, and, instead of 'Time as Chorus', Cronos supported by an allegorical tableau of Luna and the Stars (personified), sinking before the rising Car of Phoebus with all its attributes of splendour. Each figure was taken from an antique, or from the work of Flaxman.

All the leading antiquarians were called in to advise, and Kean, in his Preface, was able to inform his audience that the cornice of Leontes's palace was supported by Canephoræ, that Hermione was confined in one of the Latomiæ, and that it was in the Court of the Gynæconitis that Mamillius (played by the eight-year old Ellen Terry) told his story of the old man who dwelt by a necropolis. Presumably, instead of 'hot lavender, mints, savory, marjoram, the marigold that goes to bed with the sun', Perdita distributed 'the vegetation peculiar to Bithynia, adopted from the private drawings of George Scharf, Esq., F.S.A., taken on the spot'. Such artistic embellishment, of course, took time, and entailed some sacrifice of Shakespeare. But what though the scenes were shuffled, the text cut to half its length, and Autolycus, clown and shepherd virtually eliminated, the spectators—one can scarcely call them an audience—were compensated by the sight of 'the greatest triumph of art ever exhibited on the stage'. Kean really believed that all this nonsense added to the 'poetic effect' of Shakespeare.

One man at least disagreed with him. This was Samuel Phelps. Although, like other actor-managers of the period, Phelps was a star about whom revolved far dimmer luminaries, he did attempt to present Shakespeare with the maximum amount of text and the minimum amount of scenery, and in the course of his eighteen years at the democratic Sadler's Wells Theatre produced all but six of the plays, as well as a number of those by Shakespeare's contemporaries. Yet Phelps's virtue appears to have been, in part at least, the offspring of necessity. He too hankered after spectacle. He could not compete with Kean's five hundred performers, yet in *Henry V* his troops contrived to make a brave show on their French campaign. Eighty wax heads supplied by Madame Tussaud were fitted on wicker figures, and each man carried one of these on either side as the gallant army of forty marched a hundred and twenty strong behind the breast-high hedgerows of Agincourt—imaginary puissance, with a difference.

It was an actor who first warned the tardy Stratfordians that the year 1864 would soon be upon them. Speaking as chairman at the Shakespeare Club dinner of 1859 he called upon them to prepare to celebrate worthily the tercentenary of the great poet's nativity, and appeal to the county, nay, to the kingdom, to support their momentous undertaking. The speech was greeted with general approval and loud applause. But nothing was done. The chairman of the next Birthday celebration was even more ambitious than his predecessor: the tercentenary festivities should not be an event merely of national or even European, but of world-wide significance, appealing to Italians by their tens (Garibaldi had need of a Thousand, and was at that moment embarking for Sicily), Frenchmen by their hundreds, Germans by their thousands, and Americans by their hundreds of thousands. His speech, too, was loudly applauded. Still nothing was done, save the appointment of the President of a non-existent committee. After all, Stratford had four years in which to organise its festival and tell the world about it; moreover, there were more immediately exciting matters to occupy their attention.

Good Frend for Iesus SAKE, forbeare
To digg TE Dust Encloased HERe
Blese be TE Man ⸹ spares TEs Stones
And curst be He ⸹ moves my Bones.

'*Mr Ireland was very particular in his delineation of the monument*'

From Samuel Ireland's *Picturesque Views on the Warwickshire Avon,* 1795

'*Paynted by mee R. Burbage*'

'Poor Will Shakspere,' by P. F. Zincke, *c*. 1820

First, there was the Birthplace. When Widow Court died in 1846, rumours that an American magnate was going to buy the building and ship it across the Atlantic made Stratford act with unaccustomed expedition. A Shakespeare Birthplace Committee was formed, funds were raised and deputies appointed to bid at the auction, which took place in London in September, 1847. Among those present were Collier and Halliwell. There were cheers as the auctioneer ascended the rostrum and explained that the title to the property would descend to the purchaser from the will of the Great Poet himself. Here 'a person' demanded proof that the house really was the one in which the poet was born, but the auctioneer put him to shame by telling him that tradition was good enough for other people, and that sceptics who started doubts without foundations were advised to stay away. After the bidding had reached £2,100 the Committee stepped in, and the property was theirs for £3,000.

It was a most undesirable property. After fifty years of exploitation by the widows, the 'filthy remnant of a butcher's shamble' was in a deplorable condition, and the Committee had already considerably overspent its capital. The original plan had been to persuade the Government to take it over from them, but the Government would have nothing to do with it, and to raise the balance of the purchase price a custodian was engaged to admit visitors at a shilling a head. By 1856 there were 3,000 annual pilgrims (a century later the number is a quarter of a million) and the debt was liquidated.

The next problem was to raise money for the restoration of the property, a problem most opportunely solved by Mr John Shakespear of Worthington, Leicestershire, who claimed to be a descendant of the poet, and offered a sum of £2,500 for the purpose. At last the Committee could go spaciously ahead. The Birthplace was isolated by pulling down adjacent buildings, excrescences were removed, original features restored, and by the end of 1858 the two houses almost resembled the drawing made at the time of the Garrick Jubilee. In the same year John Shakespear died, leaving a legacy of £2,500 to the Committee. His executors refused to pay it, and the Lord Chancellor ruled that the bequest was invalid. The Committee was in even worse straits than before, but by following the example of the late widows and selling pieces of Birthplace timber, and by other ingenious devices, the debt was gradually reduced. This was the position when the tercentenary celebrations began to loom menacingly ahead.

Then there was the Shakespeare monument in the church, also the concern of the Committee. The meddling zeal of that grub Malone was still all too apparent; the grimy and ghostly effigy, disfigured by a thousand inscriptions, was a disgrace to the town. The white paint was removed, the old colours, renewed by Joseph Greene a hundred years before were, where visible, restored: the hair auburn, the eyes hazel, the complexion ruddy.

Finally, there was the railway. The new-fangled device had just reached the town, and in 1860 the Stratfordians were more interested in engines than in the drama, in the 'Will Shakespeare' that took them on jaunts to London than in the poet who took them on more imaginative excursions.

There was no mention of the tercentenary at the Birthday celebrations of 1861, and in 1862 the Hartley Colliery disaster and the distress of Lancashire, caused by the American Civil War and the consequent cotton famine, precluded any immediate appeal to the country as a whole. By the end of the year all that had been accomplished was the formation of a Committee. At last, on April 23rd, 1863, just a year before the event, a draft programme was drawn up. There was to be an Inaugural Address by the President, a Ceremonial Opening of New Place Garden, a Dramatic Reading, a Banquet and Fancy Ball. 'This scheme', the *Stratford Herald* mildly complained, 'has been pronounced rather meagre', and a general meeting of the town was called to insist on its amplification. What the ordinary folk of Stratford wanted above everything was a pageant. Many of them remembered the good old days of 1830, but from the very beginning the Committee refused to have anything to do with a piece of tomfoolery calculated to make them look ridiculous. The Festival was not for the entertainment of the masses, but for those who really understood and appreciated the works of the Immortal Bard. An Oratorio, a Concert and Theatrical Performances were added to the programme. The chairman then moved that a fund be opened for a National Memorial, to consist of a university scholarship for the Grammar School, the laying out of New Place Garden, and a triennial prize poem on the subject of Shakespeare. This was criticised, with some justice, as a parochial rather than a national memorial. The town wanted a work of art, something that they could see for their money, and amid loud cheers it was moved that a memorial statue be erected in Stratford. The motion was defeated by the casting vote of the chairman.

But, if they could not have their pageant, the people of Stratford were determined to have their monument. They insisted on the Mayor's calling another meeting, and, largely owing to the support of the Warwick phrenologist who had proposed the addition of an exhibition of pictures to the Festival programme, a motion in favour of a statue was unanimously carried. The Committee had to submit, and a monumental memorial took the place of the prize poems. Subscriptions were opened for three distinct funds: for the school, the monumental memorial, and general Festival expenses. By the end of August, when the General Committee and various sub-committees had been finally constituted, £61 had been received and £31 expended.

There were now only eight months to go, and so far from there having been an appeal to 'all the nations of the civilised world', there had been no appeal even to Birmingham. A deputation went there in September, only to find that there had been a public meeting the night before—on behalf of the rival celebrations in London. The position was growing desperate, and deputations, generally headed by the indefatigable Mayor, Mr E. F. Flower, visited Worcester, Warwick, Leamington and other neighbouring towns, and even Liverpool, Manchester, Newcastle, Edinburgh and Glasgow. At the same time an appeal for funds was addressed to the mayors of other towns, and twenty thousand copies of a letter were sent to likely private subscribers throughout the kingdom. Unfortunately there was some informality in the appeal to the Oddfellows, and the response was most unsatisfactory.

But the main obstacle to the success of the venture was London. There was no longer any talk of an international Stratford festival, but even a national festival was threatened by the rivalry of the capital. Two simultaneous national festivals were simply a contradiction in terms. Both had claims to Shakespeare, but when one thought of him it was, after all, as a native of the little town on the banks of the Avon, not as a lodger on Bankside. London had famous sons enough of her own, and could well afford to be generous. Yet there was little sign of generosity in the winter of 1863. A London Committee had been set up soon after the formation of the one in Stratford; it had four hundred vice-presidents, its resources were prodigious, and its fortunes were anxiously followed by the Stratfordians. Fortunately for them its affairs were mismanaged; when the four hundred were called together, only a fraction attended the meeting, most of them at loggerheads; there was no working committee, and no programme. Then, early in December, came the fatal blunder of refusing to accept Thackeray as a vice-president. Mr Flower seized the opportunity, and on December 8th wrote an admirable and dignified letter to the editor of *The Times*. There was no protest against the competition of the London Committee, merely a statement of the case for Stratford, and an appeal to the capital for help. There followed six weeks of suspense, and then on January 20th *The Times* declared for Stratford. It was a solemn and sonorous pronouncement. 'We do not like the idea of a monument at all. There are monuments enough. . . . Our sympathy, in so far as we have any sympathy with the movement, goes to Stratford. . . . There is nothing left for the London Committee but either to abandon their original project, or to constitute themselves into a committee auxiliary to the one at Stratford. . . . We speak with perfect impartiality, for we must repeat that the scheme of a monument finds no favour in our eyes, from whomsoever it comes.' The Editor's decision was final. Monument or no monument, the field was clear for Stratford.

The erection of a Grand Duodecagonal Pavilion had already been begun, and there remained only some matters of detail, chief of which, perhaps, was the selection of the performers. The Rev. Mr Bellew, the Committee's Corresponding Secretary in London, was able to announce that he had obtained the valuable and gratuitous services of Mlle Tietjens and other artistes for the oratorio, and that left only the actors. It was unfortunate that Mrs Fanny Kemble was going abroad in April, and would be unable to give a dramatic reading, but Miss Faucit expressed her willingness to act, provided, of course, she were given a suitable part and an assurance that there would be no other performance on the same evening. The veteran Benjamin Webster willingly accepted an invitation, but Phelps replied that, though he would be happy to assist, he was engaged to play in London on April 23rd. The Committee assured him that there would be no dramatic performance on that date, but that *Hamlet* would be presented on the 26th. They added that the Rev. Mr Bellew would call on him within a few days. That was in the middle of December. But no Mr Bellew appeared, and on January 16th Phelps wrote to the Committee to ask if the offer of his services had been rejected. On the evening of the same day he received a hearty letter from Bellew, inviting him to play Iachimo in *Cymbeline*. Phelps retorted that he had originally been invited to play Hamlet, and that he would have nothing whatever to do with the Stratford Festival.

But Phelps had not been asked to play Hamlet. It was true that the Secretary of the Committee had ill-advisedly expressed a personal wish to see him in *Hamlet* or *Othello* or *Macbeth*, but officially he had merely been informed that *Hamlet* would be presented on April 26th. He had made a simple, though pardonable, error in logic. The Committee had another Hamlet in view. This was the Frenchman, Charles Fechter, who had just caused a sensation and an unprecedented run in London by his performance of Hamlet as a blond Viking. There were some misgivings about the choice, but novelty carried the day and Fechter was invited. He accepted, and handsomely placed the whole resources of the Lyceum Theatre at their disposal.

Poor Bellew was bewildered, and by return of post wrote a conciliatory reply to Phelps's furious letter. There must have been some misconception that five minutes' conversation would set straight. He knew nothing about an offer of Hamlet, and was astonished to hear of it, as the Committee had specially requested another gentleman to play the part. This did not help matters, and the actor's broadside is worth quoting:

I claim the right, upon the following grounds, to be considered the foremost man in my profession in a demonstration meant to honour Shakespeare. I have produced worthily thirty-four of his plays, which no individual manager ever did before. They were acted in my theatre four thousand times, during a period extending over eighteen years. I have acted to the satisfaction of a large *English* public all his heroes—tragic and comic—and to that public I shall appeal, and publish this correspondence. The Stratford Committee have insulted me by asking any man in this country to play *Hamlet* on such an occasion, without having first offered a choice of characters to Yours faithfully, S. Phelps.

The attempts of the Mayor and Committee to pacify the outraged actor served only to aggravate the affront. 'I have been grossly insulted,' he repeated, and published the correspondence in the press.

The *Daily Herald* made its comment on February 8th. Nobody doubted Mr Fechter's ability as an actor, but, after all, Hamlet was the only part in which he had achieved any outstanding success, and he had no claim whatever to represent the Shakespearean drama at Stratford. Since the retirement of Mr Macready, only one man was recognised as its worthy representative by all sections of the playgoing public, and

Mr Phelps should have been accorded the highest honours within the gift of the Stratford Committee. Yet, through a want of judgment, or some not very creditable intrigue, they had managed matters so badly that they had lost the support of the greatest Shakespearean actor.

The Committee did their best to exonerate themselves, but after all their devoted labours it was bitter to be accused of a 'not very creditable intrigue'. Still, they could comfort themselves with the thought that they commanded the services of Mlle Tietjens, Miss Faucit and Messrs Fechter and Webster. Yet, not altogether so. Mr Webster was so offended by the prominence given to the upstart foreigner that he declined the honour of appearing at the celebrations.

Mr Bellew was urgently commissioned to engage substitutes for the defaulting actors, but his efforts were so hampered by the unpopular engagement of Fechter that he strongly advised the Committee to break with him if they possibly could. This was too much for the Committee. Bellew had been mainly responsible for bungling the arrangements with Phelps and the over-hasty engagement of Fechter; as a result they had lost the one, and now he was advising them to discard the other. He was brusquely ordered to make no more arrangements without further instructions, and on March 2nd it was unanimously resolved to dispense with his services. The resolution was proposed by the Mayor, who wrote to tell Bellew that nothing could make amends for the loss of Phelps. But, Phelps gone, Fechter must be retained at all costs: he was now the very sheet anchor of the Festival.

On the previous day, March 1st, the Committee had at last published their proposed Programme, with a prefatory list of their illustrious supporters. Among the two hundred and more vice-presidents were the American Ambassador, the Rev. Mr Bellew, J. Payne Collier, Esq., Victor Hugo, Herr Mommsen and Alfred Tennyson, Esq., Poet Laureate. There was a special Festival badge, ribbon and medal, all of which the Committee recommended should be worn. The celebrations were to begin at noon on Saturday, April 23rd, when, should the arrangements of the Monumental Committee be sufficiently advanced, the ceremony of laying the first stone was to take place. There were appropriate entertainments for each day of the week; Mr Fechter's *Hamlet* had been moved to the 27th, and the climax was the Fancy Ball on Friday, the 29th. At a time when the value of money was some four times greater than it is to-day, the prices were all but prohibitive; a reserved seat in the area cost a guinea, though spectators in the gallery could watch the consumption of the banquet for a modest five shillings. The Programme ended with the curt statement that on Saturday, April 30th, and the next three weekdays there would be a series of Popular Entertainments, the particulars of which would be announced later, and arrangements made for excursion trains from the neighbouring towns.

This was by no means to the liking of the people of Stratford. They had contributed their shillings towards the general fund, and the Committee had done nothing for them. You could not have a festival without a pageant; the terms were synonymous; a festival *was* a pageant, as 1827 and 1830 witnessed, and a pageant they were going to have. But the Committee refused, fearful of crushing their genteel visitors in the crowds that such vulgar and popular entertainments inevitably drew. Mr Coxwell's new balloon should go up instead. However, their hands were forced. It so happened that Mr Ginnett, the celebrated equestrian and circus manager, was in the town and, sympathising with the popular demand, made an offer as generous as it was public-spirited. 'If', he said, 'you get up a pageant, I'll find you horses, carriages and all my company to take part in it at my own expense.' A committee was formed, and on the following day a deputation waited on the Mayor, who not only surrendered, but contributed £5 towards the fund.

At last, and with six weeks to go, all was settled except the final details. The Grand Pavilion, delightfully sited in a meadow between New Place and the church, was almost finished, a wooden duodecagon that would have made Garrick's octagon look ridiculously inadequate. With a diameter of 152 feet and a height, including the lantern, of 74 feet, it had an orchestra that would accommodate five hundred and thirty performers and a stage 74 feet wide and 56 feet deep. The drop curtain was painted with a representation of Shakespeare in a vestibule. Twenty thousand cubic feet of timber, twelve tons of wrought iron, and upwards of four tons of nails were used in the construction. The interior was tastefully decorated in the Elizabethan style, with appropriate Shakespearean quotations inscribed on the front of the boxes, though for a dramatic performance some of them were, perhaps, a little ambiguous. This, for example, might be misunderstood:

> O that a man might know
> The end of this day's business ere it come.

More happily chosen, though sadder in import, were the famous lines inscribed around the walls, comparing the ephemeral structure to 'the baseless fabric of a vision'. The Committee invited Mr Fechter to come down and admire it, but were somewhat dashed when he insisted on alterations and additions so extensive that they seemed likely to cost almost as much as the original building.

The President of the Immortals had not yet finished his sport with the Committee, and March was the cruellest month of all. Mrs Keeley, who was to have played Celia to Miss Faucit's Rosalind, retired as a result of delicate health, Mlle Tietjens withdrew owing to some inexplicable misunderstanding, and the Committee's devoted Secretary, completely exhausted by his exertions and anxieties, was compelled to resign. On the same day, March 23rd, the acting manager of the Lyceum Theatre wrote a letter to the Committee. It was received on the 26th and opened by the Mayor. Fechter had resigned.

Apparently the Rev. Mr Bellew had shown him the Committee's resolution dismissing their London Secretary, and the Mayor's letter charging him with responsibility for the irreparable loss of Phelps. Irreparable indeed! Fechter chose to interpret the correspondence as a recognition of the justice of Phelps's complaint that he had been insulted, and of the truth of the report maliciously spread by a member of the Committee and published in the press as well as on the posters of Drury Lane, where Phelps was playing, that 'Mr Fechter, by undercurrent and trickery ways, forced on the choice of his *Hamlet*'. In vain the Mayor pleaded that it was all a wretched misunderstanding, and implored him to reconsider his decision. The Frenchman was not to be moved, and on April 4th the Committee had to announce in the press that the celebrated actor had broken faith, and that there would be no performance of *Hamlet*. The pecuniary loss, they explained, was not confined to the money they must offer to return to those who had taken seats for the play, for under Mr Fechter's directions the most expensive preparations had been made, and the stage enlarged expressly to allow of the scenic effects that he required. It was, therefore, particularly distressing to read the contemptuous reply in the papers a few days later: 'Mr Fechter found that the theatre had been so constructed that a large part of the audience could not possibly see the performance, and it would be absurd to dream of producing any scenic effects whatever in such a structure.' This damaging correspondence was aired in the press until a few days before the Festival began. The Frenchman had the last word: 'I withdrew, and they placarded most of the chief railway stations with my "breach of faith".'

This placard appears to have been the summit of the Committee's achievement in advertising. They were as ignorant of the art of attraction as innocent of the psychology of artists, and crammed all their information into an insignificant poster as repellent as an old newspaper. Too late they admitted ruefully that such a poster was scarcely magnetic enough to attract a visitor from Shottery, much less to arouse the attention of the world to the fête at Stratford-upon-Avon.

In their latest crisis the Committee discovered that the real sheet anchor of the Festival was genial old John Buckstone of the Haymarket, engaged to produce *Twelfth Night* with himself in his famous rôle of Sir Andrew Aguecheek. He bustled about London to find something to take the place of *Hamlet*, and succeeded in securing two of the greatest novelties of the season: *Romeo and Juliet* with Stella Colas as the heroine, and *The Comedy of Errors* with the Webb brothers as the Dromio twins. The Committee must have realised the risk they were taking, for Stella Colas was French and made fritters of English, while Miss Faucit, cast for Rosalind, was the leading tragic actress of the day, her favourite part being Juliet. As Fechter was to Phelps, so was Miss Colas to Miss Faucit, and the Committee, insensible to further blows of fortune, numbly accepted her resignation. Happily, a substitute was found, and on April 20th the Committee held its last meeting and prepared to receive its guests.

A visitor arriving by the Will Shakespeare in April 1864 would be greeted on the station platform by the information that Mr Fred Bolton, grandson of the alderman who officiated at the Garrick Jubilee, now kept the Shakespeare Hotel. On his progress towards that hostelry he would pass the Shakespearean Foundry, the Shakespearean Needle Works, the site of the proposed Shakespeare Monument at the top of Bridge Street, where, turning into High Street, just beyond the Shakespeare Printing Establishment and opposite the Shakespeare Book Shop, he would find the Shakespeare Hotel. It was here that the Rev. J. M. Jephson stayed in the autumn of 1863. The bedrooms had already been given their Shakespearean names; his was *A Midsummer Night's Dream*. The commercial room was *The Tempest*, and the coffee room, apparently less appropriately, *As You Like It*.

John Jephson was a shrewd, broadminded hunting parson who, having recently published a most encouragingly successful account of a walking-tour in Brittany, decided to make his own contribution to the Tercentenary, a preliminary report on Stratford, to be issued just before the Festival. The result is an entertaining and unprejudiced account of the town at this critical moment in its history. He did not travel on the Will Shakespeare, but on horseback, and early in the afternoon of September 3rd rode over Clopton Bridge. This and the river were delightful, but as he rode along High Street he was disillusioned; Stratford was as uninteresting as any town that he had ever seen. It had neither the neatness nor elegance suggestive of prosperity, nor any apparent sign of antiquity, but only dismal rows of mean brick cottages. The bridge, the Gild Chapel, the church, the Birthplace and the house of Williams the breeches maker (now known as Harvard House) were the only visible remains of the period when Shakespeare lived there. There was no half-timbering on the Grammar School, Hall's Croft, Nashe's house or the Garrick Inn, for the present Elizabethan appearance of Stratford is a post-festival phenomenon. Even of the apparent antiquities, only two met with the parson's comparatively unqualified approbation: the bridge and the church. He had read his Ruskin, and disapproved of anything much later than Decorated Gothic. The Town Hall—'the noble structure in the Tuscan Order', of which the Stratfordians were so proud—was 'an ugly modern building', and the Gild Chapel with its clumsy tower was in the debased style of the reign of Henry VII. The Birthplace was 'restored', a word to strike terror into the heart of a man of taste. New Place presented a forlorn and miserable appearance. Nothing was to be seen but a newly-made garden, and the rubbish and foundations of a house. On the far side was an unsightly and apparently abandoned shed. This was 'The Theatre', the foundation stone of which had been so solemnly laid to the music of *Macbeth* at the Jubilee of 1827.

The church was better, though even here there were signs of restoration. The lines on Shakespeare's grave were, of course, foolish doggerel that could not have been written by the poet, but the monument was not in bad taste, except for the naked little boys at the top. The bust, however, with its restored colours, exceeded all expectations. Judging from the smirk upon the features, the poet was engaged in penning a comedy, and the whole face expressed high intelligence and genial good humour. That all Englishmen are fond of manly out-of-door sports was a fundamental tenet of the good parson's creed, and he was overjoyed to see that the bust represented the Shakespeare that he had always imagined, the honest, manly, unsentimental Englishman —the typical John Bull. After this, it is only to be expected that the reasons for the poet's hasty marriage and his exploits in the deer park should be defended, almost commended, as pardonable frolics.

Jephson's judgment was generally more acute than this. One cause of Shakespeare's excellence, he suggested, was that he wrote to please his public, not to please posterity. He had no patience with the spectacular stage productions of the period; a play's effect, he maintained, remarkably anticipating Granville-Barker, could be produced only by the words of the poet, and not by costume and scenery. But actors were more concerned with themselves than with Shakespeare, like Garrick in the picture in the Town Hall, embracing Shakespeare's bust, and looking as if he really believed the nonsense that people talked about his rivalling the genius of the poet himself. Then, Garrick had been responsible for that ridiculous mummery in the streets of Stratford, and he devoutly hoped that no such folly would be repeated in April. He had, indeed, little sympathy either with the forthcoming Festival or its objects. Stratford he saw as a town living upon the memory of its great poet, and ironically suggested that it should appoint a high priest to preside over the Cult of the Bard and regulate the devotions of the pilgrims. As for a statue, what sense was there in encumbering another public place with stone or bronze? But to found a theatre in which the Shakespearean drama could be acted, and a school of acting maintained, would be a work really worthy of the occasion. Having delivered himself of these memorable sentiments, the Rev. John Jephson retired into the obscurity of his rectory. But his words were read by those in authority in Stratford, and remembered.

When the Festival Committee held its last meeting on April 20th, all was ready for the visitors. Since the departure of Jephson much had been done to give the town that appearance of elegance and neatness, the lack of which he had so much deplored; vacant premises had been decorated and furnished as temporary hotels, and almost every house newly painted. The exhibition of three hundred pictures in the Town Hall was perhaps the finest that had ever been arranged in a town the size of Stratford. Pride of place went to Sir Thomas Lawrence's portrait of John Kemble as Hamlet, graciously lent by the Queen herself. In addition to paintings by Reynolds, Maclise, Frith and other famous artists, there were pictures by the local Sketching Club and Etching Club, and twenty-five portraits of Shakespeare, as well as his walking-stick and jug. At one end of the hall were stalls for the sale of photographs, statuary and Festival badges, medals and ribbons.

The morning of the 23rd dawned brilliantly fine. The display of bunting was superb, and never had the town appeared so festive and inviting. Nothing, indeed, was lacking but the visitors. Though there was a fair sprinkling of gentry, ordinary people felt, with some justice, that the Festival was not for the likes of them, and the crowds that were expected to pour into the town simply failed to appear. There were no vulgar bands or common cannon to be heard, and all was a genteel silence when the church clock struck two and announced the beginning of the festivities. But before the first official ceremony, the banquet, a significant event took place. An unexpected German delegation, bringing greetings from the Goethe Society, waited on the Mayor. The Corporation was hastily convened and, as soon as a sufficient number had assembled, the delegates delivered their speeches. They were long, but their burden was lucid enough. The Angles and Saxons had delivered Britain from the tyranny and corruption of the Roman occupation; English and Germans alike were sons of the same great mother, and it followed that, next to Goethe and Schiller, there was no poet so truly loved by the German people, so thoroughly their own, as Shakespeare. It was a point of view that had not occurred to the Stratford councillors, and they were unusually thoughtful as they joined the procession to the pavilion and the banquet.

The Festival, despite the disappointing attendance, went with a swing. The banquet was followed by Shakespearean fireworks, and the fireworks by Shakespearean sermons. Monday was devoted to the *Messiah* and Shakespearean song, including Garrick's 'Sweet Willie, O'. Mr Buckstone's *Twelfth Night* was a great success, though the afterpiece, *My Aunt's Advice*, was not much admired. On Wednesday, 27th, the night on which *Hamlet* should have been presented, a hilarious performance of *The Comedy of Errors* was followed by *Romeo and Juliet*, 'remarkable only for the presence of Miss Stella Colas', an ambiguous observation that was slightly amplified by the dramatic critic, 'who did not understand Miss Stella Colas'. It was a pity that Mr Tennyson had to decline the honour of writing the Festival Ode, as it was felt that Mr Brougham's sonnet scarcely reached laureate level, but that evening's performance of *As You Like It* more than made amends for any shortcomings in the morning's concert. The last item arranged for the gentry was the Fancy Ball on Friday. It was a brilliant affair, and dancing was kept up with indefatigable vigour till five o'clock in the morning, when, as was generally admitted, the Shakespeare tercentenary celebration proper came to a splendid conclusion.

The 'People's Week', or rather half-week, had a more uproarious splendour. There were more visitors in one day than in the whole of the previous week. The celebrated equestrian, Mr Ginnett, arrived with his circus, and pitched his rival pavilion by the river. The pageant, headed by a carriage containing Mr Ginnett's band, and augmented by his equestrian troupe caparisoned in Shakespearean costume, out-pageanted anything that Stratford had ever seen before, and was repeated on the following day. The performances of *Othello*, *Much Ado* and the trial scene from *The Merchant of Venice*, for which the most expensive seats cost only three shillings, were crowded. The only disappointment was the failure of 'Coxwell's monstre Balloon' to ascend. There was insufficient gas in Stratford to inflate it.

Financially, the Tercentenary Festival was a failure. Preparations that should have been begun two or three years before the event were crammed into little more than six months. Nobody on the Committee had any experience of international, or even national, propaganda, all were equally innocent of the ways of celebrated artistes, and they were exceptionally unfortunate. Yet in spite of opposition and adversity they had carried through a festival on a scale never before attempted by a small provincial town. More important, they had kindled an enthusiasm that nothing now could extinguish, and John Jephson's modest 'Contribution to the Tercentenary' had inspired them with an ideal. 'To found a theatre in which the Shakespearean drama could be acted,' he had written, 'would be a work really worthy of the occasion.' Although no statue was erected in Stratford in 1864, the foundation stone of a more important monumental memorial was laid thirteen years later, and at the Birthday celebrations of 1879 the Shakespeare Memorial Theatre was opened with a performance of *Much Ado About Nothing*. This was primarily the result of the vision, exertions and generosity of Mr Charles Edward Flower, son of the Mayor who had been Chairman of the 1864 Committee.

XI

SHAKSPERE DISINTEGRATED

THE Tercentenary inspired more immediate memorials than the Stratford theatre. The Germans piously founded their own Society, the Deutsche Shakespeare-Gesellschaft. Then there was the nine-volume edition of Shakespeare edited by the Cambridge scholars, W. G. Clark and W. A. Wright, and published between 1863 and 1866. Aided by Capell's priceless legacy of quartos to Trinity College library, they produced a text that for long remained the standard one, and the *Cambridge Shakespeare* must be reckoned among the major monuments of Victorian scholarship. There was no longer any excuse for the maltreatment of Shakespeare in the theatre, yet the bad old ways continued.

It was not that Shakespeare was still travestied by the performance of the refined versions of the seventeenth and eighteenth centuries. The star-actor-manager of the Victorian theatre produced what Shakespeare had written, though this was not necessarily the same thing as how it had been written. The refined version had given place to the acting version. A Shakespeare play must be a spectacle; that was axiomatic, for words and characters and plot were of themselves in-sufficiently enthralling to attract the audiences that would make a profitable run. Profitable runs were also axiomatic. If the scene was Rome it must look like Rome, Alexandria like Alexandria, and the battle of Shrewsbury like a battle, not a brawl. But as a battle could scarcely be won in less than ten minutes, and Rome built in under a quarter of an hour, text had to be sacrificed to action, and scenes re-arranged to suit the sets. One could not for ever be putting up and pulling down Rome; Roman scenes had to be run together and fol-lowed by an Alexandrian sequence, even though the play demanded alternations between the two. Each manager, therefore, had his own acting version according to his particular fancy: Shakespeare's text it is true, but only half of it, turned inside out. How far this shuffling with the order was carried may be illustrated by a late Victorian production of *Twelfth Night*: scene 1 combined Shakespeare's II.1 and I.2; scene 2 was I.1 and I.4; scene 3 a compound of I.3, I.5 and II.2, and so on.

Charles Kean died in 1868, Phelps ten years later, by which time a new star had arisen, and in 1878 Henry Irving took over the management of the Lyceum Theatre. He had neither the voice nor the presence to make a really great actor, but he was a great teacher and producer, and his leading lady was the incomparable Ellen Terry. Nor did he produce a large number of Shakespeare's plays, but those he did produce he mounted with an increasing splendour until they culminated in the pageantry of *Henry VIII* with its sensational fourth act, in which the audience was ravished by a reproduction of a genuine Tudor street, every casement of its three-storied half-timbered houses thronged with citizens as the royal procession went by. In his production of *Macbeth* he could not resist reintroducing Davenant's flying witches, and the chief spectacle of the play was the host of withered hags engaged in their aerial frolics, singing, as they used to sing over the stage and over the pit of the old theatre in Lincoln's Inn Fields,

> O what a dainty pleasure's this!
> To sail i' the air,
> While the moon shines fair.

Yet *Macbeth* was not a success, mainly because of Irving's physical inadequacy for the part of the tragic hero.

Irving rarely produced a play with another part that competed with his own. *Hamlet*, therefore, was the ideal medium for the display of his talent, and his acting version of the tragedy is particularly instructive. Shakespeare wrote a ferocious tragedy of revenge, but Irving transformed it into a tragedy of love, a romantic drama in which the accident of the King of Denmark's murder wrecked the happiness of Hamlet and Ophelia. Claudius and Laertes, therefore, were played down and their speeches ruthlessly cut, while the fourth act was devoted almost entirely to the pretty madness of Ophelia. Unfortunately Hamlet himself had to be tamed. Here could be no place for the gentle lover to talk of lugging guts into the neighbour room, or of killing uncles in the incestuous pleasures of their beds. However, to compensate for these unavoidable, though minor, omissions, Hamlet was allowed the full range of his other soliloquies, and the play ended with his death. 'The rest is silence.' It was. What need of further words, even of Horatio's valediction, when the last of the star-crossed lovers was dead? It was not *Hamlet* without the Prince, but it was perilously like *Hamlet* without the other characters. This sentimental and popular version of

M

the play, Irving's first Shakespearean production at the Lyceum, was symptomatic of the period.

The advent of Irving—he was playing at the Lyceum before he became its manager—coincided with the formation of the New Shakspere Society in 1873. This was the work of F. J. Furnivall, an inveterate promoter of literary companies who had already floated the Early English Text, Chaucer, Wycliff and Ballad Societies, and now, feeling that something was rotten in the state of Shakspere, paused to give a hand to that poet before passing on to promote Societies for Shelley and Browning.

Furnivall's jaunty self-confidence is reflected in the eccentricity of his spelling, though there was some justification for his version of the poet's name. All the signatures that we possess, he reminded his fellow students, read 'Shakspere', and, he added severely, 'though it has hitherto been too much to ask people to suppose that Shakspere knew how to spell his own name, I hope the demand may not prove too great for the imagination of the Members of the New Society'. The admonition was submissively received, and for the last quarter of the nineteenth century the authoritative reading was 'Shakspere'.

As a matter of fact Furnivall was not quite accurate. The principal signature on the will is 'Shakspeare', the spelling adopted in the second half of the eighteenth-century and established by Steevens and Malone. Before that 'Shakespear' had been the favourite form, though Theobald preferred 'Shakespeare', which led to Pope's pillorying that punctual man of letters for his insistence on three *e*'s. Coleridge preserved the eighteenth-century 'Shakspeare', but Hazlitt, who always delighted in disagreeing with him, reverted to 'Shakespear'. The spelling on the monument in Stratford church is 'Shakspeare', but 'Shakespeare' is inscribed on the graves of his wife and daughter, and this is the spelling of the folio and nearly all the quartos. Collier's Shakespeare Society established the modern usage, and to escape the obloquy associated with that body was doubtless one reason why Furnivall produced his neat, though less euphonious, variation. 'Shakspere' disappeared with the New Shakspere Society in 1894, and 'Shakespeare' it has been ever since.

Collier, it will be remembered, was still very much alive in 1873, and that Furnivall was at pains to dissociate his New Society from the old one is clear from his explanation of its objects. 'Antiquarian illustration, emendation, and verbal criticism—to say nothing of forgery, or at least, publication of forg'd documents—were of the first school.

The subject of the growth, the oneness of Shakspere, the links between his successive plays, the light thrown on each by comparison with its neighbour, the distinctive characteristics of each Period and its contrast with the others, the treatment of the same or like incidents etc. in the different Periods of Shakspere's life—this subject, in all its branches, is the special business of the present, the second school of Victorian students.'

It was lamentable that the ordinary Englishman had no notion of the characteristics, the periods, or succession of Shakspere's works, humiliating that he did not even know whether *Love's Labour's Lost* was written before or after *The Tempest*. And it was a disgrace to England that the study of Shakspere was still so narrow that there was no book by an Englishman dealing in any worthy manner with Shakspere as a whole. They ordered these things better in Germany; the *Commentaries* of Gervinus—an honour to a German to have written, a pleasure to an Englishman to read—was the only book that could be put into the hands of the student who wanted to know the mind of Shakspere.

Furnivall disarmingly disclaimed any pretension to being a Shaksperean scholar, nor had he any wish to be the President of the Society; the post was vacant, but it was to be hoped that it would soon be filled by one of their most celebrated poets, Mr Tennyson perhaps, or Mr Swinburne. He was merely the Director of Studies, but he knew what was to be done. He had founded the Society in the same way that he had founded all his other Societies; that is, having a special work to get done, he asked people to come forward and help him to do it. He did not ask people to come forward and tell him what to do; he was going to tell them; he knew. And at the opening meeting, on March 13th, 1874, he told them.

The first thing was to establish the order in which Shakspere wrote his plays. Malone had made a memorable attempt to do this, but his method was woefully inadequate, his conclusions deplorably erroneous. The new scientific method must be employed; statistics, derived from rigorous metrical tests, would yield the final answer. The verse of each play must be analysed, and the proportion of rhyme, run-on lines, double endings and other metrical devices calculated and tabulated. Then from these percentages, on the reasonable assumption that the subtler the versification the later the play, the correct chronological sequence would reveal itself. This was to be the special task of Mr

Fleay, and fortunately Mr Fleay had already prepared the very first paper to be read to the Society, on 'Metrical Tests as applied to Dramatic Poetry'.

The order in which the plays were written having been established, it would be found that they fell naturally into a number of well-defined groups corresponding to the various Periods of Shakspere's life (Mr Halliwell would discover and correlate all biographical information); thus, a group of comedies would suggest a happy phase, and a sequence of tragedies indicate a period of more profound and serious thought, perhaps even a personal tragedy. Gervinus found three distinct periods, but Furnivall favoured four, though the final decision would lie with Professor Dowden, whose assignment was to make a special study of the subject, based on the findings of Mr Fleay.

All this, of course, was merely the prelude to higher aesthetic criticism. But only when the Chronology and the Periods had been determined would it be possible to study the growth, the oneness of Shakspere; 'to study the progress and meaning of Shakspere's mind, the passage of it from the fun and word-play, the lightness, the passion of the Comedies of Youth, through the patriotism (still with comedy of more meaning) of the Histories of Middle Age, to the great Tragedies dealing with the deepest questions of man in Later Life; and then at last to the poet's peaceful and quiet home-life again in Stratford, when the daughters he saw there, the sweet English maidens, the pleasant country scenes around him, passt as it were again into his plays. So we get him at last down quietly in his country home again, with the beauty of that country, wife and girl, and friends around him; with sheep-shearings to be talkt of, and Perdita with the Spring flowers to be lovd, and everything else serenely enjoyd; and so he ends his life.'

Thus briskly directed, and production speeded by a positively industrial division of labour, the work of the Society went rapidly ahead, and in his first Report, in the summer of 1875, Furnivall was able to announce very satisfactory progress. 'It has led the revival of interest in Shakspere that the theatres and press bear witness to; it has enrolld nearly 450 Members; it has establisht Branch Societies, and helpt to form many reading parties; it has forc't on the notice of the English public that most powerful and useful instrument in Shakspere criticism, "Metrical Tests"; it has procurd the publication of a new and cheaper edition of the Englisht *Gervinus*. Its members Mr Halliwell and Prof. Dowden have publisht valuable works on Shakspere.' Halliwell's publication was the first part of his *Illustrations of the Life of Shake-speare* (he risked the Director's derision, but as a member of the original Shakespeare Society he claimed the right to retain their spelling), Dowden's contribution was *The Mind and Art of Shakspere*. He had kept abreast of, almost ahead of, Mr Fleay.

He found, as Furnivall had thought, that there were four distinct Periods in the twenty years of Shakspere's writing life. In his earlier plays, the poet wrote 'concerning young men and maidens, their loves, their mirths, their griefs, as one who is among them', of Rosalind, for example, 'a gallant curtle-axe upon her thigh, and the bright, tender, loyal womanhood within'. Then after the patriotic phase of the histories, and the bitter depths of tragedy, Shakspere returned to the young men and maidens, not now, however, as one who was among them, but 'tenderly bending over the joys and sorrows of youth', and creating heroines 'made up of beauty, and love, and womanly pity'. And 'over the beauty of youth and the love of youth, there is shed, in these plays of Shakspere's final period, a clear yet tender luminousness, a beautiful, pathetic light'. It was just as Furnivall had foreseen. Shakspere himself, after the tempest of the tragic period, sailed into harbour, beaten and storm-tossd, but yet with sails full-set, to anchor at peace. After this it is strangely prosaic to learn, when considering Shakspere as a whole, his oneness, his mind, that, if not exactly 'a Tory and a gentleman, he had within him the elements of English conservatism'.

This sentimental view of Shakspere and his heroines, his tender maidens and their loyal womanhood, was in part a reflection of the spirit of the age, with its idealised conception of woman, in part a development of the teaching of Coleridge. He had shown that Shakspeare's art was equal to his genius, and it followed, therefore, that all things were possible with him. Shakespeare could do no wrong; he was beyond all criticism, o'ertopping knowledge. There was nothing left but to adore, and see who could shout the loudest. The floods of adulation were loosed, and the weighty waters of romantic German professors augmented the torrent. Carlyle, like Furnivall, a disciple of the Germans, joined in the general paean: 'There rises a kind of universal Psalm out of this Shakspeare too; not unfit to make itself heard among the still more sacred Psalms.' Carlyle was concerned with Hero-Worship, with Shakspeare as Hero, but a few years later Mrs Cowden Clarke developed the parallel theme of Heroine-Worship, with Shakspeare's maidens as Heroines. The three volumes of her reconstruction of *The Girlhood of Shakespeare's Heroines* were published in the middle of the century. Then there was Mr Swinburne, particularly Mr Swinburne on *Cymbeline*: 'Here above all is the most heavenly triad of human figures that ever even Shakespeare brought together; a diviner three, as it were a living god-garland of the noblest earth-born brothers and love-worthiest heaven-born sister. . . . The very crown and flower of all her father's daughters,—I do not speak here of her human father, but her divine—the woman above all Shakespeare's women is Imogen . . . the woman best beloved in all the world of song and all the tide of time.' A few years later came the popular, though anonymous, *Shakspeare's Garden of Girls*, with its seductive Introduction, 'At the Wicket'. Small wonder that Irving preferred to exalt the love interest in *Hamlet* at the expense of the sordid revenge motif, and that Furnivall and Dowden were able to distil sentiment from Mr Fleay's hard-boiled statistics.

Sentimental and exclamatory criticism of the school of *O altitudo* was not confined to heroines and heroine-worship. The age of Beauties, Gems and Keepsakes had begun, as is witnessed by the list of publications in the Transactions of the New Shakspere Society for 1875. Apart from a forbidding *Shaksperean Statistics* the catalogue is an alluring one: Dodd's *Beauties of Shakspeare*; *Religious and Moral Sentiments*: Gems gathered by G.; *Shakspeare Daily Gem Book*: a Journal for Birthdays; *Household Words*; *Cupid's Birthday Book:* one Thousand Lovedarts from Shakspeare, gathered and arranged for every Day in the Year; and half a dozen Shaksperean Almanacs, Calendars and Daily Companions. What exactly were Warburton's *Shakspeare Copy Books*, for School Use, is not very clear.

For Furnivall, airborne with optimism, Shakspere was merely another natural phenomenon, the heart of whose mystery could be plucked out by Victorian science along with other secrets of nature. Although he breezily underrated the difficulty as much as he overrated his scientific statistical method, he and his well-disciplined team did much useful work in the service of Shakspere. Metrical tests at least helped to confirm the chronology of the plays, and the Society published a series of parallel texts, source books, allusion books and so on, as well as their own Transactions. And there was Mr Halliwell's (now Halliwell-Phillipps) *Outlines of the Life of Shakespeare*. Yet it was all very confusing; a handful of facts were expanded into a thousand pages, and it was not easy to reconcile Mr Halliwell's portrait of the man with Professor Dowden's revelation of his mind and art. How could the son of illiterate parents, withdrawn from school at the age of thirteen to work as a butcher's apprentice in his father's decaying business, be the poet who sailed into harbour at last, with sails full-set? The Stratford peasant, as Carlyle called him, must indeed have been a natural phenomenon to have been the author of the thirty-six plays of the canon. Or was he the author? Mr Fleay with his statistics seemed to be intent on proving that he was not; at least, that he did not write by any means all the matter in the folio.

Of course, there had always been those, like Pope and Hanmer, who maintained that the more disgusting passages in the plays were actors' interpolations, but this was something altogether different. The eighteenth-century editors had only nibbled; Mr Fleay was positively gnawing. With the aid of his metrical tests he had already proved that Shakspere wrote no more than half of *Henry VIII*, *Pericles*, *Timon of Athens* and *The Taming of the Shrew*. It was as easy as lying, this separation of Shaksperean gold from anonymous dross. It was, indeed, as easy as science. 'We must adopt', wrote Fleay, 'every scientific method from other sciences ['other' is excellent] applicable to our ends. From the mineralogist we must learn to recognize a chip of rock from its general appearance; from the chemist, to apply systematic tabulated tests to confirm our conclusions; from the botanist we must learn to classify; finally, from the biologist we must learn to take into account, not only the state of any writer's mind at some one epoch, but to trace its organic growth from beginning to end of his period of work. When these things are done systematically and thoroughly, then, and then only, may we expect to have a criticism that shall be free from shallow notions taken up to please individual eccentricities.'

Systematically and thoroughly, then, Mr Fleay continued his experiments. Chunks of *Macbeth* proved to be the work of Middleton, *Julius Caesar* merely Ben Jonson's adaptation of a Shaksperean play. Moreover, others were beginning to join in the game: New Shakspere Society professionals, armed with their fool-proof scientific method, and amateurs, armed only with hypersensitive ears that detected false Shakspere as easily as Holofernes detected false Latin. *Henry V* was originally written by Marlowe and others, revised by Peele and others, given comic relief by Chapman, and finally revised by Shakspere and others. *Hamlet*. . . .

The New Shakspere Society had much to answer for. They had

given official sanction to exclamatory criticism and the sentimental evaluation of Shakspere and his works. To make a miracle out of the quite unremarkable story of a successful genius, whose higher education had been the conversation of poets and the companionship of courtiers, they exaggerated the poverty of his origin and the illiteracy of his environment. 'Removed prematurely from school;' Halliwell-Phillipps had written, 'residing with illiterate relatives in a bookless neighbourhood; thrown into the midst of occupations adverse to scholastic progress, it is difficult to believe that when he first left Stratford, he was not all but destitute of polished accomplishments.' How was it possible to reconcile this with Professor Masson's estimate? 'In Shakespeare's plays we have Thought, History, Exposition, Philosophy, all within the round of the poet. It is as if into a mind poetical in form there had been poured all the matter which existed in the mind of his contemporary Bacon. The only difference between him and Bacon sometimes is that Bacon writes an Essay and calls it his own, while Shakespeare writes a similar essay and puts it into the mouth of Ulysses or a Polonius.' Even their orthography proved unfortunate, for by adopting the 'Shakspere' spelling, which was the old-fashioned form of the early Stratford records, they tended to divorce the Stratford man from the London poet, whose name was generally spelt 'Shakespeare'—as, it is worth remarking, it *always* is in the records of his acting. Finally, though with the best intentions in the world, by the wholesale disintegration of the plays, they added to the general bewilderment, and almost prepared the way for those who were ready to go a step further and maintain that Shakspere, the Stratford actor, was quite distinct from 'Shakespeare', the London dramatist; that Shakspere, in short, wrote not a single line of the plays attributed to him.

In 1886 the Baconian Society was founded. A few years later the New Shakspere Society was disbanded. Halliwell-Phillipps was dead; Furnivall, having systematised Shakspere, felt that Shelley and Browning were in need of similar scientific study and Societies, Dowden, that their minds and arts were in need of appraisal, and Fleay, metrical tests exhausted, dedicated his talents to Egyptology and Assyriology. The cause of Shakspere was left to the Germans and the Shakespeare-Gesellschaft.

XII

SHAKSPERE UNMASKED

HAD they known it, the Baconians were celebrating their centenary when they founded their Society. Just a hundred years before, the solution of the Shakespeare mystery had been revealed to the Rev. James Wilmot, an ardent admirer of the works of the great Lord Verulam. Like Shakespeare himself, tired of London, Dr Wilmot had sought the quiet and seclusion of his native Warwickshire, and settled as rector of Barton-on-the-Heath, near Stratford, where his books, particularly those of Shakespeare and Francis Bacon, formed his principal distraction. That was in 1781, when he was fifty-five. The more he read, the more he was impressed by the similarity of knowledge displayed by his two favourite authors. There was, for example, a reference in *Coriolanus* to the circulation of the blood, and in *Love's Labour's Lost* an apparently intimate knowledge of the Court of Navarre at the time when Anthony Bacon, Francis's brother, had stayed there. Shakespeare must have been an exceptionally knowledgeable man with an extensive library, though there was nothing in the scanty records of his life to suggest that he was. The rector began to investigate. He covered himself with the dust of every private bookcase for fifty miles around, but could find no more trace of Shakespeare's books in the course of twenty years than could Samuel Ireland in ten days. Nor could he find in the plays any trace of the legends and folklore retailed by John Jordan and his cronies, or of the scenes that their author must have frequented in his youth. Apparently the rector overlooked the fact that he himself lived in the native village of Christopher Sly of *The Taming of the Shrew*, 'old Sly's son of Burton-heath', incidentally the village of Shakespeare's aunt and uncle, Joan and Edmund Lambert.

By the time he was eighty, Dr Wilmot had compiled volumes of manuscript notes on his researches. But he told no one. Stratford remembered only too well the havoc wrought by another clergyman, and he had not even been a Warwickshire man. To reveal his secret would be to court ostracism, and worse. Yet he did reveal it—to one man.

In 1803 Mr James Corton Cowell of Ipswich agreed to read a

paper on the Life of Shakespeare to the local Philosophical Society. As he knew very little about the subject and Malone's *Life* had not yet appeared, he paid a visit to Stratford to gather material. He was dismayed to find so little, astonished to be met everywhere by a strange and perplexing silence. And then he met Dr Wilmot.

On February 7th, 1805, Mr Cowell read his promised paper on the Life of Shakespeare. He was apologetic. He was, he confessed, a pervert, nay a renegade to the faith he had professed, and was prepared, as he unfolded his surprising story, to be greeted with cries of disapproval and even of execration. The truth was that he had met an ingenious Warwickshire gentleman who had convinced him that 'the real author of the Plays attributed to Shakspeare was Sir Francis Bacon'. The Ipswich Philosophers were thrown into confusion, and not unnaturally demanded the name of the author of this outrageous story. Mr Cowell, having pledged them to secrecy, told them, elaborated the rector's arguments, and concluded with a modification of his original assertion: 'Dr Wilmot does not venture to say definitely that Sir Francis Bacon was the author; but, through his great knowledge of the works of that writer, he is able to prepare a cap which fits him amazingly.'

Soon after this memorable meeting Dr Wilmot ordered all his papers to be burned, and died. In 1813 Olivia Wilmot Serres published a Life of the Rector of Barton-on-the-Heath. It is an interesting work, although there is no mention of Bacon. Not only does Dr Wilmot prove to have been the author of the *Letters of Junius*, but also the husband of the King of Poland's sister. Secret marriages to royalty ran in the family, for their daughter was the wife of the Duke of Cumberland, and Olivia herself the child of this union, Princess Olive of Cumberland.

The Ipswich Philosophers kept their word, and it is only the comparatively recent discovery of the manuscript of Cowell's epoch-making address that has revealed the first Baconian.* The founders of the Society in 1886 knew nothing of Dr Wilmot and the priceless manuscripts that had perished with him, though they knew of an even earlier exposure of the Stratford pretender. This was *The Life and Adventures of Common Sense: an Historical Allegory*, published in 1769. According to this fanciful history, soon after the defeat of the Armada, Wisdom, Genius and Humour went to London, where they formed a friendship

---

* See *The Times*, 25 Feb. 1932 'The first Baconian', by Prof. Allardyce Nicoll. It should be unnecessary to add that Prof. Nicoll is *not* a Baconian.

with 'a person belonging to the Playhouse', one who had been a profligate in his youth, and 'some say a Deerstealer'. Such a confirmed thief was the plausible rogue that he robbed Wisdom of his commonplace book, Genius of the mirror that reveals the souls of men, and Humour of the mask that transforms the words of the wearer into incomparably graceful wit. It was with these materials, and a profound genius stolen from nobody, that he began to write plays. The thief's name was Shakspeare. The author of this allegory was Herbert Lawrence, Garrick's friend, the year of its publication that of the Stratford Jubilee, and one would have thought his humorous sally a contribution to the festivities, similar to Thomas King's whimsical speech on Shakespeare as an underbred bully of our passions. But no; for the Baconians 'Wisdom' was obviously Bacon, and it is with the treasures of his commonplace book that the plays are stored. The Baconians forget to add the conclusion of this episode: how Wisdom, Genius and Humour refused to take any action against Shakespeare because they were 'apprehensive that we could not distress this Man without depriving his Country of its greatest Ornament'.

But Lawrence, after all, did not overtly claim Bacon as the author of the plays. Nor did that sceptical sportsman, Joseph C. Hart, United States Consul at Vera Cruz, in his unexpected outburst in his *Romance of Yachting* of 1848. After watching a bullfight at Cadiz he describes how he took a turn along the banks of the Guadalete, which inspired him to quote the passage in *The Winter's Tale* about the deserts of Bohemia and the storm. Falling into a reverie, he began, 'Ah, Shakespeare—Immortal Bard,' and then, sharply—'Who were you?' Certainly not the Stratford actor. That man was merely the factotum who put the smut into plays which he eventually acquired after they had been left with him at the Globe by starving poets. Then, a hundred years after his death, said Rowe to Betterton, 'I want an author for this selection of plays.' 'I have it,' Betterton replied; 'call them Shakespeare's.' And so on for thirty-five pages before returning to the romance of yachting. Although he came to no conclusion, Joseph C. Hart has the honour of being the first openly to ask, 'Who wrote Shakespeare?'

Two years later, in the *Gentleman's Magazine*, James Spedding more modestly inquired, 'Who wrote Shakespeare's *Henry VIII*?' As Spedding's life-work was the editing of the works of Bacon, his answer was read with some excitement by ardent admirers of Bacon who found

Halliwell's recent *Life of Shakespeare* distinctly flimsy and unconvincing. His conclusion, however, was quite unsensational. There was not a word about, not a suggestion of, Bacon; Shakespeare and Fletcher had written the play in collaboration. Spedding was to become a distinguished member of the New Shakspere Society, and one of Mr Fleay's first metrical tests happily confirmed his findings as to the authorship of *Henry VIII*. Shakespeare scholars had themselves made a breach in the solid-seeming façade of the canon. Yet the broader question of the nautical and literary Consul, 'Who wrote Shakespeare?', remained unanswered. He had not long to wait.

Delia Bacon was the daughter of a missionary among the American Indians. Proselytising, pioneering and teaching were in her blood, and after conducting classes for women in history and literature, according to her own original methods, she left New for Old England to discover who really wrote Shakespeare, and why. Thanks to the good offices of the Vicar of Stratford she was allowed to spend whole nights beside the grave in the church, where Samuel and William-Henry Ireland had lingered half a century before. Apparently her vigils were disappointing and uninspired. There was no revelation as to how the Stratford actor acquired the political sagacity and experience exhibited in the plays, particularly in the Roman plays, particularly in *Coriolanus*, full of the 'new philosophic statesman's ripest lore, the patient fruits of observation strange'. Her own patient fruits appeared in 1857 as *The Philosophy of the Plays of Shakespeare Unfolded*. Having rejected the authorship of Shakespeare, it was perhaps inevitable that she should discover the hand of her namesake, the impress of the master mind of the new philosophic statesman, Francis Bacon. He was certainly there, the principal author, though she generously conceded that he was only the leader of a coterie, which included Sir Walter Raleigh and Edmund Spenser, jointly engaged in formulating a revolutionary, and therefore dangerous, politico-philosophic system, so dangerous that they dared do it only in the shadowy form of plays, ascribed to one 'Shakespeare'. Miss Bacon was the first martyr to the cause. Her devotion to this one idea had unbalanced her mind, and whilst she was in England it became completely unhinged. She died insane in 1859, the year of the Collier exposure.

In England there were other sceptics working along similar lines. There was, for example, the anonymous contributor to *Chambers's*

Journal, who, after an ingenious discussion of the question, 'Who wrote Shakespeare?', concluded that Shakspere 'kept a poet'. Mr William Henry Smith was more definite, though not altogether so. In 1857 he followed up a privately printed pamphlet with his *Bacon and Shakespeare,* in which he modestly suggested that Bacon was the most likely author of the plays. It is a dull little book, its main burden being that there is nothing in the little that we know about Shakespeare to suggest that he could have written the plays, while Bacon possessed all the necessary qualifications. Yet in its detail it pointed the way for further advance. One great impediment, of course, was Ben Jonson's lines in the folio, 'To the memory of my beloved, the author Mr William Shakespeare, and what he hath left us.' At first glance that seems to suggest that Shakespeare was the author of the plays, that he was dead, and that Jonson was referring to him. But a careful perusal of the poem raises doubts. Bacon was still alive when the folio was published, and the lines,

> Thou art a Monument, without a tomb,
> And art alive still, while thy Book doth live,

seem much more applicable to a living than to a dead person. Then again, 'Soul of the age' seems more applicable to Bacon than to Shakespeare, as does the famous line, 'And though thou hast small Latin and less Greek', for there is reason to suppose that though Bacon was well acquainted with Latin, he was not greatly proficient in the Greek language. Here Smith was being culpably careless; Jonson wrote 'thou *hadst* small Latin and less Greek'.

Mr Smith found the portrait in the folio equally ambiguous, for, as it does not resemble the Stratford monument, it may be that the lines of the engraver 'shadow forth Bacon, or Shakespeare, indifferently', a supposition that is strengthened by the fact that the pose of a youthful portrait of Bacon is similar to that of the folio engraving. Then there is the parallel passage test:

Bacon: Poetry is nothing else but feigned history.
Shakespeare: The truest poetry is the most feigning.
Bacon: He wished him not to shut the gate of your Majesty's mercy.
Shakespeare: The gates of mercy shall be all shut up.
Bacon: . . . which I have called Essays. The word is late, though the thing is ancient.
Shakespeare: I hope he wrote this but as an essay or taste of my virtue.

Mr Smith was getting out of his depth. Yet what are we to make of the mysterious note from Bacon's Catholic friend, Tobie Matthew: 'The most prodigious wit that ever I knew of my nation, and of this side of the sea, is of your lordship's name, *though he be known by another*'? If this does not mean that Bacon was known by the name of Shakespeare, what does it mean?

It is not, perhaps, very convincing, but the nibbling process had begun, the seeds of doubt were sown. Judge Nathaniel Holmes of Kentucky wrote seven hundred octavo pages in support of Mr Smith's thesis, reinforcing it with the peculiarly injudicial evidence that 'it is historically known that Bacon wrote plays and poems'.* Mr Appleton Morgan of Cincinnati entered the lists with his *Shakespeare Myth* as the champion of Miss Bacon. 'My theory is', he wrote, 'that Delia Bacon became insane—if at all—(for that she died in a mad house is one of the many fictions of that irresponsible magazine writer Richard Grant White) from the reception and treatment of her theory. I should be very unwilling to admit a disbelief in W.S. as prima facie insanity.' When Dr Thompson of Melbourne, Australia, joined the fray, even Lord Palmerston, Disraeli, Cardinal Newman, Walt Whitman, Mark Twain, John Bright, Emerson and A. P. Sinnett began to waver, even the Iron Chancellor, Prince Bismarck, and Mrs Henry Pott.

That, however, is not quite accurate. Mrs Pott arrived independently at the conclusion that Bacon wrote Shakespeare. For years she had been engaged on her great work of editing the manuscript of Bacon's *Promus of Formularies and Elegancies*. This *Promus*, or Storehouse, contains some sixteen hundred entries in various languages: quotations, proverbs, memorable phrases and even single words. Doubtless it was the commonplace book that 'Shakespeare' stole from 'Wisdom', for how otherwise are we to account for the correspondence between passages in the *Promus* and in the plays? For example, six entries in the *Promus* which occur very near together are found in eleven consecutive lines in *Romeo and Juliet*:

---

* There is no record of a play by Bacon, though he paid for, helped to devise or wrote speeches for a number of masques, entertainments and dumb shows. The only verse definitely known to be his is a metrical version of seven of the Psalms, in the manner of Sternhold and Hopkins.

Promus	*Romeo and Juliet*
Rome.	Romeo.
Good morrow.	Good morrow.
Sweet for speech in the morning.	What early tongue so sweet saluteth me?
Lodged next.	Where care lodges.
Golden sleep.	There golden sleep doth reign.
Uprouse.	Thou art uproused by some distempera-
	ture.

This parallelism can scarcely be mere coincidence; the writer of *Romeo and Juliet* must surely have had Bacon's *Promus* at his elbow. Then, on the very same page (Folio 112) Bacon makes the note, 'The Cock; The Larke'. Shakespeare often mentions these birds: the former in *Hamlet*, *Macbeth* and *The Tempest*, the latter (significantly) in *Romeo and Juliet* as well as in *Cymbeline*. And compare Bacon's 'Wyld tyme on the grownd hath a sent like a Cypresse chest', with *A Midsummer Night's Dream*, 'I know a bank where the wild thyme blows'. It cannot, of course, seriously be supposed that any borrowing was the other way round, that Bacon made these notes from the plays, for use in his philosophical writings. One can forgive the Baconians much, but it is not easy to forgive Mrs Pott when, in order to equate her hero with the author of the plays, she writes in a note to the *Promus*: 'From the entries which refer to women we see that Bacon formed very un-favourable views regarding them, views which unhappy passages in his own life probably tended to confirm. The Shakespeare Plays seem to exhibit the same unfavourable sentiments of their author.'

When Mrs Pott published the *Promus* in 1883, she appealed for helpers to read, mark and annotate all the literature from about 1461 to 1661, in order to prove to the public that the entries apply to 'Shake-speare' and Bacon's prose works alone. She herself, of course, had long been satisfied that this was so. But when further examined, the *Promus* entries were found not to be confined to 'Shakespeare', and it began to look as though Bacon wrote most of the Elizabethan drama, as well as other classics such as Florio's translation of Montaigne's *Essays* and Burton's *Anatomy of Melancholy*. This, however, was not altogether surprising, for there are allusions in the *Anatomy* to Bacon's Secret Society for the Advancement of Learning, and, though Mrs Pott did not claim this, there is reason to believe that before assuming the pseudonym of Shakespeare, Bacon wrote under the name of Spenser, Watson, Greene, Lodge, Peele, Marlowe, Lyly and Nashe, *Euphues* and *Piers Penilesse*, of course, being autobiographical. It was a stiffish assignment. The *Faerie Queene* alone is a tolerably long poem. But as we know little more about Bacon's life from 1579 until at least 1590 than we do about Shakespeare's, we may assume that he had plenty of time.

The Baconians were becoming a force to be reckoned with; the evidence was accumulating, and things were beginning to look black for Shakespeare. A few years earlier a number of late Elizabethan manuscripts had been discovered at Northumberland House in London, twenty-two doubled sheets, the outer one forming the title-page. Some of these were copies of minor compositions by Bacon, a short essay and a few speeches for delivery at tilts and entertainments, others were letters and tracts by various authors. On the title-page was part of a list of contents, most of them Bacon's and some of them missing, then, after a space, four plays: 'Rychard the second', 'Rychard the third', 'Asmund and Cornelia' and the 'Ile of Dogs'. None of the plays was in the folder. The rest of the page was covered with scribbles in another hand, including repetitions of the whole or part of the names 'Mr ffranncis Bacon', 'William Shakespeare', 'Philip Sidney', writer of one of the letters, and 'Thomas Nashe', author of the *Isle of Dogs*. One would have thought that the doodler was airing his knowledge of the authors. But no! The names of Bacon and Shakespeare on the same page! Moreover Bacon's *Essays*, *Richard II* and *Richard III* were all published in 1597, the last two *anonymously*! It was virtually documentary proof that Bacon was Shakespeare. Then, one of the scribbles was the word 'honorificabilitudine', a variation of 'honorificabilitudinitatibus' in *Love's Labour's Lost*. This horrific word, cited by Dante as difficult to employ in poetry, must have some special significance. Suppose it were an anagram! It *was* an anagram! The ingenious Dr Platt of New Jersey discovered that simply by reversing the first eleven letters we get Bacifironoh', from which it is not difficult to pick out 'Bacon'. But this was mere child's play compared with the rearranging of all the twenty-seven letters: *hi ludi tuiti sibi, Fr Bacono nati*. Perhaps the Latin was a little shaky, the translation a little forced, but it would serve: *These plays intrusted to themselves proceeded from Fr Bacon*.

The revelations of Mrs Pott and Dr Platt shook even the Germans. Up till now Baconism had made no impression on them, but in March, 1883, the *Allgemeine Zeitung* published an article saluting the 'industrious and courageous lady', and appealing to the English aristocracy to

F. J. Furnivall

Charles Kean's *Macbeth*, 1853

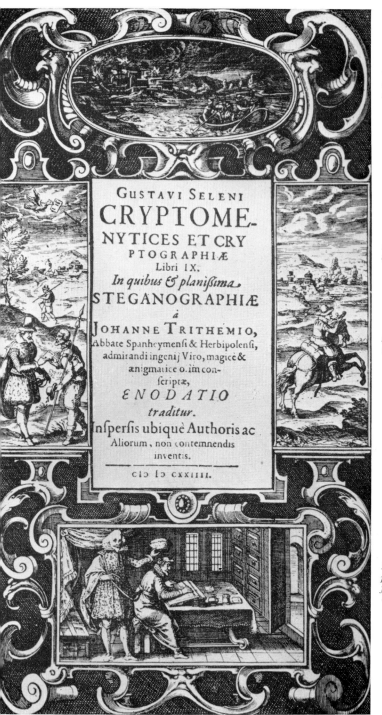

'The Tempest,' a play that is filled with Beacon (Bacon) lights

Bacon gives a play to a Spearman

Shake-spur rides away (note the spur)

GVSTAVI SELENI
CRYPTOME-
NYTICES ET CRY
PTOGRAPHIÆ
Libri IX.
In quibus & planiſſima
STEGANOGRAPHIÆ
à
JOHANNE TRITHEMIO,
Abbate Spanheymenſi & Herbipolenſi,
admirandi ingenij Viro, magicè &
ænigmatice o. im con-
ſcriptæ,
ENODATIO
traditur.
Inſperſis ubiquè Authoris ac
Aliorum, non contemnendis
inventis.

cIↃ IↃ cXXIIII.

Bacon writing the plays, while the Stratford actor, masked and overdressed, takes his chapeau

Bacon is Shake-speare!

The revealing title page of *Cryptomenytices*, by Gustavus Selenus, 1624

follow the example of the Duke of Northumberland, and search in their family papers for hidden treasures of the 16th and 17th centuries. 'May the internal evidence, which speaks so repeatedly in favour of this hypothesis', the article concluded, 'be, ere long, established by the finding of documentary evidence, which will be required before the public will be induced to accord to the great Thinker, Bacon, that open recognition as a *Poet* also.' With this European support behind them, the Baconians formed their Society for the study of Bacon, and of the evidence in favour of his authorship of the plays commonly ascribed to Shakespeare.

At the beginning of 1886, therefore, there were two Societies, the New Shakspere and the Bacon, each claiming to represent the real Shakespeare. The Baconian technique was quite simple, merely an exaggeration, or caricature, of current orthodox scholarship and criticism. Shakspere of Stratford is beneath contempt, 'a mean, drunken, ignorant and absolutely unlettered rustic', while the author of the plays is universally recognised as the greatest genius of all the ages; 'Classical scholars are amazed at the prodigious amount of classical lore which they display. Lawyers declare that their author must take rank among the greatest of lawyers. His knowledge is so extensive that there is not a single living man capable of perceiving half of the learning in the plays.' Thus, by abusing the Stratford actor and beating the orthodox bardolaters at their own game of rhapsodical hyperbole they so widened the gap between Shakspere and the author of the plays that, their premises granted, it became impossible to accept both as the same man. It only remained to show that Bacon was the greatest genius who had ever lived, and the only possible author of the plays.

An attempt was made to seduce Spedding from his allegiance to Stratford. As the greatest Bacon scholar of the age, he should have been the first to see the light. However, Spedding replied courteously but firmly: 'If there were any reason for supposing that the real author was somebody else, I think I am in a condition to say that, whoever it was, it was not Francis Bacon.' Furnivall was distinctly coarser: 'The idea of Lord Bacon's having written Shakspere's Plays can be entertaind only by folk who know nothing whatever of either writer, or are crackt, or who enjoy the paradox or joke.' The Bacon Society could afford to smile. They knew that the final proof was at hand. The Hon. Ignatius Donnelly, of Hastings, Minnesota, had almost finished his

N

Great Cryptogram: Francis Bacon's Cipher in the so-called Shakespeare Plays.

For many years the ex-Senator of Minnesota had been puzzled as to why Bacon had fathered his immortal works on a dissolute player, without leaving a clue to such a sacrifice. Then one day he came across an elaborate Baconian cipher in *Every Boy's Book*. Like a flash came the thought, 'Could Bacon have put a cipher into the plays?' He searched the text for likely words. *Henry IV* sounded promising, with *Francis, gammon of bacon, great, seal, commonwealth, England.* He counted and he calculated, but there seemed to be no arithmetical relationship between the words; though he was convinced that the cipher was there, he could not find it. Then came another flash of inspiration. The key, if anywhere, would be in the folio. He bought a facsimile copy and began again. He was struck by the word *Volume* in the first scene of 2 *Henry IV*. It was the 208th word in the first column of page 75. The number of words on page 74 was 532. Add 208 to 532 and we get 740. Divide by the number of the page, 74, and the result is 10. *And there were ten words in brackets in the first column of page 74!* This made him realise that the bracketed, italicised and hyphenated words were all part of the cryptogram, and at length he was able to work out the formula indicating the words that made up the hidden story. The system was in two parts. By the first process, the words that were to compose the narrative were selected; by the second, they were marshalled into terse, graphic and truly Baconian prose. It was Mrs Pott who persuaded the author not to publish his second clue. He had had time to decipher only *Henry IV*, and she wished to protect him from any unscrupulous adventurers who might rob him of the fruits of eight years' labour by working through the remainder of the folio.

It would certainly have been a temptation to decipher the rest of the plays after the revelations made by Bacon in *Henry IV*. We learn that Bacon first wrote under the name of Marlowe: 'These plays are put forward at first upon the stage in the name of More-low, a woe-begone sullen fellow', but as 'he had engaged in a quarrel with one Arch-or' and awkwardly got himself killed, Bacon had to find another dummy in Shakspere. Unfortunately Robert Cecil, Elizabeth's chief minister and no friend of Bacon, knew the truth: 'Seas-ill said that More-low or Shak'st-spur never wrote a word of them. . . . He was in a state of the greatest wrath, and would prove that the counterfeit image shown

upon the title-leaf of his volume is but a mask to hide my own face.'
And so he told the Queen that the face of Shakespeare in the folio con-
cealed that of the real author, Bacon. To prove his assertion, Seas-ill
described Shakspere's profligate youth, how he robbed Sir Thomas
Lucy's park, froze the fish in his pond, and fled to London leaving 'his
poor young jade big with child'. How could this infamous 'son of a
poor peasant, born in a hole', an even more woe-begone wretch than
More-low, have written the plays? The real author was Bacon, who
had written the histories to encourage rebellion and treason on behalf
of James VI of Scotland. However, the Queen refused to believe
Seas-ill and defended Bacon, though she ordered Shakspere's arrest on
the old charge of robbery, threatening to make a carbonado of him if
he refused to reveal the authorship of the plays.

Bacon was at St Albans when he heard the dreadful news, and
knowing that the craven Shakspere would confess the truth, took rats-
bane. He staggered into his orchard, fell and cut his head, and when
found and carried into the house feigned death to give the poison time
to work. But his stomach rejected it.

Meanwhile the unsuspecting Shakspere was lying ill in Stratford,
and Bacon's servant, Percy Hotspur, was sent on a swift horse to urge
him to fly the country. He found the sick actor sweating out his fever
in a fur-trimmed cloak, and when Percy convinced him that he could
not save himself by betraying Bacon he consented to fly. There followed quite a scene. Mrs Shakspere hung upon her husband's neck and
wept; his sister, Mrs Hart, bawled; her children howled, and his
brother Gilbert, who was drunk, assaulted Percy with a rusty old
sword. But Percy felled him with a bung-mallet and knocked him into
the malt cellar. Then Bedlam was let loose. . . .

The story is left teasingly incomplete, for after a thousand pages of
analysis, calculation and exposition the Great Cryptographer progressed
only far enough to discover that Shakspere ran away to sea. Yet here,
with a vengeance, was new light on Shakspere—and the rest of the
folio still remained to be deciphered. But there seemed to be no convincing some people; some were sceptical, others positively hostile, and
there were even those who were inclined to laugh. Perhaps, however,
Bacon did seem sometimes to be confused in his narrative. He appeared
to think that the folio was published before the death of Queen Elizabeth, and that Henslowe, the manager of a rival company of actors, was
Shakspere's colleague. And it was unfortunate that he should have

made the nineteenth-century error of misreading the name of Marlowe's murderer, Ingram Frizer, as Francis Archer. Then his equivalents for people's names, 'hence-low', 'shak'st-spur' and the rest, although imaginative, somehow failed to carry conviction. And Mr Donnelly's arithmetic constantly let him down. Sometimes it was merely a mistake in the number of the column, sometimes an error in addition, sometimes a faulty calculation. Perhaps, after all, the cipher was over-ingenious and not altogether reliable, the cryptographic revelation just a little too sensational; perhaps it proved too much. From being a source of pride to the Baconians, it became a source of embarrassment; it was not insisted on, and was allowed to fade into the background. The episode was one to be forgotten.

The resilient Senator, however, was in no way disconcerted. In 1892 he founded the American Baconian Society with its headquarters in Chicago, and Mrs Pott contributed an article to the first number of its magazine. There was no mention of the Great Cryptogram. But two years later the author of a Retrospective Review in the English *Baconiana* wrote sadly: 'Unfortunately, far from offering help to sift truth from error, and to forward a discovery which if true is a very great one, the public voice combined to belittle Mr Donnelly's efforts, to laugh him down, and to prove him wrong. The result was, for a time, to injure him and the Baconian cause in one.' Thirty-four of the folio plays still remain to be deciphered.

Two other cryptograms emanated from America at about the same time. Mrs Windle of San Francisco modestly disclaimed any discovery or labour on her part; her cipher was merely a mysterious revelation from the unseen world, from the spirit of Bacon himself. Mrs Elizabeth Wells Gallup's *Bi-literal Cipher* was equally mysterious, for apparently it proved that Bacon had made use of Pope's translation of Homer. In one matter, however, she was able to confirm, and even advance, the Senator's findings, for her cipher revealed that, 'Francis of Verulam is author of all the plays published by Marlowe, Greene, Peele and Shakspere'. She also found good reason to suspect the chastity of the Virgin Queen, and hinted that Bacon was of even greater lineage than had previously been imagined. But by now the cryptographic approach had been somewhat overworked, and Sir George Greenwood more moderately urged the relatively simple thesis that the Stratford actor could not have written the plays, without pressing the claims of Bacon,

But the publication of Sidney Lee's *Life of Shakespeare* roused the Baconians to further activity. The book, or as they called it, 'romance', was admittedly not a very inspiring work, and they simply could not understand how anybody could still seriously advance the quaint theory that Shakspere of Stratford was the author of the plays published in his name. This phase of their offensive culminated in the most rollicking of all the Baconian treatises, Sir Edwin Durning-Lawrence's *Bacon is Shake-speare*. Here, as the uncompromising title suggests, was no boy's play, but a mature and skilful deployment of all the deadly evidence that would deliver the coup de grâce to the Stratfordians.

Sir Edwin first disposes of the monument and the folio engraving. It will be remembered that in the middle of the eighteenth century, thanks to the efforts of Joseph Greene, the monument was repaired, and it was then, we are told, that the present bust was substituted for the original one, for the purpose of fraudulently supporting the Stratford myth. The old bust represented the real Shakespeare, the miserly-looking rascal hugging a sack to his belly, as depicted in Dugdale's *Warwickshire* of 1656. As for the folio portrait, that is merely a cunningly drawn cryptographic picture, showing two left arms and a mask. This is clear not only from the drawing, but also from Ben Jonson's lines referring to it, for simply by changing 'out-do' to 'do-out' and 'hit' to 'hid', we arrive at the correct meaning, which is that the artist was concealing the real face behind a mask. Incidentally, the number of letters in Jonson's lines is 287, showing that the author of the plays intended to reveal himself 287 years after the publication of the folio in 1623; that is, in 1910, the very year of Sir Edwin's book.

The possibility of the Stratford usurer's having written the plays is dismissed with equal ease. The only writing of his that we possess is the so-called signatures, but those on his will were written by his solicitor, as had been conclusively proved by Magdalene Thumm-Kintzel in a Leipzig magazine. So far from his being able to write the plays, there is a probability, practically amounting to a certainty, that the Stratford money-lender could not so much as write his name. There is the evidence of the plays themselves. In *As You Like It*, for example, when Touchstone, who of course is Bacon, asks William, who of course is Shakespeare, 'Art thou learned?', he replies, 'No, sir.' This means, unquestionably, that William Shakespeare could not read one line of print.

Shakespeare, then, was not Shake-speare. That Bacon was, is clear as daylight and champain. Consider Sonnet 81:

Or I [Bacon] shall live your epitaph to make,
Or you [Shakespeare] survive when I in earth am rotten . . .
Your name [Shakespeare] from hence immortal life shall have,
Though I [Bacon], once gone, to all the world must die . . .
Your monument shall be my [not your] gentle verse,
Which eyes not yet created shall o'er-read,
And tongues to be your being [which as an author was not] shall rehearse,
When all the breathers of this world are dead;
You [Shakespeare] still shall live, such virtue hath my pen [not your own pen,
    for you never wrote a line],
Where breath most breathes, even in the mouths of men.

The Tempest was written expressly to afford a clue to his identity. Bacon, of course, is Prospero (each had a brother Anthony) and Shakespeare the drunken Stephano (Shakespeare died of drink). At the end of the play, the falsely crowned king of the island who had stolen the wine (the poetry) flings away the crown (stephanos is Greek for crown), and Caliban exclaims, 'What a thrice double ass was I to take this drunkard for a God!' *The Tempest* was a favourite medium whereby Bacon's contemporaries so thoughtfully revealed his authorship of the plays on the title-pages of their books.

It is, however, in *Love's Labour's Lost* that Bacon most clearly reveals his authorship. Sir Edwin boldly resorts again to cipher. Bacon himself frequently used numerals as equivalents for letters, and if we reckon A as 1, B as 2, and so on, the equivalent of Bacon's name is 33, and of the all-revealing word, 'honorificabilitudinitatibus', 287, a number we have met before. Sir Edwin gives an improved solution of the anagram: 'Hi ludi F Baconis nati tuiti orbi', meaning, 'These plays, F. Bacon's offspring, are preserved for the world'. Now, the numerical value of the first and last letters of the seven Latin words is 136, while that of the intermediate letters is 151. This shows quite clearly that the revealing word is the 151st on page 136 of the Comedy section in the folio, as indeed it is, italic words, of course, being omitted. Moreover, six lines further down we find, 'What is Ab speld backward with the horn on his head?' The Latin for *horn* being *cornu*, the answer of course should be, '*Ba corn*-u fool'. And this question occurs on line 33, the numerical signature of Bacon! It is worth noting that, as 33 too obviously represented Bacon, 53 was frequently used instead. This is the numerical value of *Sow*.

These are only some of the more convincing proofs adduced by Sir Edwin; others are, perhaps, a little far-fetched and open to question. But almost inevitably he clinches his thesis with a reference to *Hamlet*, to Rowe's statement that 'the top of Shakespeare's performance was the Ghost'. 'The moment we realise', writes Sir Edwin, 'that Bacon is *Ham*let, we perceive that the purpose of the rumour is to reveal to us the fact that the highest point to which the actor, Shakespeare of Stratford, attained was to play the part of Ghost to Bacon, that is to act as his "Pseudonym", or in other words, the object of the story is to reveal that Bacon is Shakespeare.'

'Men of great intelligence in other matters', concludes the author of this remarkable book, 'seem, when the life of Shakespeare of Stratford is concerned, quite prepared to refuse to exercise either judgment or common sense, and to swallow without question any amount of preposterous nonsense.'

Twenty years later, in *Shake-Speare's Sonnets Unmasked*, Mr B. G. Theobald proved, by similar methods and with equal ingenuity, that Bacon wrote the poems as well as the plays. Sometimes he revealed himself in quite a simple acrostic, as in Sonnet 14:

> *B*ut *f*rom thine eies my knowledge I deriue
> *A*nd *con*stant stars in them I read such art.

But the main proof is much more complex than this. By adding and arranging the number of roman and italic words and letters on the page, and by using three ciphers, Mr Theobald was able to show that Bacon wrote the *Faerie Queene* as well as the *Sonnets*. It is true that the author reveals himself indifferently as Bacon, Shakespeare, Spenser, Greene, Peele, Marlowe and Puttenham, in various forms, and that even Mr Theobald admits an element of truth in the objection that there is no end to the feats of juggling if once we begin playing with figures. But these are not the book's main weaknesses. The Baconians had become guilty of the very vice of which they had accused the Stratfordians, the vice that had indeed been largely responsible for their own original apostasy—that of idolatry.

'The mighty author of the immortal plays was gifted with the most brilliant genius ever conferred upon man,' is the judgment of Sir Edwin. 'In the whole history of literature, by far the most brilliant figure is that of Francis Bacon,' is the opinion of Mr Theobald. These are large claims, rivalling the exclamatory superlatives of Swinburne.

Yet they are not all. In some of the *Sonnets* Bacon reveals himself by the signature Francis Tudor. And in the very year in which Mr Theobald unmasked the *Sonnets* a book appeared with the title, 'Shakespeare Unmasked: the self-named William Shake-Speare, the Prince of Wales, born legitimate and unacknowledged: son of H.M. Queen Elizabeth and the Earl of Leicester: baptised in the false name of Francis Bacon: Philosopher, Dramatist, Poet and Arch-Martyr.' Bacon's royal birth has not yet been conclusively proved, but it is the most fascinating topic discussed to-day in the Baconian magazine, *Baconiana*.

XIII

SHAKE-SPEARE IDENTIFIED

JAMES GREENSTREET was as dissatisfied with the cryptographic revelations of Bacon as he was with Halliwell-Phillipps's portrait of Shakespeare as a young man 'all but destitute of polished accomplishments'. The author of the plays was above all things polished and accomplished; not necessarily a philosopher like Bacon, but an aristocrat, travelled and highly educated, a brilliant courtier, one who would not dare to put his name to such a paltry thing as a play, which would certainly be interpreted as treasonous by his enemies. He looked round for a likely candidate, aired his views in *The Genealogist* in 1892, and died. Though his work was frigidly received and quickly forgotten, it had not been in vain; twenty-five years later it was discovered by Professor Abel Lefranc, who was working along similar lines and in 1919 published *Sous le Masque de William Shakespeare: William Stanley, VIe Comte de Derby*. As is always the way, one schism had led to another; the original anti-Stratfordian heresy had produced the Derby recusants. And the Derby recusants encouraged still further apostasy.

In the following year Thomas Looney identified Shakespeare as Edward de Vere, 17th Earl of Oxford. After all, Oxford was a poet, his poems were extant, which was more than could be said about Bacon or Derby. It was true that nobody had thought them worth editing and publishing separately, but Mr Looney soon remedied this and made them available for all to read. Nobody, however, read the poetry of another candidate for fame, a third member of the growing group of noble earls with Shakespearean pretensions, Roger Manners, 5th Earl of Rutland. Although he might be said to have had literary contacts— his wife was Sir Philip Sidney's daughter, and Shakespeare helped to design a heraldic device for his successor, the sixth earl,—there was nothing whatever to suggest that he wrote a single line of verse in his life.

Sir Edward Dyer was a more promising candidate; he again was a poet and, according to Mr Alden Brooks, had all fifty-four necessary qualifications for being Shakespeare; he was, for example, an undistinguished courtier, fond of flowers, of giving advice, and died before 1608. His famous poem, 'My mind to me a kingdom is', is in itself almost a sufficient proof that he was Shakespeare. And consider the verbal parallels: Sonnet 114 has 'My great mind most kingly drinks it up', while 'No worldly waves my mind can toss' is virtually repeated in *The Merchant of Venice*, 'Your mind is tossing on the ocean'. Of course William in *As You Like It* is the martext Shakspere, and Touchstone, 'honest Ovid among the Goths', is Dyer. Dyer's coat of arms displayed three goats. Finally, Sonnet 111 tells us in so many words who the author really was: 'my nature is subdu'd / To what it works in, like the Dyer's hand'. Not 'dyer', mark you, but 'Dyer', with a capital D.

If anybody remained unconvinced by the claims of Dyer, Bacon, Derby and the rest, there was Sir Walter Raleigh, or Anne Whateley, or John Florio's father. . . . There was no end to exciting possibilities, and 'true Shakespeares' became almost as abundant as authentic like-nesses. All sects, however, were united in one article of belief, or dis-belief: the Stratford actor did not write the plays; and in 1922 the Shakespeare Fellowship was formed, under the neutral presidency of the 'agnostic' Sir George Greenwood, to 'investigate the question of the authorship of Shakespeare's plays and poems'. One of the vice-presidents was Professor Lefranc, but the emphasis was all on the claims of the Earl of Oxford.

Professor Lefranc patiently pursued the claims of his own candidate, and by 1950 completed his monumental treatise on Derby, the two volumes of *À la Découverte de Shakespeare*, an erudite and immensely detailed work, full of valuable information about sixteenth-century England and France. Slighter and more popular books have been written on the same theme.

What, ask the Derbyites, are the characteristics of the man who wrote the plays? Unquestionably he was an aristocrat, scholar, linguist, musician, hunter, traveller, and of course a rare poet. The grammar school boy from Stratford is at once ruled out. But so are the other candidates as well. As a writer of prose Bacon is superb, but decidedly inferior as a poet. There is no evidence that Rutland was a poet at all, yet if he was Shakespeare he must have written *Venus and Adonis* when he was sixteen, which is absurd. Then, although Oxford had almost all the necessary qualifications, his poetry lacks the majestic and flowing rhythm, the humour and *joie de vivre* of Shakespeare. His poems are those of an unhappy, frustrated man. Here they have good authority on their side; according to Professor C. S. Lewis, 'Oxford shows here and there a faint talent, but is for the most part undistinguished and verbose.' Besides, his name was Edward, not William, nor were his initials W.S. . . . But, ah, William Stanley, 6th Earl of Derby!

William Stanley was three or four years older than Shakspere, and probably, we are told, spent much of his youth at Meriden Manor, near Stratford, which accounts for the numerous Warwickshire references in the plays. (One of the Baconian arguments against Shakspere is the absence of such references.) After going to Oxford and Gray's Inn he travelled abroad, and could not have failed to visit the Court of Navarre, where he acquired the information that enabled him to write *Love's Labour's Lost*. It is a pity that there is no evidence to show that he really did visit the Court of Navarre. But, although admittedly some of the reports of his travels are legendary, Stanley had ample time to pick up the staggering knowledge of northern Italy revealed in the plays. For example, the first act of *Othello* is thoroughly Venetian in spirit and atmosphere, and Portia was obviously the true red-golden-haired Titian type found in Venice.

Stanley returned to England, probably with the drafts of a number of plays in his pocket. This was about the middle of 1587, when Shakspere may have joined the Earl of Leicester's company of actors who played at Lord Derby's house in July. It was there, doubtless, that the two W.S.s met, and Shakspere's duty would then have been, for a monetary consideration of course, to introduce Stanley's plays to the professional stage, under the *nom de plume* of Shakespeare, or Shake-speare, aristocratic variations of the vulgar Shakspere. The hyphenated Shake-speare is, of course, an obvious pseudonym, distinguishing the real author from the mere actor, a fact that all anti-Stratfordians stress, though for some reason or other they fail to make the point that it must have been Derby (or Bacon or Oxford or Rutland etc.) who was the Will. Shake-Speare who played in Jonson's *Sejanus* in 1603.*

But how do we know that Stanley was the author? Well, we know that he was a poet because Spenser, writing probably in 1594, when

---

* See the Actors' list in the Jonson Folio, 1616 'This Tragœdie was first acted, in the yeere 1603. By the Kings Maiesties Servants. The principall Tragœdians were, Ric. Burbadge, Will. Shake-Speare. . . .'

William Stanley succeeded his brother Ferdinando as Earl of Derby, says so:

> And there though last not least is *Aetion*,
> A gentler shepheard may no where be found:
> Whose *Muse* full of high thoughts invention,
> Doth like himselfe Heroically sound.

Aetion is a Greek proper name meaning eaglet. The Earl of Derby bore an eagle in his crest. Therefore there can be little doubt that Aetion, the poet, was the Earl of Derby, a supposition that is strengthened if we assume that Spenser knew the secret of the pseudonym, for no name sounds more heroically than Shake-speare. Then, we know that Derby was a dramatist because a letter of 1599 describes him as 'busy penning comedies for the common players'. Of course there is no record of any play of his. They are all in the folio.

As we should expect, the major incidents of Derby's life are mirrored in the plays. He wrote *A Midsummer Night's Dream* as a wedding present for his bride, the Earl of Oxford's daughter, Elizabeth de Vere, whom he married in 1595, while his financial difficulties are reflected in *The Merchant of Venice*, his jealousy in *Othello*, *Cymbeline* and *The Winter's Tale*. His public life, however, was uneventful, and about 1623 he retired to Chester, leaving much of the management of his affairs to his son. He would have plenty of leisure for writing, yet, though he lived for nearly twenty years after the publication of his folio, he wrote no more. The secret of his authorship died with him in 1642. Why it should have done is not very clear. As a result, there is no record of his life in the *Dictionary of National Biography*.

The Derbyites do not necessarily maintain that William Stanley wrote everything in the plays. There is, for example, evidence of a woman's hand. Could a mere man have written, 'All the yarn that Penelope spun in Ulysses' absence did but fill Ithaca with moths'? Such feminine touches were most probably contributed by the Countess of Pembroke, Sir Philip Sidney's sister, and mistress of Wilton House, near Salisbury. Wilton was the centre of a brilliant circle of courtiers and poets, and there we may imagine them, each making his peculiar contribution to the plays. The eclectic approach has distinct advantages. Oxford, of course, had much to give, and would help out his son-in-law with his topography and duelling terms. Then Rutland, who went to Denmark in 1603, supplied a few vivid details about Elsinore, changing, for example, 'Walks over yonder mountain top' to 'Walks o'er the dew of yon high eastern hill'. There were no mountains, he discovered, near Elsinore. Raleigh was invaluable as a source of nautical information, while Bacon added his unparalleled knowledge of science, law and philosophy. All these, however, formed but the circumference of the circle; at the centre was the master mind and shaping hand of William Shake-speare, 6th Earl of Derby.

It is an idyllic picture, this of the brilliant group of aristocrats composing plays for the common players in London, as they lay beside the river that flowed through the gardens of Wilton House. Ben Jonson knew the scene well, and celebrated it in his lines 'to the memory of my beloved the author', printed in the folio twenty years before Derby's death:

> Sweet Swan of Avon! what a sight it were
> To see thee in our waters yet appeare,
> And make those flights upon the bankes of Thames,
> That so did take Eliza, and our James!

Jonson, of course, could not have meant the Warwickshire Avon, a mere tributary. He meant unquestionably the Wiltshire Avon, which, though admittedly small, is a river in its own right, receiving the waters of the stream beside which so many of the plays of Shake-speare had been composed.

Thomas Looney, however, was not satisfied. Although he entirely agreed with the Derbyites that Shakspere did not write the plays, they were running the wrong man. He knew the real Shake-speare; he had traced him by following the clue of the *Venus and Adonis* stanza, and then by his deductive reasoning, confirmed by unanswerable evidence, demonstrated that he was Edward de Vere, 17th Earl of Oxford. Professor Freud was impressed by Looney's case; Mr Percy Allen, the dramatic critic, was convinced. Oxford was indeed the hidden dramatist, though not necessarily sole author of all the plays, and his *Life Story of Edward de Vere as William Shakespeare* appeared in 1930. The case for Oxford is as enthralling and convincing as those for Derby, Bacon and the rest.

Edward de Vere succeeded to the Earldom of Oxford in 1562 at the age of twelve, when he became a ward of Queen Elizabeth and entered the household of William Cecil, Lord Burghley. There he fell in love with Burghley's daughter, Anne, a situation reflected later in *Hamlet*, with himself as the Prince, Anne as Ophelia, Burghley as

Polonius, and his favourite cousins Francis and Horace Vere as Francisco and Horatio. In 1571 the young couple were married, but the union proved an unhappy one. The Queen was jealous, made love to Oxford, exactly like Venus in *Venus and Adonis*, and in 1574 became his mistress. In the following year she bore him a son, and as the Countess of Southampton had opportunely given birth to an illegitimate child at about the same time, the Queen's baby was substituted for hers, growing up to be known as the 3rd Earl of Southampton, the 'lovely boy' of his father's *Sonnets*, published as 'Shake-speares'.

Meanwhile Oxford was abroad, storing up memories of the French court to be dramatised in *Love's Labour's Lost*, in which Southampton played Moth, as can be seen by the appearance of the four letters in his name. His Italian journey was precisely that of Bassanio in *The Merchant of Venice*—and of course Portia is Queen Elizabeth besieged by suitors. While he was abroad Anne gave birth to a daughter whose legitimacy he suspected, partly because of the slanders directed against his wife by his cousins Charles Arundel and Lord Henry Howard. But he soon discovered their treachery and pilloried them in *Much Ado About Nothing* as the slandering villains Conrade and Borachio. This is obvious, as Conrade is an anagram of C.Aronde(l), Dogberry incidentally being a near-anagram of Borachio—we have only to change the D to an O to get Borregyo—though the relevancy of this is not very clear. *Cymbeline*, *The Winter's Tale* and *Othello* all dramatise the same episode.

After a short disgrace Oxford was restored to the Queen's favour and flattered by two critics of the time as being the most excellent poet among the noble lords and gentlemen at Court, and in 1598 Francis Meres was to mention him (along with sixteen others) as being one of 'the best for comedy amongst us' (at the same time giving three paragraphs to Shakespeare, 'the most excellent' both in comedy and tragedy). Most of Oxford's great tragedies, then, were written after 1598. But this is to anticipate.

In 1589 Oxford retired from Court, and may have gone to live in his Manor House of Bilton, about twenty miles from Stratford in the Forest of Arden, where he wrote *As You Like It*. He, of course, is the courtly Touchstone, who makes game of the rustic William, the illiterate Stratford actor on whom he fathered his plays. Anne was now dead, and he repaired his dissipated fortunes by a second marriage, moving in 1596 to King's Place, Hackney, where he wrote most of the *Sonnets* and his last three tragedies, *Macbeth*, *King Lear* and *Antony and Cleopatra*. Kent in *Lear* is Oxford, for Kent tells us that he is forty-eight, Oxford's exact age in 1598, the date of the play. It is astonishing how the biographical details fit into the pattern of the plays.

Oxford died at King's Place in 1604, and most of the later plays of 'Shakespeare' are by various hands: Fletcher, for example, being the chief author of *Henry VIII* and Raleigh of *The Tempest*. But when Fulke Greville moved into King's Place in 1608 a number of Oxford's manuscripts were discovered, including *Lear*, *Troilus and Cressida*, *Pericles* and the *Sonnets*, all of which were published in the following year. Incidentally, this clearing-up of the mystery of King's Place led to the clearing-up of the mystery of 'Mr. W. H.' to whom the publisher of the *Sonnets*, Thomas Thorpe, dedicated the volume.* The late Colonel B. M. Ward discovered that a William Hall was married in Hackney parish church in 1608, and the conclusion is obvious that this was the man who secured the manuscripts during the removal and handed them over to Thorpe. No wonder the grateful publisher wished 'Mr. W. H. ALL. HAPPINESSE'.

Mr Allen, however, will have nothing to do with this William Hall. For him Mr. W. H. is Henry Wriothesley, Earl of Southampton, the son of Queen Elizabeth and the Earl of Oxford. His portrait is even in the centre of the ornament at the top of the *Sonnets* title-page, and below are two hares symbolising the 'lovely boy', or 'heir', as he is so often called by his father in the poems.

* 'TO . THE . ONLIE . BEGETTER . OF . THESE . INSUING . SONNETS . MR . W . H . ALL . HAPPINESSE . AND . THAT . ETER-NITIE . PROMISED . BY . OVR . EVER . LIVING . POET . WISHETH . THE . WELL . WISHING . ADVENTURER . IN . SETTING . FORTH . T . T .'

Thorpe's dedication is equally clear; it is in fact signed in the phrase
'OVR . EVER . LIVING. POET', for of course *Ever* is E.Ver,
Edward Vere. If confirmation is required for anything so patent, we
have only to turn to sonnet 76:

> Why write I still all one, *ever the same,*
> And keepe invention in a noted weed,
> That *every word* doth almost tell my name,
> Shewing their birth and where they did proceed?
> O know, sweet love, I alwaies write of you . . .

'Eword Very' does indeed almost spell Edward Vere. Moreover, 'E.
Ver the same' in Latin is *Semper Eadem*, the Queen's favourite motto,
so that with exquisite subtlety Elizabeth, Oxford and their son, 'sweet
love', are brought together.

Another particularly illuminating sonnet is number 33 ('Full many
a glorious morning have I seen') when read as an open reference to the
birth of Southampton, for the imagery of the sun breaking through the
clouds symbolises Southampton and his mother, an emblem repeated in
visual terms in the famous Ditchley portrait of the Queen standing on
a map of England, with the city of Oxford between her feet and
Southampton immediately below. The sun, or son, however, was Oxford's 'but one hour' before the 'region (regina) cloud' masked him
from his view. The so-called 'Will' sonnets (134–6) are a further
confirmation of Oxford's authorship, for though his name was Edward,
Will is an old form of *well* or *spring*, and *spring* (the season that is) in
Latin is *Ver*.

And so, from the first sonnet to the last, the story is revealed of the
'dark lady' Queen Elizabeth, the lovely boy Southampton and his
father Oxford: from the opening line of sonnet 1 to the closing lines
of sonnet 154, with their reference to the pregnant Elizabeth's visit to
take the waters of Bath in 1574, and Oxford's reconciliation with her
there. Nobody would deny that the poet of the *Sonnets* is also the poet
of the plays, and as Oxford is unquestionably the author of the *Sonnets*
so is he as unquestionably the author of the plays.

Fifteen years after his study of Oxford's life Mr Allen was in a
position to offer a still perversely sceptical world a final solution of the
Shakespeare mystery, a solution that could scarcely be contested, since
he had it from the lips, if that is the correct expression, of the principal
characters themselves. And it was a very satisfactory solution, for with

one important qualification and some modification of detail, it confirmed his own conclusions, at the same time adding a wealth of new and delightfully exciting information.

During the war he became interested in spiritualism, and in the course of conversation with his communicant on the other side inevitably touched on the subject that was always close to the surface of his mind, the Shakespeare mystery. These talks proved so absorbing that he began to wonder if he could get into contact with the Elizabethans themselves, a scheme in which he was encouraged, through his medium, by Walt Whitman, William Archer and Marie Lloyd. And had not Mr Alfred Dodd just published a book reporting Bacon's revelation from the spirit world that he was Shakespeare? At length, therefore, he asked the medium's Control if it would be possible to bring Bacon to speak to him. It was possible, Bacon would be pleased to speak, or rather his words would be recorded by the medium in automatic script. So it came about that he had his first sitting with the quondam Lord Chancellor.

After the preliminary courtesies Mr Allen went straight to the heart of the matter. Did Bacon write any or all of the plays of Shakespeare? No, he wrote none of the plays, though he revised *Love's Labour's Lost* (leaving in it a number of Baconian clues to mystify posterity), and, as one of a circle of interested people, was frequently asked for his opinion, which, however, was rarely accepted. So far so good, but now the crucial question: Was the Earl of Oxford the author? Yes, he was the author—that is, the principal author, but it had to be remembered that he always collaborated with William Shakspere the actor. This was a staggering revelation, but Bacon was quite firm; Shakspere normally suggested the plot and provided the framework which Oxford filled in with his poetry and peopled with his characters. Still, it was puzzling; it was a very different story from the one he had recently told Mr Dodd. But Bacon explained. Mr Dodd had not spoken to him directly, but through a Deputy who, convinced that he, Bacon, had written the plays and poems, had reported to this effect without troubling to consult him. It was all a mistake: 'I am no poet, nor did I write a play.' 'I shall be glad', Bacon added, 'to refute Dodd.'

He was able to refute others equally decisively. When asked if there was any truth in the assertion that the Earl of Derby was Shakespeare, he replied with a contemptuous and triple negative: Derby wrote plays of a sort, but was not what you would call a dramatist. As for the Earl of Rutland, he was not even a member of the Shakespeare circle. The original group was composed of Oxford, Bacon, Raleigh and a few others, all of whom worked incognito or under the general pseudonym of 'Shake-speare', so masking their identity behind the name of Stratford William, who, however, was himself part author of many of the plays. After Oxford's death in 1604 another Shakespeare group was formed, in which Fletcher played an important part, being mainly responsible for *Cymbeline*, *The Winter's Tale*, *The Taming of the Shrew* and *Titus Andronicus*, published apparently when he was fifteen.

The rest of the conversation with Bacon was mainly concerned with topical detail about the plays, though he did divulge the priceless information that three original manuscripts were preserved in a tomb, 'a stone tomb', about which he suggested consulting Oxford, whom he promised to ask to come and speak. Finally, he agreed to write a short Preface to Mr Allen's proposed book on his revelation of the Shakespeare mystery.

However, it was not Oxford who next came to be greeted, but the Stratford man, a somewhat surly Shakspere, for until Bacon had disclosed his collaboration with Oxford Mr Allen had always thought him merely a mask for the others and something of a fool. There is a subtle change of tone in the initial catechism of Shakspere, the result no doubt of a natural embarrassment, and Shakspere in turn was correspondingly guarded in his replies. But the stiffness wore off, for Shakspere proved a merry rogue, by no means a fool, and by the end of the third sitting the two were on such good terms that he readily agreed to write his biography through the hand of the medium. It is a fascinating document.

He was born at the 'Birthplace', though his parents soon moved elsewhere, and was brought up a Protestant. At the grammar school he was a dull boy, for after seeing two plays in Stratford his thoughts were always with the theatre, so that when his father insisted on his becoming a butcher he ran off to London, where he got a job at the first Globe theatre, a converted inn, as cleaner and ostler. That was in 1581 when he was seventeen. In the following year he was persuaded by his father to marry Anne Hathaway, who, however, did not live in the famous cottage at Shottery. On his return to London he was given a few comic parts at the Globe, and it was there that he met the Earl of Oxford. The two soon became friends, and as the merry Shakspere was full of good stories, and Oxford a poet, they began to collaborate in the writing of plays, the former sketching the plot and the latter supplying the characters and dialogue. Shakspere, however, created most of the comic and villainous characters, and it was he who produced the plays on the stage.

The collaborators used to work, and drink, in a quiet room in the Mermaid, and it was there that Shakspere, who was no poet, made a wager with the company of wits that he could nevertheless write a good poem. The result was the very inferior *Lucrece*, into which a number of Baconian clues were inserted, though much against the wishes of Bacon himself.* Shakspere's companions, of course, knew that he was not the poet of the plays; they suspected Oxford, though they could not be quite sure.

Oxford's death was a catastrophe. Shakspere retired to Stratford, where he continued to write a little, but his fluency was gone. The fire was burned out, and, though he had no hope of a future life, he was resigned to his departure. When asked if he was not surprised to find himself alive after death, he replied, 'I was not surprised, my dear sir; for in nature there are no surprises. I accepted what *was* nature—I died of a disease of the liver.'

Mr Allen had to wait six months before he was honoured by an interview with Oxford. The Earl's first words were not encouraging: 'Very willing, but embarrassed by difficult conditions. O!' Nor did he prove to be nearly as interesting as the other two informants, being mainly concerned with corroborating their evidence and confirming leading questions or the answers to his counter-questions. Thus, when asked to explain an obscure allusion to a 'sun-tree', he countered, 'Yes —well, I should like first to know how you have interpreted it.' Mr Allen was helpful: 'I took the sun-tree to mean the Queen and her son.' 'Yes,' the Earl admitted, 'you are right.' However, he helped to find a title for Mr Allen's book, suggesting *Talks with Elizabethans*, agreed to write an Epilogue to it, and even offered to compose a sonnet that would be irrefutable proof of the authenticity of the conversations.

* For example, the first words of the first two lines are '*F*rom', '*B*orne', while in the last two lines '*con*sent' is immediately above '*b*anishment', with '*Finis*' directly below.

Again, in the fifteenth stanza we read of 'subtle-shining secrecies / Writ in the glassy margents of such books'. And sure enough, the marginal letters are B-C-N-W-S-N-M, which is, of course, 'Bacon, William Shakspere's name'.

The single sonnet was generously increased to four, so that when the book appeared it was with a Preface by Bacon, an Envoi by Shakspere and an Epilogue by Oxford, immediately following three of the new sonnets by 'Shake-speare'. The fourth was printed on the title-page. It begins:

> Enshrinèd in this tomb a secret lies,
> Mark ye! The body must to dust decay;
> The soul immortal is, it never dies,
> A living flame that burns by night and day.

The reference is to the manuscripts buried in a 'stone tomb'.

Oxford, Bacon and Shakspere had all agreed that it was time to reveal where these manuscripts lay hidden, as verifiable evidence for the satisfaction of unbelievers. They were buried with Shakspere at Stratford, one bundle as his pillow, another between his hands, and a third at his feet. The plays are *Hamlet*, *Macbeth*, *Lear*, *Othello*, *Henry V* and *Richard II*, and are in the handwriting of the joint authors, Oxford and Shakspere. Yet after all, it was felt that it would be impossible to get permission to open the grave; 'You might more easily disturb the Holy Sepulchre,' was the opinion of the ex-Lord Chancellor, remembering perhaps the abortive efforts of Dr Ingleby. So Mr Allen had to be content with convincing himself. He arranged with his shadowy friends to go to Stratford and stand above the grave in the parish church, where Oxford and Shakspere would meet him and touch him as a sign of their presence. And so, one morning in May, as he stood there with hands outstretched towards the head and feet, he felt a glow, accompanied by a tingling sensation, creep up his arms. Only a few feet below him was the manuscript of *Hamlet* lying on Shakspere's breast. It is one more alarming example of the extremes to which the cult of Shakespeare may lead its devotees.

Another and younger dramatic critic, this time an American, has been more successful in the matter of opening tombs. In the middle nineteen-thirties Mr Calvin Hoffman began to study the Elizabethan drama, and the more he read of Marlowe the more he was struck by the similarity between his work and Shakespeare's. This should not have surprised him. Marlowe was born in the same year as Shakespeare, went to Cambridge, and revolutionised the drama with half a dozen blank verse plays before being killed in a brawl in 1593. It was only to be expected that the early verse of Shakespeare would be influenced by the man who had got the start of him by his university education. But

Mr Hoffman finds more than this; the echoes are in the later plays as well. For example: *Marlowe*, 'Shape we our course to Ireland'—*Richard II*, 'To-morrow next we will for Ireland'. *Marlowe*, 'breakers of the peace'—*Romeo and Juliet*, 'disturbers of the peace'. *Marlowe*, 'To cast up hills against the face of heaven'—*Hamlet*, 'And bowl the round knave down the hill of heaven' (an allusion, doubtless, to that whoreson round man, Falstaff). *Marlowe*, 'I arrest you of high treason' —*Henry VIII*, 'I arrest thee of high treason'. *Marlowe*, 'Here is my dagger'—*Julius Caesar*, 'there is my dagger'. Such parallelisms can scarcely be coincidental. Yet long before most of Shakespeare's plays were written Marlowe was dead. Or was he? In 1931 Dr Gilbert Slater had suggested that Marlowe was not killed, but lived to collaborate with Oxford, Derby, Rutland, Bacon, Raleigh and the Countess of Pembroke in the writing of the plays. Mr Hoffman turned to the recently discovered contemporary documents describing the killing, and found that Dr Slater was quite right. Any objective mind could see that the coroner's report was a patent fraud.

After twenty years of patient research Mr Hoffman closed the last gaps in his case for Marlowe, and published it. Shakespeare, of course, was merely a semi-literate actor about whom we know next to nothing, and whose death passed unnoticed. Yet Mr Hoffman himself offers a startling piece of biographical information that has somehow escaped all previous research. Apparently Shakespeare's son-in-law, Dr John Hall, noted in his Diary, 'My father-in-law died on Thursday.' His reconstruction of events is as sensational as Ignatius Donnelly's cryptographic revelations. We know that in 1593 Marlowe was arrested, probably at the house of Thomas Walsingham, on a charge of atheism, and released on bail. Then, according to the coroner's detailed report, he was killed in a house in Deptford by one Ingram Frizer, acting in self-defence. But what really happened, Mr Hoffman tells us, was this. Thomas Walsingham, a wealthy and influential man, was not only Marlowe's patron but also his lover, so that the young poet was faced with the double charge of atheism and homosexuality. It was as much as his life was worth; he must fly the country. But Walsingham has an additional plan to make all sure. He talks to his creatures Ingram Frizer and Nicholas Skeres, each of whom has 'an odorous reputation'. They are to kill a man—any man—and will be well paid. The money bag flashes on the table; its mouth spills sovereigns, and the two bullies pocket the first instalment of their pay. Meanwhile Marlowe packs his books—his Holinshed, his Halle, his Ovid, Seneca and Virgil, says good-bye to his lover, and on the night of the 29th reaches Dover in disguise. The morning of the 30th dawns. Frizer and Skeres are at Deptford. They see a likely looking victim, probably a foreign sailor who wants a woman. They entice him inside a house, and when all are drunk stab him to death. The next day he is buried in an unknown grave as Christopher Marlowe. Walsingham bribes the coroner, who writes his false report, and Frizer is freed. Meanwhile, 'the figure on the Channel ship watches the tender outlines of the French coast as they emerge out of the morning mist, purple and gold in the rising sun. . . .'

Marlowe had left the manuscript of his recently written 'epic poem *Venus and Adonis*' with his lover, as he tells us in Sonnet 48:

> How careful was I, when I took my way,
> Each trifle under truest bars to thrust.

Soon afterwards it was published, the first work to bear the name of Shakespeare. Walsingham had lost no time. He had made the round of the London theatres and discovered 'a steady, not too imaginative' actor, who would lend his name to anything for money. And so began the flow of wonderful poems and plays that Marlowe wrote in exile, and Walsingham published under the name of Shakespeare—some of them at least, for some were issued anonymously, others only in the folio. Of course Walsingham did not part with the original manuscripts, but kept them for sentimental and security reasons, and had them copied for distribution to the theatres. There is evidence for this in the fact that in his will he left forty shillings to a scrivener.

From France Marlowe must have gone to Italy, where he picked up the staggering knowledge of that country revealed in the plays. He was a reformed character, a lonely exile doing penance for his sinful pride, and the *Sonnets*, transposed into a probable order of succession, reveal, as we should expect, his story:

> How heavy do I journey on the way . . .
> My grief lies onward, and my joy behind,

and so on. When published, they were of course dedicated to his lover, 'Mr. W. H.'—Walsing-Ham.

There is no lack of further proof, if further proof be needed, that Marlowe was Shakespeare. There is, for example, that amazing play

As You Like It. Touchstone, of course, is Marlowe, and William the rustic actor. But what is the significance of that enigmatic character, Sir Oliver Martext? It is through his name that Marlowe chose to reveal the secret of his authorship: Martext, Mar-text, or in full, Marlowe's-text.

There remains the conclusive, scientific proof. Some seventy years ago Dr T. C. Mendenhall, an American professor who must have heard of Furnivall and Fleay, counted each letter of every word in the representative works of half a dozen authors, from Percy Shelley to John Stuart Mill. From these figures, computed to the minutest decimal, he was able to construct graphs showing their peculiarities of style and the average length of words in their vocabularies. Some time later a wealthy Baconian commissioned him to test the works of Bacon and Shakespeare by his mechanical method. Women, hired for the research, counted 200,000 words from Bacon, 75,000 from Jonson, 400,000 from Shakespeare, all the words in Marlowe's plays, and over a million more from other authors. Then the professor began to plot the characteristic curves of Bacon and Shakespeare. 'He didn't have to finish the job. A single glance ruled out any possibility of similitude.' Shakespeare's average word was one of four letters, a length that Dr Mendenhall had never met with before. Bacon's was considerably longer. But then came a sensational discovery. The characteristic curve of Marlowe agreed with Shakespeare as well as Shakespeare agreed with himself.

The Stratfordians are now driven behind their last rampart of belief, the folio. But Mr Hoffman has no difficulty in overrunning this and scattering the defenders. Anyway, its authority has always been doubted; Sir Thomas 'Hamner', for example, disavowed *The Two Gentlemen of Verona*. The truth is, of course, that Walsingham supplied the manuscripts and financed the publication. Heminge and Condell, grocer and publican, had nothing to do with the volume. The Dedication and Preface to which they lent their names, for a consideration, were almost certainly written by one of the syndicate of publishers, Edward Blount, Marlowe's friend. Although the Preface is a tissue of lies, the offence of Blount, whose aim was to stimulate sales, is understandable. As for Jonson's elegy on 'My beloved the author Mr William Shakespeare', it was 'made to order—for money . . . Jonson would have written anything for money.' Mr Hoffman quotes Jonson's severely critical estimate of Shakespeare, but it is a pity that he failed to notice the lines, 'I lov'd the man, and do honour his memory (on this side idolatry) as much as any. He was (indeed) honest, and of an open, and free nature, had an excellent *Phantsie*; brave notions, and gentle expressions.' Perhaps, however, they are not relevant to the argument, which leads us to the conclusion that 'if anything, the First Folio is a compelling reason for denying Shakespeare's authorship of it, and for affirming Christopher Marlowe's.'

The final proof would be the discovery of Marlowe's manuscripts. Perhaps Walsingham carried his lover's written works to the grave. On May 1st, 1956, his tomb at Chislehurst, Kent, was opened. There was nothing but sand. That, of course, does not affect the case for Marlowe's authorship. The manuscripts may still turn up among the Walsingham papers.

A hundred years ago, even seventy or sixty years ago, there was some excuse for wondering how the romantic and sentimentalised conception of Shakespeare as an inspired but virtually uneducated peasant could be reconciled with the extravagant claims made for the knowledge and learning displayed in his work. To-day there is no excuse for posing such a paradox. Modern scholarship has revealed Shakespeare as a man of no great learning, but as a genius with a sound grammar school education, who went to London where his higher education was among the poets and wits of the theatre, the Inns of Court and the Court of Elizabeth and James itself. There is no more reason to believe that he was incapable of writing the works published in his name than there is to believe that Jonson, Keats and Hardy, all of whom were the sons of working men and left school at sixteen, were incapable of writing theirs. Anti-Stratfordians, of whatever sect, all start from the premise, uncritically accepted, that Shakespeare was a semi-literate rustic who could do little more than con an actor's part and write his own name, if he could do even that. Such a premise is merely a distortion of a long-obsolete view that attributed too little culture to the man and too much to the plays.

Why people should still persevere in this antiquated pastime of bard-baiting and bard-questing is matter for a psychologist and a May morning. Some, the hard core of the movement, probably see themselves as the champions of an unrecognised, or insufficiently recognised, genius—Bacon, Derby, Oxford, the Countess of Pembroke, or whoever takes their fancy—against the Stratford impostor. They must have a cause to which they can attach themselves, one for which they can fight, and even the most intelligent people may be carried away by this irrational compulsion. Others, though not so many to-day as formerly, may be impelled by snobbery, a blind refusal to admit that a provincial grammar school boy should be the national poet of England. Others again may find it an easy way to publicity and even celebrity of a sort. It would, for example, be no very difficult task to cook up a case for James I as the author of the plays—no doubt it has already been done. After all, James was a writer; he was notoriously fond of young men like the 'lovely boy' of the *Sonnets*; Stuart, like Shakespeare, begins with an S; then there is the 'marvellous falorous' Captain Jamy in *Henry V*, and another most satisfactory self-portrait in *Macbeth*, while *Hamlet* is a very palpable hit at James's rival brother-in-law, Christian IV of Denmark. Touchstone, of course, is James, 'the wisest fool in Christendom'. . . . One is almost tempted to begin on the anagrams and parallel passages. Which offers us another reason. A man must have a hobby, and what more fascinating hobby for a winter's evening than the ingenious game of tracing in the plays an Elizabethan-Jacobean hand other than Shakespeare's? If Sir Thomas Hanmer had been alive to-day it is a hobby that he would almost certainly have preferred to the more exacting pastime of editing the plays, one that would give even more scope for his celebrated intuition. But for the great majority of professed anti-Stratfordians the whole business can be no more than a joke; they cannot seriously believe the frivolous fantasies that they write and read in their peculiar publications.

o

SHAKESPEARE REINTEGRATED

TAME rabbits that nibbled the grass of the sylvan Athenian scene brought nineteenth-century productions of Shakespeare to a triumphant conclusion. Yet this was only the beginning of the sumptuous realism purveyed by Beerbohm Tree at His Majesty's, and his Edwardian presentations were even more opulently upholstered. *The Tempest* opened with a complete ship wallowing in a roaring sea, waves breaking over its deck and a hurricane shredding its sails. Then, though they had to wait the best part of an hour to see them, audiences were ravished by the rural beauty of the rose-embowered cottage, waterfall and willow in *The Winter's Tale*, by the gorgeous palaces, solemn temples and palm trees of *Antony and Cleopatra*, and by the hammer-beam roofs and fan vaulting of *Henry VIII*. Tree had out-Irvinged Irving, and the logical conclusion of this oriental ostentation was the inanities of *Chu Chin Chow*, which, put on in the summer of 1916, ran for five years.

The nineteenth century lasted longer in England than on the Continent, but even here it came to an end with the great war of 1914–18. The breakdown of the old political order coincided with a second industrial revolution; oil was superseding coal as a source of power, and motor-car and aeroplane were beginning to compete with steam engine and steamer. Moreover, a new and unexpected world had been discovered, though it remained to be explored, the vast dark world of the unconscious mind. All these things added up to a revolution comparable to that which brought the Middle Ages to an end.

The breakdown of the old order had been foreshadowed in the arts. The impact of the new painting struck England with the Post-Impressionist Exhibition of 1910, when the art of Manet, Cézanne, Van Gogh and Gauguin, as well as that of Matisse and the other Fauves, was characterised as one that stops where a child would begin. In the following year came the new art of the Russian Ballet. This, with its décor by Bakst, was more to the liking of London, though it was by no means sure of the music of Stravinsky, who seemed positively to take pleasure in flouting conventional rhythms, harmonies and forms. Then there was the queer new poetry of Mr Eliot: *The Love Song of J. Alfred Prufrock*, so very different from *The Idylls of the King*, and the new and so unreticent prose of Mr Joyce. There can have been few in England who were aware of the strange abstractions being carved by Brancusi, or even of the airy simplifications being erected by Le Corbusier, who proclaimed the disturbing doctrine that a house was a machine to live in. But even though the great mass of people were unaware of what was happening, a movement violently hostile to the romantic, sentimental, rhetorical neo-baroque Victorian-Edwardian art had set in. Artists impatient of decoration and trimmings were concentrating on essentials, and, instead of reproducing variations of old forms, were inventing new ones, often inspired by the austere and functional streamlining of the new machines. The effect was soon felt in the theatre.

In the autumn of 1912 Harley Granville-Barker produced *The Winter's Tale* at the Savoy. *The Times* was startled by its audacity, ironical in its reception, yet on the whole approving: 'Here, like it or lump it, is post-impressionist Shakespeare. . . . The costumes are after Bakst, the busbies and caftans come from the Russian ballet, and . . . squads of supers have symmetrical, automaton-like movements . . .' This was soon followed by *Twelfth Night*, and at the beginning of 1914 by *A Midsummer Night's Dream*, with its famous golden fairies. Self-conscious and arty though these productions, as seen in photographs, appear to-day, they swept away the accumulated false conventions of centuries. Not that Granville-Barker was the first reformer. In Stratford and the provinces F. R. Benson and his company had played fairly full texts with a minimum of stock scenery, and in 1900 shocked London by staging *Hamlet* in its entirety. At the same time, though in the uncommercial theatre, William Poel was presenting Shakespeare and the other Elizabethans on a stage approximating to that for which they wrote. The importance of Granville-Barker is that he challenged the Kemble–Kean–Irving–Tree tradition on its own ground, the West End of London, and defeated it. By removing the footlights, pushing the stage forward and raising it at the back, he restored the contact between audience and players. By using simple formalised sets and curtains, by insisting that speeches should be spoken trippingly on the tongue, and by cutting out all otiose stage business, he was able to present an unabridged text, with only one interval, in little more than two hours. Tree's production of rather more than half of *Julius Caesar* had lasted from eight o'clock to midnight. Shakespeare was restored in the theatre, and the age of the producer, the artist responsible for every detail of the presentation, had arrived. It was not without its own new dangers.

The attack on the false conception of Shakespeare, and its attendant bardolatry, was delivered at about the same time. The aged Tolstoy was the first to get in his blow. Shakespeare, like Beethoven, did not fit into his philosophical system, and he saw him as one who despised the working classes, repudiating both religious and humanitarian efforts to alleviate their lot (Dowden's 'Tory gentleman' apparently). His view of life was essentially immoral, and the sooner people freed themselves from his foolish worship the better. This was a little hard on Shakespeare, but then it was scarcely literary criticism. Croce, the Italian, was less brutal, more ironical: 'Shakespeare stands, either beside Dürer and Rembrandt, or on a spur of Parnassus, facing Homer and Aeschylus on another spur, sometimes permitting Dante to stand at his side—Dante was of German origin—while the impotent crowd of poets of the Latin race seethes at his feet.'

In England, Sir Walter Raleigh, rejecting the ecstasies of nineteenth-century romantic criticism, returned to what he called the 'cool and manly' utterances of Johnson. At the same time Lytton Strachey demolished the cosy Furnivall–Dowden dream of Shakespeare in his retirement babbling of spring flowers and sheep shearings to sweet English maidens. Instead he saw the man who created Leontes as well as Perdita, Caliban as well as Ariel, a writer of ethereal songs who, half bored to death, burst from time to time into violent and bitter speech. As for his learning, scholarship revealed that, though he knew no Greek, he was schooled in the grammar, logic and rhetoric of the period, and could and did read some of the Latin classics in the original. It was a strange reversal of the situation; realism had been banished from the stage and established in the study.

The most original contribution of the twentieth century to Shakespearean criticism has been in the field of imagery. As early as 1904 A. C. Bradley had remarked on the way in which the animal imagery of *King Lear* intensified the atmosphere of horrible monstrosity, and thirty years later Caroline Spurgeon showed that there was a similar 'iterative imagery' in all Shakespeare's later work. This was the product of his unconscious mind, its effect being to emphasise the peculiar atmosphere of each play, as, for example, the disease imagery in *Hamlet* reinforces the theme of rottenness in the state of Denmark.

This is not the place in which to attempt to survey all that the last fifty years have contributed to the study of Shakespeare, but now that we are well past the middle of the century perhaps we should pause to ask ourselves what our descendants will think of our efforts a hundred years hence. Our own age, like Shakespeare's, is one of transition from an old order to a new; novelty and experiment are its keywords, and it may be that we shall be accused of follies comparable to those that we find among our predecessors. And we must remember that we are on record, both aurally and visually, as never before. However, it is not suggested that we should interpret our Shakespeare with an eye to the approval of posterity. Posterity may be wrong. Each age must redis-cover and reinterpret the plays for itself, and if we are true to our own age we cannot be far out.

We pride ourselves, quite rightly no doubt, on a saner view of Shakespeare and his work; at least we attach more importance to the poetry and to the plays as works of art. But have we fallen into the New Shakspere Society error, and overvalued the new science of psychoanalysis as an aid to understanding? Does Shakespeare really reveal himself unconsciously in his imagery, as Caroline Spurgeon sug-gested, as 'a compactly well-built man, probably on the slight side, extraordinarily well co-ordinated, lithe and nimble of body, quick and accurate of eye, delighting in swift muscular movement . . . probably fair-skinned and of a fresh colour, which in youth came and went easily, revealing his feelings and emotions'? Or, by an analysis of their imagery, are we to conclude, with M. M. Morozov, that Iago was once a sailor, and Hamlet a tough realist? Dr Ernest Jones, by a pro-cess of Freudian analysis, finds the solution of the Hamlet mystery in the Oedipus Complex. Claudius succeeded in doing the two things that Hamlet unconsciously wished to do—kill his father and marry his mother—so that his power to act against his hated rival was paralysed by his own sense of guilt. It may be so, though the solution seems just a little over-sophisticated for the age of *The Anatomy of Melancholy*. And are we really to believe, with the leader of the new interpretative school of criticism, that 'Macbeth and Lear are created in a soul-dimension of primal feeling', that 'Prospero is shown as giving his Miranda, the feminine aspect of his own self, or soul, to mankind', and that Shakespeare so loved the Fair Youth of the *Sonnets* that 'an inward bisexuality, already dormant, was rapidly developed within the poet's soul or mind, or rather "soul-mind"'? Or again, are we to believe with the critic of the realist school that 'a true interpretation of *The Taming of the Shrew* depends on our considering it in relation to the doctrine of the harmonious hierarchical universe'? Perhaps, after all, 'twere to consider too curiously to consider so.

We can also congratulate ourselves on producing Shakespeare far more frequently and intelligently than ever before. The Old Vic has become his London home, and at Stratford-upon-Avon Garrick's celebration of the firm of Garrick and Shakespeare has become an eight-month Festival at which a repertory of half a dozen plays and more is annually performed. Moreover Samuel Daniel's prediction that

> worlds in th' yet unformed Occident
> May come refined with th' accents that are ours

has been fulfilled, and summer festivals are now held at other Stratfords, in Ontario and Connecticut. The producer has come into his own, and, freed from the encumbrance of Victorian apparatus, can present the plays with simple sets and curtains on a stage similar to the Elizabethan, with an Elizabethan tempo that makes it possible to give the whole text as Shakespeare wrote it.

He can also present them in a manner as foreign to the Elizabethan as was the Victorian, for the imposition of a producer's whimsicality may be every whit as distracting as the old stuffy realism, and posterity may accuse us of exploiting novelty for novelty's sake, of adding yet another folly to the cult of Shakespeare. The freakish can more easily be assimilated by comedy than by tragedy, but even comedy rejects the Duke's playing with a yo-yo while Portia pleads with Shylock. Modern dress productions are another matter, in a sense old-fashioned rather than a novelty. The Elizabethans appear to have had certain conventional costumes for Greeks and Romans, but as far as we know Burbage played Hamlet and Macbeth in Elizabethan dress, as Betterton and Garrick played the parts in the costume of their own times. The early nineteenth-century antiquarian productions were the real innovation, so that when Sir Barry Jackson produced 'Hamlet in plus fours' in 1925 he was merely reverting to the old tradition. It was a revelation to those who were fortunate enough to see it, so immediate, so much more real than Victorian realism did it seem. But it does not follow that all the other tragedies lend themselves to similar treatment.

Finally, we may ask ourselves what we are making of the new media of film, wireless and television, all of which can so admirably reproduce the speed and fluidity that Shakespeare had in mind when he wrote. May it not be that the coloured film is in danger of returning to the worst excesses of the Victorian stage, of cutting Shakespeare to make time for spectacle, of making Westerns out of the histories, even of improving them 'with interpolations from Garrick, Cibber, etc.'? The television screen is still too small for the satisfactory presentation of a play, which is as yet an uneasy series of diminutive scenes and close-ups. Yet, if I may finish on a personal note, I recently saw a production of *Twelfth Night* that was as fresh and natural as if it had never been played before. The pity was that about a quarter of it was missing. Apparently the B.B.C. have decided that an hour and a half of Shakespeare is as much as an audience can be expected to endure (Kemble was rather more flattering to his audiences). Perhaps they are right. I saw the performance in the lounge of an hotel; viewers returned for the last verse of Feste's last song and the beginning of the next parlour game.

A hundred years ago that 'excellent actor and estimable man, Mr Harries Tilbury', was warning the members of the Shakespeare Club in Stratford that 'Time with his stealing steps will quickly bear you to the year 1864', and asking them how they were preparing to celebrate the event. We know what happened. The quatercentenary of Shakespeare's birth will soon be upon us. We shall order things better this time, but it will be interesting to hear what the Festival Committee proposes to contribute to the Cult of Shakespeare. No doubt it will be something more than an Inaugural Address, a Dramatic Reading, a Banquet and a Fancy Ball.

LIST OF BOOKS

Th is list gives the main sources on which I have drawn. For convenience it is arranged according to chapters, though some of the books cover a wider field and more than one episode.

In particular, there is *Amazing Monument* by Ivor Brown and George Fearon, published in 1939 and now out of print. It is an entertaining account of the Shakespeare Industry, but as it is mainly concerned with Stratford it coincides with my book only in two or three of its episodes.

For chapters XII and XIII the list is arranged chronologically instead of alphabetically.

I

Brooke, C. F. T. (editor). *The Shakespeare Apocrypha*. 1908.
Chambers, E. K. *William Shakespeare*. 2 vols. 1930.
Hotson, Leslie. *The Commonwealth and Restoration Stage*. 1928.
Kirkman, Francis. *The Wits: or Sport upon Sport*. 1672.
Shakespeare. *The First Folio*, in reduced facsimile. 1876.

II

Dramatists of the Restoration. 15 vols. 1874. (Gives most of the early adaptations.)
Evelyn, John. *Diary*. 4 vols. 1889.
Odell, G. C. D. *Shakespeare, from Betterton to Irving*. 2 vols. 1921.
Pepys, Samuel. *Diary*. 2 vols. 1924.
Spenser, Hazelton. *Shakespeare Improved*. 1927.

III

Cibber, Colley. *Dramatic Works*. 4 vols. 1760.
Dryden, John. *Dramatic Works*. 6 vols. 1725.
Tate, Nahum. *The History of King Lear. Reviv'd with Alterations*. 1681.

IV

Edwards, Thomas. *The Canons of Criticism*. 1747.
Lounsbury, T. R. *The First Editors of Shakespeare*. 1906.
Pope, Alexander. *The Dunciad*. Editions of 1728, 1743, 1751.
Shakespeare. Editions of:
    Nicholas Rowe. 6 vols. 1709.
    Alexander Pope. 6 vols. 1725.
    Lewis Theobald. 7 vols. 1733.

Thomas Hanmer. 6 vols. 1744.

William Warburton. 8 vols. 1747.

The Variorum Editions of 1803, 1813 and 1821 give the editorial prefaces and most of the important essays of the 18th century.

THEOBALD, LEWIS. *Double Falsehood.* 1728.

Shakespeare Restored. 1726.

V

ANGELO. *Reminiscences of Henry Angelo.* 1828.

BROWN, IVOR, and GEORGE FEARON. *Amazing Monument.* 1939.

DAVIES, THOMAS. *Memoirs of the Life of David Garrick.* 1780.

WHELER R. B. *History and Antiquities of Stratford-upon-Avon.* 1806.

VI

BOADEN, JAMES. *The Life of John Philip Kemble.* 1825.

INCHBALD, ELIZABETH. *The British Theatre.* 25 vols. 1806–9.

IRELAND, SAMUEL. *Picturesque Views on the Warwickshire Avon.* 1795.

Miscellaneous Papers and Legal Instruments under the Hand and Seal of William Shakspeare. 1796.

A Vindication of his Conduct. 1796.

IRELAND, WILLIAM-HENRY. *The Confessions of William-Henry Ireland.* 1805.

Henry II. 1799.

Vortigern. With an Original Preface. 1832.

JORDAN, JOHN. *Welcombe Hills.* 1777.

MAIR, JOHN. *The Fourth Forger.* 1938.

MALONE, EDMOND. *An Inquiry into the Authenticity of Certain Miscellaneous Papers and Legal Instruments.* 1796.

NICHOL, JOHN. *Literary Anecdotes of the Eighteenth Century.* 1812–15.

PRIOR, J. *The Life of Edward Malone.* 1860.

RITSON, JOSEPH. *Letters.*

SHAKESPEARE. Editions of:

Samuel Johnson. 8 vols. 1765.

Edward Capell. 10 vols. 1768.

George Steevens. 10 vols. 1773.

Edmond Malone. 10 vols. 1790.

VII

BOASE, T. S. R. *Illustrations of Shakespeare's Plays in the 17th and 18th Centuries.* Journal of the Warburg and Courtauld Institutes, Vol. 10. 1948.

BOYDELL, JOHN. *The Shakespeare Gallery.* 2 vols. 1803.

INGLEBY, C. M. *Shakespeare's Bones.* 1883.

NORRIS, J. PARKER. *The Portraits of Shakespeare.* 1885.

SUMMERSON, JOHN. *Sir John Soane's Museum.* 1955.

Waterhouse, Ellis. *Painting in Britain, 1530–1790.* 1953.

VIII

BOWDLER, THOMAS. *The Family Shakspeare.* 1818.
HORNBY, MARY. *The Tragedy of the Battle of Waterloo.* 1819.
IRVING, WASHINGTON. *The Sketch Book.* 1820.
MONCRIEFF, W. T. *Excursion to Stratford-upon-Avon.* 1824.
WHELER, R. B. *History and Antiquities of Stratford-upon-Avon.* 1806.

IX

COLLIER, J. P. *New Facts regarding the Life of Shakspeare.* 1835.
HALLIWELL-PHILLIPPS, J. O. *Curiosities of Modern Shakespearian Criticism.* 1853.
INGLEBY, C. M. *A Complete View of the Shakspere Controversy.* 1861.
SHAKESPEARE SOCIETY. *Papers.* 1844–49.

X

HUNTER, ROBERT E. *Shakespeare, Stratford, and the Tercentenary Festival.* 1864.
JEPHSON, J. M. *Shakespere: A Pilgrimage to Stratford-on-Avon.* 1864.

XI

DOWDEN, EDWARD. *Shakspere, his Mind and Art.* 1875.
HALLIWELL-PHILLIPPS, J. O. *Illustrations of the Life of Shakespeare.* 1874.
NEW SHAKSPERE SOCIETY. *Transactions.* 1874–92.
SWINBURNE, A. C. *A Study of Shakespeare.* 1880.

XII

LAWRENCE, HERBERT. *The Life and Adventures of Common Sense.* 1769.
SERRES, OLIVIA WILMOT. *The Life of the Author of the Letters of Junius.* 1813.
HALLIWELL-PHILLIPPS, J. O. *The Life of William Shakespeare.* 1848.
HART, JOSEPH C. *The Romance of Yachting.* 1848.
BACON, DELIA. *The Philosophy of the Plays of Shakespeare Unfolded.* 1857.
SMITH, W. H. *Bacon and Shakespeare.* 1857.
SPEDDING, J. *The Works of Francis Bacon.* 1857–74.
  The Letters and Life of Francis Bacon. 1861–72.
  The Conference of Pleasure. 1870.
HALLIWELL-PHILLIPPS, J. O. *Outlines of the Life of Shakespeare.* 1881.
POTT, MRS HENRY. *The Promus of Formularies and Elegancies, by Francis Bacon.* 1883.
Baconiana. The magazine of the Francis Bacon Society. 1886 onwards.
THEOBALD, R. M. *Dethroning Shakspere.* A selection of letters contributed to the Daily Telegraph shortly before the publication of Donnelly's 'Great Cryptogram'. 1888.

DONNELLY, IGNATIUS. *The Great Cryptogram: Francis Bacon's Cipher in the so-called Shakespeare Plays.* 2 vols. 1888.

MARTIN, THEODORE. *Shakespeare or Bacon?* (anti-Bacon). 1888.

LEE, SIDNEY. *A Life of William Shakespeare.* 1898.

GALLUP, MRS E. W. *The Bi-literal Cypher of Sir Francis Bacon.* 1899.

GREENWOOD, GEORGE. *The Shakespeare Problem Restated.* 1908.

BEECHING, H. C. *William Shakespeare. A Reply to Mr George Greenwood, M.P.* 1908.

DURNING-LAWRENCE, EDWIN. *Bacon is Shake-Speare.* 1910.

ROBERTSON, J. M. *The Baconian Heresy. A Confutation.* 1913.

THEOBALD, B. G. *Shake-Speare's Sonnets Unmasked.* 1929.

EAGLE, RODERICK. *Shakespeare: New Views for Old.* 1930.

PENDERED, MARY L. and J. MALLET. *The Strange Story of Olivia Wilmot Serres.* 1939.

EAGLE, RODERICK. *Bacon or Shakspere.* 1955.

XIII

LEFRANC, ABEL. *Sous le Masque de William Shakespeare.* (Derby). 2 vols. 1919.

LOONEY, THOMAS. *Shakespeare Identified* (Oxford). 1920.

The Shakespeare Fellowship News-Letter, the organ of the Oxfordian Society founded in 1922.

ALLEN, PERCY. *The Life Story of Edward de Vere as William Shakespeare* (Oxford). 1930.

SLATER, GILBERT. *Seven Shakespeares.* 1931.

BROOKS, ALDEN. *Will Shakspere and the Dyer's Hand* (Sir Edward Dyer). 1943.

LEFRANC, ABEL. *À la Découverte de Shakespeare* (Derby). 2 vols. 1945, 1950.

ALLEN, PERCY. *Talks with Elizabethans.* (Oxford). 1945.

HOFFMAN, CALVIN. *The Man who was Shakespeare* (Marlowe). 1955.

EVANS, A. J. *Shakespeare and his Magic Circle* (Derby). 1956.

XIV

Shakespeare Survey. Edited by Allardyce Nicoll. 1948 onwards.

SPURGEON, C. *Shakespeare's Imagery.* 1935.

INDEX